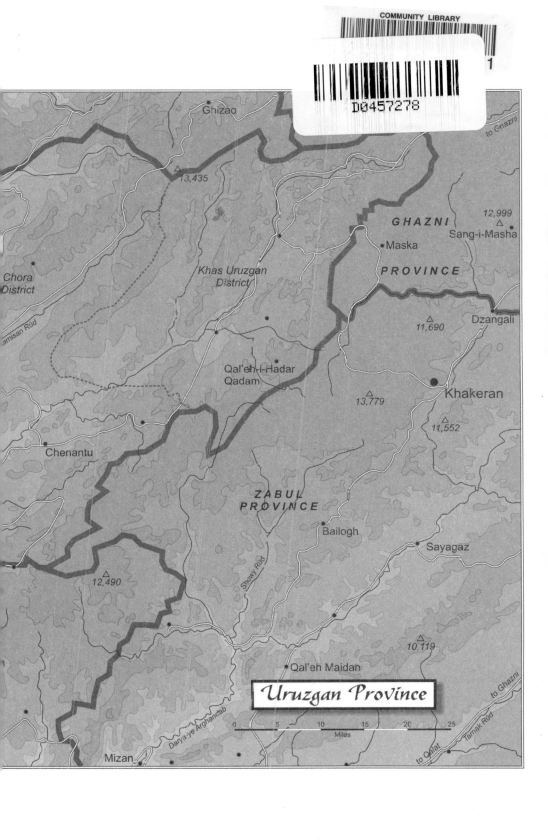

Ghizao

to Ghazni

△
13,435

GHAZNI

12,999
△
Sang-i-Masha

• Maska

PROVINCE

Chora
District

Khas Uruzgan
District

△
11,690

Dzangali

amisan Rūd

Qal'eh-i-Hadar
Qadam

△
13,779

△
11,552

● Khakeran

Chenantu

ZABUL
PROVINCE

• Bailogh

• Sayagaz

△
12,490

Showy Rūd

△
10,119

• Qal'eh Maidan

Uruzgan Province

to Ghazni

0   5   10   15   20   25

Miles

Tarnak Rūd

Darya-ye Arghandab

to Qelat

Mizan

THE VALLEY'S EDGE

Related Titles from Potomac Books

The Other War: Winning and Losing in Afghanistan
—Amb. Ronald E. Neumann

After the Taliban: Nation-Building in Afghanistan
—Amb. James F. Dobbins

Simple Gestures: A Cultural Journey into the Middle East
—Andrea B. Rugh

THE
VALLEY'S EDGE

A YEAR WITH THE PASHTUNS IN THE
HEARTLAND OF THE TALIBAN

DANIEL R. GREEN

Foreword by AMB. RONALD E. NEUMANN (RET.)
Afterword by BRIG. GEN. H. R. MCMASTER, USA

Dish Couch,
Thanks again for all of your
help and support!
Daniel R. Green
11/4/1

Potomac Books
Washington, D.C

Library of Congress Cataloging-in-Publication Data
Green, Daniel R.
    The valley's edge : a year with the Pashtuns in the heartland of the Taliban / Daniel R. Green; foreword by Ronald E. Neumann; afterword by H. R. McMaster.—1st ed.
      p. cm.
    Includes bibliographical references and index.
    ISBN 978-1-59797-694-7 (hardcover; alk. paper)
    ISBN 978-1-59797-864-4 (electronic edition)
    1. Afghan War, 2001—Personal narratives, American. 2. Afghan War, 2001—Campaigns—Afghanistan—Uruzgan. 3. Postwar reconstruction—Afghanistan—Uruzgan. 4. Counterinsurgency—Afghanistan—Uruzgan. 5. Political stability—Afghanistan—Uruzgan. 6. Taliban. I. Title.

    DS371.413.G74 2012
    958.104'742—dc23

                                           2011023383

Potomac Books
22841 Quicksilver Drive
Dulles, Virginia 20166

First Edition

10 9 8 7 6 5 4 3 2 1

"Whom shall I send, and who will go for us?"
Then I said, "Here am I. Send me."
    —Isaiah 6:8

When you break bread with people and share their troubles and joys, the
barriers of language, of politics and of religion soon vanish. I liked them and
they liked me, that was all that mattered.
        —Julien Bryan, quoted in *Britain and the Arabs: A Study of Fifty Years,*
        1908 to 1958 by John Bagot Glubb

To enable one country to appreciate what another people really thinks and
desires is both the most difficult and the most vital task which confronts us.
        —John Bagot Glubb, *Britain and the Arabs: A Study of Fifty Years,*
        1908 to 1958

He did not expect to be looked after and rarely asked permission to do
anything. His kind of American still had a bit of the frontier in him.
        —Mark Etherington, *Revolt on the Tigris: The Al-Sadr Uprising and the*
        Governing of Iraq

It is not a question of being liberal or conservative, or soft or tough, it is a
question of being effective.
        —David Halberstam, *The Making of a Quagmire: America and Vietnam During*
        the Kennedy Era

This book is dedicated to the following:

SGT. TAMARA THURMAN,
killed in action, Pentagon, September 11, 2001

FIRST LT. LAURA M. WALKER,
killed in action, Afghanistan, August 18, 2005

STAFF SGT. CLINTON T. NEWMAN,
killed in action, Afghanistan, February 13, 2006

KERRY GREENE,
United States Agency for International Development,
who died in Germany following a brief illness
contracted in Afghanistan, May 7, 2010

And to my fellow U.S. Department of State,
USAID, and other colleagues in the field:

U.S. Embassy staff
U.S. Army Civil Affairs
Twenty-fifth Infantry
Iowa National Guard
Texas National Guard
Connecticut National Guard
Third and Seventh Special Forces Group
The Australian government
The government of Netherlands

CONTENTS

Foreword by Amb. Ronald E. Neumann (Ret.)   xi

Preface   xvii

Uruzgan Province Time Line   xxi

List of Abbreviations   xxiii

1   Welcome to the U.S. Government   1

2   Afghanistan   11

3   Uruzgan: The Heart of Asia   21

4   A Provincial Affair (Tarin Kowt—Spring 2005)   39

5   A Visit to the Green Zone (Chora—Spring 2005)   67

6   The New Regime (Tarin Kowt—Summer 2005)   79

7   Journey to Chenartu (Chora—Summer 2005)   89

8   The Thin Black Line (Tarin Kowt—Summer 2005)   95

9   Bringing Democracy to the Pashtuns (Tarin Kowt—Fall 2005)   115

10 Uruzgan's Bloody Past (Tarin Kowt—Fall 2005)   127

11   The War Returns (Tarin Kowt—Summer 2006)   147

12   The Good Samaritan (Chora—Summer 2006)   165

13   The Dutch Take Over (Tarin Kowt—Summer 2006)   177

14   Interregnum (2006–2008)   183

15   Afghanistan (2009–2011)   189

Epilogue   213

Afterword by Brig. Gen. H. R. McMaster, USA   217

Appendix A.   Tarin Kowt: Some Ideas on Leadership
              Change in Uruzgan Province   221

Appendix B.   Counterinsurgency in Uruzgan Province:
              The Political Dimension   227

Notes   235

Index   237

About the Author   245

FOREWORD

Following the collapse of the Taliban in 2001, the U.S. government adopted a new and innovative approach of bringing good governance, reconstruction, and development efforts to Afghanistan's rural countryside. In 2002 it created Provincial Reconstruction Teams (PRTs), which were combined civil-military platforms charged with partnering with local communities and Afghan officials to achieve these goals and to extend the reach of the central government. Each PRT had a U.S. military civil affairs team, a military force protection element, police mentors, a development adviser, and a diplomat. These teams brought together a number of different skills and resources to work with local residents and provincial government officials. They provided development dollars and expertise; diplomatic skills, including conflict resolution and cultural understanding; technical knowledge, such as in the fields of agriculture, construction, and engineering; political skills, like fostering government institutions and mentoring leaders; and management and policing skills, among a host of other capabilities.

The PRTs in Afghanistan were always an experiment, and they differed significantly from those later set up in Iraq. In the Iraqi case, there was an existing, although frequently inefficient, local government and the PRT's main task was to make local Iraqi structures more effective. While largely comprising members of the military, the Iraq PRTs were led by civilians and comparatively well resourced. In Afghanistan there were really no functioning local governmental structures, as the machinery of government had completely broken down after years of warfare. Competent civil servants were largely nonexistent, not only at the local level but also throughout Afghanistan, and the PRTs frequently ended up functioning as parallel governments whose resources overshadowed what the locals could do, even though the PRTs lacked the sovereign authority to govern. This was an awkward arrangement and not one with any immediate solution until the passage of years could allow Afghanistan to regrow its own cadre of educated professionals.

However, while the PRTs had more resources than the Afghan state, they were significantly underresourced for their own mission. The police advisers were extremely limited in scope and numbers. Approaches to improving governance were experimental and lacked the personnel needed to reach below the provincial level to the districts where most Afghans lived. The single State Department and United States Agency for International Development (USAID) officer in each PRT was a very light civilian presence with little funding and no support staffs. Various efforts to strengthen their numbers went largely without response during my time in Afghanistan (2005–2007) when Iraq was consuming the preponderance of Washington's attention and resources. Although I did secure approval for language training for nineteen State officers for PRTs, the lag time from establishing the positions to selecting officers and giving them a year of training meant that none of those trained ever reached Afghanistan before my departure, and Washington continued to deny additional requests for USAID provincial funding.

The work in PRTs took diplomats out of the relatively safe environment of the embassy and the normal routine of diplomatic relations and put them in harm's way in Afghanistan's countryside. Suits and ties were set aside for combat boots and dungarees, and regular meetings with urbane central government officials were replaced with illiterate tribesmen in dusty villages. These diplomats also had to work with the U.S. military to a degree not seen since the Vietnam War. The world of ambassadors and senior diplomats working with generals and admirals to craft strategy was supplemented by young diplomats partnered with sergeants and captains, and tactical considerations were the norm. For many of these officials, the threat of insurgency was a visceral reality where every dry riverbed could potentially conceal an improvised explosive device and where every looming plateau or valley edge could hide insurgent forces ready to launch an ambush. As a military veteran of the Vietnam War, I knew all too well the challenges many of our U.S. Department of State personnel were experiencing as they confronted an enemy that hid among the population and used the country's natural terrain to its advantage.

As ambassador to Afghanistan from 2005 to 2007, I came to rely upon these diplomats scattered across the country at military task forces, regional commands, and PRTs to keep me informed of local events and leaders. These officers were often the only diplomats in a whole province and served as my eyes and ears for the key challenges confronting the United States outside Kabul. They frequently gave me their complete and unvarnished views on the leading personalities of their province as well as on the obstacles to achieving the U.S. goals they confronted. I always made a point of meeting alone with the State and USAID officers in the PRTs during my weekly trips into the provinces to ensure I was getting their frank views. Their reports were snapshots of our collective effort of building a viable Afghan government that met the hopes and aspirations of its people. They also documented the growing threat of the Taliban insurgency and the effects it had on the rural communities of Afghanistan.

Too frequently, these reporting cables, as they are called in the U.S. Department of State, detailed the deteriorating security situation as previously friendly villagers became neutral or hostile, how local allies were gunned down or fled their home villages, and how the Taliban overran district centers and began to hold territory. They supplemented the broader analytical reports done in the embassy, sometimes drafted by me, that began to predict as early as the fall of 2005 the larger insurgency we would face beginning in 2006 and to the present. Unfortunately, many of these trends failed to make an impression on Washington, where the continuing violence of Iraq dwarfed the increase in Afghanistan's violence in 2006. This was dramatically illustrated when my recommendation for almost $600 million in additional economic assistance for 2006, including an additional $100 million for PRT projects, was reduced to $43 million in Washington. It was only when violence had started to decrease in Iraq that the U.S. government was jolted into action in Afghanistan.

Dan Green's personal memoir of his service with the U.S. Department of State in the Tarin Kowt PRT (2005–2006), as well as his military service with the U.S. Navy in Kabul at the U.S. Embassy (2009–2010), provides a rare and valuable look at the challenges of working in Afghanistan. His book is a story of not only his individual experiences, but also of the U.S. experience in Afghanistan as seen through the lives of the residents of Uruzgan Province from 9/11 to 2011. By focusing on two of Uruzgan's districts and three main villages, you become directly acquainted—as much as one can without being there—with the unique demands of simultaneously conducting reconstruction, development, and good governance programs while fighting an insurgency. He also documents how he and his colleagues navigated the complicated relationships they had with local officials who intermittently helped as much as hindered the achievement of their shared efforts. In recounting this work, Dan underlines the critical importance of an individual's work in a war fought at the "street level." Talented individuals who remain long enough to learn something of the local complexities are essential to success. Unfortunately, it is a lesson still largely unlearned by our short tours and rapid personnel turnover.

While I do not agree with all of Dan's criticisms of USAID and the State Department, they are valid as he saw things from the field. Many of the difficulties U.S. government civilians experienced in Afghanistan stemmed from deeper structural problems within USAID and the Department of State that continue to hamper our work in Afghanistan and elsewhere. USAID in 2008, for example, numbered only 2,200 personnel worldwide. It remains much too small for the work it is asked to do, even though in 2011 500 more personnel were added. It is also hampered by U.S. laws that make it extremely difficult to operate small programs effectively, forcing USAID to rely on expensive foreign contractors who are difficult to monitor while understaffed.

Unless and until the U.S. Congress agrees to properly staff and train USAID, it will remain incapable of supervising contractors or working rapidly and flexibly in fast-changing situations such as Afghanistan.

The State Department has grown more since the period covered in Dan's book but remains significantly understaffed. The problems he notes in recruiting temporary personnel to fill difficult field positions have many causes, but at the root is the lack of financing to build and train a permanent cadre of officers with the necessary experience. Even the best of the temporary hires, and there are many, leave after a few years, so the department loses their expertise and the knowledge they have gained. Only when Congress alters its persistent refusal to recognize that diplomacy and development work are part of national security will it be possible to address the fundamental and under-lying structural problems.

Dan's account does provides a distinct perspective on how things had changed and, regrettably, stayed the same upon his return to Afghanistan in 2009–2010. However, on my last visit to Afghanistan in 2011, I did find that the civilian-military teamwork in Kabul and the relations between the two seemed, finally, to be improving. Our nation will be better served if that trend continues.

Moreover, Dan's ability to act tactically, think strategically, and write glob-ally is a strength. His experiences of working at the Pentagon and the State Department have also broadened his perspective. He is as comfortable in a dusty Afghan village sharing lamb and rice with local tribal elders as he is with the most senior leaders of our government. Very few accounts of Afghanistan have given attention to the work of numerous civilians in the field. What they contribute and the challenges they face are widely ignored by the public at large. His book helps to fill this gap and is an important contribution to our collective understanding of the challenges of Afghanistan. It is also, in his own words, a contribution to understanding "the enduring need to remember the attacks of September 11 and to honor those victims as we seek to prevail in Central Asia."

—Amb. Ronald E. Neumann (Ret.)
President, American Academy of Diplomacy

PREFACE

The mortar round slammed into the village, announcing the presence of the Taliban, and the white-and-gray plume of smoke shot upward in a vertical column. Our Humvee was perched on a desert knoll behind and slightly to the right of the main element, keeping an eye on the flank while the sun began to set from its midday high. Within what seemed like a millisecond of the explosion, Sergeant Gibinski gunned the engine, launching the Humvee into the air as the several-ton truck leaped over dry riverbeds and hills en route to a plateau overseeing the village. We started to hear radio chatter from Captain Black, who was leading the main convoy in the valley, and as he directed our men we could hear the whoosh of rocket-propelled grenades and the clack-clack of AK-47s. Our turret gunner, Private First Class Dean, rotated his 50-caliber machine gun toward the village on the left, scanning for targets, as our vehicle anchored the high ground. Just as soon as he had set his turret, Dean dove into the Humvee, chuckling nervously. His face was beet red and beads of sweat hugged his closely cropped hair. "Man, that was close," he yelled, as he sat back up in the turret. "The bullets were all over me, buzzing my head." I told him to be careful as I passed a water bottle to him, then quickly slashed the ropes that held our ammunition boxes together. As I handed him a box, I couldn't believe this firefight was happening in a village I had passed through countless times the previous year. The war had changed since I had left seven months ago, but so had I.

The Valley's Edge is a personal memoir of my service in Afghanistan with the U.S. Department of State and the United States Navy. It is principally an account of my experiences as a political adviser to a U.S.-led Provincial Reconstruction Team (PRT) in the southern Afghanistan province of Uruzgan from 2005 to 2006 and my return to Afghanistan in 2009–2010 with the U.S. Navy. Because it is a memoir of my time at the Tarin Kowt PRT, it must inevitably give greater emphasis to my own actions, yet I could not have achieved half of what I did without the great team of people I worked with in the province. I have endeavored to write as complete and fair an account of my time in Afghanistan as possible. Although I have gained much in perspective as the years have gone by and after military service in Iraq, I realize people of good will can still have different views about the same events and their participants. Most of this book is drawn from a journal I kept, as well as from reports I drafted for the military and diplomatic cables I wrote for the U.S. ambassador. I have changed the names of some people in order to protect their identities or their reputations. When it comes to describing other people's actions and motivations, I have very consciously sought to be fair. However, as with many things in war, the consequences of bad decisions, leadership, and planning can sometimes be quite dire; therefore, I think it is important for readers to see the war as it is and not as we would like it to be. I am incredibly grateful to the dozens of friends and colleagues who generously gave their time in reviewing previous drafts of this book and making sure I saw things from as many vantage points as possible.

The opportunity to serve your country during war, whether in uniform or as a civilian, confers a special responsibility on those who have deployed, a responsibility to tell others about your experiences as forthrightly and comprehensively as possible. It is only through a better understanding of the conflict we are involved in that we can achieve victory and a safer world. The desolate patch of land that constitutes Uruzgan Province, a province on the edge of the Hindu Kush Mountains to the north and the sprawling wasteland of the Margow and Khash Deserts that dominate the south, is an excellent place to study the U.S. experience in Afghanistan. From the earliest part of the war when Hamid Karzai rallied the southern Pashtuns there against the Taliban, to the continuing challenge of safeguarding the province from repeated insurgent incursions, Uruzgan has functioned as a bellwether of U.S. efforts to prevent Afghanistan from becoming a safe haven for Islamic jihadism again. Thus, the experience of the United States in Uruzgan serves as a case study of the evolving nature of the American mission in Afghanistan and showcases how unrealistic expectations, a surface-level understanding of the Afghans, and a lack of both resources and bureaucratic imagination contributed to the resurgence of the Taliban in the area.

This memoir focuses on the villages of Tarin Kowt and Chora—the former is the capital of Uruzgan Province and the home of the governor; the latter is where the governor's main political opponent lives. One of my chief goals is to humanize the Afghan people and show how our collective work of improving their communities through good governance, reconstruction, and development activities set aside religious, ethnic, and societal differences and allowed us to see the struggle against violence and intimidation as a common one. While U.S. personnel grieved when our soldiers died, a deep sadness also enveloped us when our Afghan friends lost their lives violently. I have also tried to explore the themes of duty, courage, friendship, betrayal, selfishness, and alienation, discussing my own maturing beliefs on what service and sacrifice mean, and my general disappointment with our war strategy. I hope my colleagues at the PRT will see that I accurately reflected the collective joys and frustrations of working in Afghanistan because it is their respect and esteem that motivated me as we fought on that valley's edge several years ago in the heartland of the Taliban.

URUZGAN PROVINCE
TIME LINE

September 11, 2001	Al Qaeda attacks the United States.
November 2001	U.S. Special Forces arrive in Uruzgan Province.
January 21, 2002	Jan Mohammed Khan is appointed governor of Uruzgan Province.
Spring 2002	Provincial capital is shifted from Khas Uruzgan District to Tarin Kowt District.
July 1, 2002	A wedding is bombed in Deh Rawud District.
Summer 2002	Forward Operating Base (FOB) Tycz is established in Deh Rawud District.
March 28, 2004	Uruzgan Province is divided in two, creating a predominantly Hazara Dai Kundi Province in the north.
April 2004	Twenty-second Marine Expeditionary Unit arrives.
Summer 2004	FOB Ripley is established in Tarin Kowt.
Summer 2004	Tarin Kowt Provincial Reconstruction Team is established.
Summer 2004	Twenty-fifth Infantry Division arrives.
Fall 2004	FOB Anaconda is established in Khas Uruzgan District and FOB Cobra in Char Chena
October 9, 2004	Afghan presidential election is held.
December 22, 2004	Permanent PRT site is opened.
March 2005	Uruzgan Provincial Shura is reestablished
September 18, 2005	Provincial Council and Wolesi Jirga elections are held.
Summer 2005	Australian forces arrive in Uruzgan.
January 5, 2006	First suicide vest attack occurs.

March 2006	Jan Mohammed Khan is removed as governor of Uruzgan.
March 18, 2006	Abdul Hakim Monib is appointed governor of Uruzgan.
May 2006	Dai Kundi Province district of Gizab is given to Uruzgan.
May 1, 2006	First suicide car bomb attack takes place.
June 2006	Taliban overrun Chora District Center.
June 3, 2006	Coalition and Afghan forces repel Taliban from Chora District Center.
June 2006	Wife of Achikzai tribal leader Haji Malem Abdul Khaliq Khan is shot and blinded by Coalition Forces troops.
August 2006	Dutch forces assume control of Uruzgan.
August 2006–2010	Series of patrol bases are established throughout Tarin Kowt and Chora Districts.
December 19, 2006	Mullah Aktar Mohammed Osmani is killed by Coalition Forces air strike.
June 15–19, 2007	Taliban attempt to overrun the District Center of Chora. Dutch, Australian, and U.S. troops repulse the attack with assistance from Rozi Khan's Barakzai tribesmen. This event would eventually be called the Battle of Chora.
September 2007	Abdul Hakim Monib is removed as governor of Uruzgan.
September 2007	Asadullah Hamdam is appointed governor of Uruzgan.
May 2008	Governor Hamdam holds election for district chief of Chora. Former Provincial Police chief Rozi Khan is elected.
September 2008	Rozi Khan is accidentally killed by Australian Special Forces. His son Daoud Khan replaces him as district chief.
November 2008	Chairman Mullah Mawlawi Hamdullah resigns from the Provincial Council.
August 20, 2009	Presidential, Provincial Council, and Wolesi Jirga elections are held.
January 2010	Construction on new Provincial Council building begins.
February 2010	Taliban leader Mullah Abdul Ghani Berader is arrested in Pakistan.
March 21, 2010	Asadullah Hamdam is removed as governor of Uruzgan.
August 2010	Dutch forces depart from Uruzgan.
September 18, 2010	Wolesi Jirga elections are held.
November 2010	Daoud Khan is removed as district chief of Chora.
November 13, 2010	Rozi Khan mosque opens.
December 13, 2010	Mohammed Omar Shirzad appointed governor of Uruzgan.
March 25, 2011	New mosque in Sar Marghab opens.
May 1, 2011	Al Qaeda leader Osama bin Laden is killed.
July 17, 2011	Former Uruzgan governor Jan Mohammed Khan is assassinated in Kabul along with Uruzgan member of parliament Mohammed Hashim Watanwall.

ABBREVIATIONS

ACM	Anti-coalition Militia
ACS	Afghans for Civil Society
AHP	Afghan Highway Police (deactivated, redesigned in 2007)
AMF	Afghan Militia Force
ANA	Afghan National Army
ANDS	Afghan National Development Strategy
ANP	Afghan National Police
ANSF	Afghan National Security Forces (i.e., ANA, ANP, and NDS)
AO	Area of Operations
AOR	Area of responsibility
APC	Armored personnel carrier
ARG	Afghan Reconstruction Group
ASF	Afghan Security Force
BAF	Bagram Air Field
BDA	Battle damage assessment
BUB	Battle update brief
CA	Civil affairs; civic action
CADG	Central Asia Development Group
CAFE	Compound across from embassy
CAT	Civil Affairs Team
CERP	Commander's Emergency Response Program
CF	Coalition Forces

CFT   Cross-functional team
CIA   Central Intelligence Agency
CIVCAS   Civilian casualties
CJSOTF   Combined Joint Special Operations Task Force
CMOC   Civil Military Operations Center
CO   Commanding officer
COIN   Counterinsurgency
CONOP   Concept of operations
COP   Chief of police
DFAC   Dining facility
DDP   District Delivery Program
DDR   Disarmament, Demobilization, and Reintegration
DIAG   Disarmament (alt., Disbanding) of illegally armed groups
DST   District Support Team
EOD   Explosive ordnance disposal
ETT   Embedded Training Team
FAO   Foreign Affairs Officer
FOB   Forward Operating Base
FRAGO   Fragmentation order
FSO   Foreign Service Officer
GIRoA   Government of the Islamic Republic of Afghanistan
GOA   Government of Afghanistan (later GIRoA)
HA   Humanitarian assistance
IC   International community; intelligence community
IDC   Information Dominance Center
IDF   Indirect fire
IDLG   Independent Directorate for Local Governance
IED   Improvised explosive device
IJC   International Security Assistance Force Joint Command
IPA   Interagency Provincial Affairs
ISAF   International Security Assistance Force
JCMB   Joint Coordination and Monitoring Board
JEMBS   Joint Electoral Management Body Secretariat
KAF   Kandahar Air Field
KAIA   Kabul Area International Airport
KBR   Kellogg, Brown and Root
KIA   Kabul International Airport (later KAIA)
KLE   Key leader engagement

KTD	Key terrain district
MEDCAP	Medical civil affairs project
MJ	Meshrano Jirga (House of Elders; upper house of Afghan parliament)
MOD	Ministry of Defense
MOI	Ministry of Interior
MRAP	Mine-resistant ambush-protected
NATO	North Atlantic Treaty Organization
NDS	National Directorate of Security
NGO	Nongovernmental organization
ODA	Operational Detachment Alpha
OGA	Other government agency
OSD	Office of the Secretary of Defense
PRT	Provincial Reconstruction Team
QIP	Quick Impact Program
QRF	Quick Reaction Force
RC	Regional Command
SF	Special Forces (U.S. Army)
SOF	Special Operations Forces
SOIC	Stability Operations Information Center
SVBIED	Suicide vehicle-borne improvised explosive device
TB	Taliban
TCAPF	Tactical Conflict Assessment and Planning Framework
TF	Task Force
TIC	Troops in contact
TOC	Tactical Operations Center
TTP	Tactics, techniques, and procedures
UN	United Nations
UNAMA	United Nations Assistance Mission in Afghanistan
USAID	United States Agency for International Development
USDA	United States Department of Agriculture
USFOR-A	U.S. Forces–Afghanistan
USO	United Service Organization
VBIED	Vehicle-borne improvised explosive device
WJ	Wolesi Jirga (House of the People; lower house of Afghan parliament)
XO	Executive Officer

1 WELCOME TO THE U.S. GOVERNMENT

I believe that the pulse of government should be strong and steady, and the men at the helm imbued with missionary zeal.

—Philippine president Ramon Magsaysay, whose government successfully defeated the Huk Communist insurgency in the Philippines in the 1950s

I joined the Bush administration on Wednesday, January 24, 2001. I was twenty-four years old at the time and showed up at the Metro entrance to the Pentagon wearing the only suit I had other than one I still owned from high school. Full of excitement about the opportunities that awaited at the Pentagon, I had the zeal that could only come from having worked on a hard-fought political campaign. For the last year I had been working seven days a week at the Republican National Committee as a researcher studying environmental and small business issues and helping with the odd assortment of research tasks that presidential campaigns inevitably bring. During the last month of the 2000 presidential campaign, I returned to my home state of Florida and helped manage the get-out-the-vote effort in Broward County, eventually participating in the recount effort. The whole experience had been searing, and my generally balanced nature had become markedly more partisan. After landing a temporary job as the director of archives for the Inaugural Committee in December, I had been told to expect a job sometime in the middle of the next year. To my surprise, I received a very welcome call from the transition team on January 19 informing me that I had received a political appointment and should report to the Pentagon the following week. When I showed up at the Department of Defense on that cold Wednesday morning, I felt that I had gone through a crash course in national-level politics, was a somewhat-savvy political operator albeit still quite young, and strongly supported the president's goals for the country and the department. I considered myself extremely fortunate to be working with an obviously experienced administration and with a secretary of defense whom I admired as a serious and thoughtful person.

The other young appointees and I settled into the Transition Office, which was a recently converted cafeteria, and began helping the senior leaders vet resumes by doing background research on prospective appointees. In the interim, I purchased three new suits, started taking my first courses for a PhD in political science at George Washington University, and set about learning what exactly was available for me at the Pentagon. Most everyone told me that I should try to get a job in what was called "Policy" or "OSD Policy," which stood for Office of the Secretary of Defense (Policy), because, as one person put, it was the "little State Department." After interviewing around, I eventually ended up as an "action officer" in OSD Policy, which is a fancy way of saying I was the lead person for my portfolio, which was nuclear nonproliferation policy. I was in charge of reading government messages, staying abreast of issues at the International Atomic Energy Agency, participating in interagency meetings with the U.S. Department of State, and providing support to my boss in the form of writing read-aheads for meetings, drafting talking points, and providing advice. When I think back to that time, I was clearly over my head; the closest colleague in age was at least forty to forty-five. But I tried my best to know the issues, learn what I could from my coworkers, and avoid the watchful eye of my boss who was quite quick to point out my deficiencies. From January to when I finally received my permanent political job in September, I managed to begin my graduate studies, navigate the shoals of finding a new job, and get an issue area that was interesting. The adrenaline of working on the campaign had dissipated by this stage, and the slow rhythm of government had become my routine.

When American Airlines Flight 77 slammed into the Pentagon on September 11, 2001, I was sitting at my desk in room 4A873 watching the attacks take place in New York on CNN. The shock wave that coursed through the building felt like a quiet rumble, as if the building had exhaled after a deep breath. I quickly ran to the window with my colleagues because our office spaces looked into the courtyard of the Pentagon, and we saw the fireball and smoke from the flight spill over the top of the wall directly across from our office. I ran back to my desk and called my best friend, telling him "they" had hit the Pentagon and I was getting out. We then rapidly filed into the hallway, joining the mass of people making their way to the opposite side of the building. One employee was crying uncontrollably, saying another plane was on the way, which added to the sense of pandemonium. We eventually made our way outside, near the Metro entrance, and I circled around the building to my right, winding my way through the parked cars to see the damage. People were desperately trying to call their families; because I didn't have a cell phone, I started to make my way up to the Sheraton Hotel that overlooked the Pentagon from a nearby hill, hoping to find a pay phone. As I neared the highway that ran by the Pentagon's western side, I finally made out the billowing scar that the plane had carved into the building. Someone in the crowd called for all of the military personnel to line up and push people back from the site. At that, I crossed the road, made my way up the side of an underpass, and sat down to take in all of what had happened.

As I sat there, I felt an amazing sense of detachment from the whole experience, as if I was watching a movie of the events I had just experienced. The lights of the emergency vehicles were flashing and people were rushing around as the black, acrid smoke continued to pour from the building. There was also a strange silence and sense of calm that descended upon me, and then I realized, with a start, that I hadn't yet called my family to tell them I was still alive. I pulled myself up, managed to get back on the road to the Sheraton, and joined a group of people climbing the hill.

The line to the pay phones proved far too long at the hotel, but a woman I had worked with, and who I had the good fortune of running into, offered to give me a ride home just as soon as her daughter was able to get through the traffic. I fell in with her group and we sat in a small eatery a further ways up the road, watching the news reports of the day's momentous events. Nearly two hours after the attack, I was able to call my parents on a pay phone near the restaurant. My mom sounded strangely stoic but was clearly relieved I was still alive. We spoke for a few minutes and I told her my plans to wait out the mayhem at a friend's house in Alexandria, to which I had an extra set of keys. I then rejoined the group, and not too long after the woman's daughter showed up and graciously drove me to my friend's apartment. Collapsing into his easy chair with the lights out and the blinds drawn, I felt grateful for the networks' twenty-four-hour coverage, and simply let the day's events sink in.

I had been so focused on the immediacy of what was happening around me, it was only then, in the quiet of the apartment, that I could reflect on what it all meant for the country and for me. We had been attacked. It is simple to write but psychologically more difficult to understand. The last time I had ever associated those words with an event in my life, it was tied to my grandfather's service in World War II. The attack aroused in me an unfettered sense of patriotism and singleness of purpose. We had to not only punish those who had killed our fellow Americans but had to so thoroughly decimate them that they would know what it meant to constantly feel the fear of looming death. It is an emotion I still feel strongly, and no words can really capture its animating energy.

On September 12, I arrived at the Pentagon ready for the new day in a new world that had changed in less than twenty-four hours. As I stepped off the Metro at the Pentagon stop, I could feel the eyes of my fellow passengers bearing down upon my back and could almost hear their questions: What is going on in the building? Did that man know anyone who had been killed? What will we do? I was returning to work but it was also a crime scene, a symbol of a new era, and the last resting place of more than two hundred Americans. I flashed my badge to the new soldiers who lined the Metro exit and made my way back to my office. A thin film of soot covered the hallway and my office was among the last still manned; a no-man's-land had been declared from the eighth corridor where I worked forward to the impact site between the third and fifth corridors. I dropped off my things and slowly walked to the side that had been struck by the plane. A few corridors later, the hallways became dark, and small driblets of water fell from the ceiling. A string of soldiers lined the hallway and dirt that had been tracked in from the courtyard formed small clumps of mud. I looked down the corridor I had walked down numerous times before when I had worked in the army for a few months as a civilian. It was now a dark and lifeless concrete tomb. The slow dripping of water and the darkness created a strange sense of isolation, even though pictures of this building were being flashed across the television screens of billions of people. It was a disquieting feeling to simultaneously be alone and yet completely known by the entire world. I finally returned to my office, noticing all of the sign-in sheets on the doors indicating a time and date for September 11 but no signature or record of exiting, and saw a series of white body bags lining the center of the building. I couldn't tell if they had been used yet but they reminded me of a row of white tombstones at Arlington National Cemetery, waiting for their final cargo.

Little did I know that within a week of the attacks and half a world away, a Pashtun tribal chief named Hamid Karzai would motorcycle across the desert from Quetta, Pakistan, to a small village named Tarin Kowt in the middle of Afghanistan seeking to spark a Pashtun uprising and how it would directly impact my life. In the interim, I hungrily followed the news of our military campaign, hoping that I would have a chance to participate in some manner.

As the weeks passed, the deadly toll of the Pentagon attack became more evident as the final list of victims was compiled. One name stuck out: Sgt. Tamara Thurman. I instantly remembered her from the transition team where she had worked—a convivial data entry specialist helping the team collect, organize, and process resumes for high-level positions at the Pentagon. Her name would be the first of many I would come to know in the years ahead, of people killed in the global war on terror. I felt extremely fortunate to be at the epicenter of our country's response to this war of my generation. I also believed that Secretary Rumsfeld and President Bush were the right men to relentlessly pursue those who had attacked us and that collectively the administration had the right mix of experience, savvy, wisdom, and determination to prevail in the new conflict.

At the same time, I felt disconnected from the war and now sought a means of contributing to it in a meaningful way. While I had already begun the process of joining the military, the terms of the program would keep me away from the front lines for at least two years. Additionally, the opportunity to witness my country's response firsthand at the Pentagon was a once-in-a-lifetime chance that I couldn't pass up. As the Taliban resistance collapsed and the war in Afghanistan seemed to end altogether more quickly than I had anticipated, I felt I had lost my chance to participate I never imagined that my way to war would come through the heart of American diplomacy, the U.S. Department of State.

In October 2003 I started work at State, hoping to expand my experiences in the federal government. I was still working in the nonproliferation policy field and had added disarmament and arms control to my portfolio, and I was happy to experience a different part of the government and serve in a somewhat higher position. While the work was certainly more interesting, I was still hoping to get overseas to Afghanistan. Not long after I arrived, a colleague, Michael Coulter, mentioned he was going to Afghanistan for six months to work with a Provincial Reconstruction Team as their political adviser. The PRT, as I soon learned, focused on working with local government officials to help them develop their capabilities as part of a general good governance effort and to conduct reconstruction and development projects. The idea was immediately intriguing to me because it seemed like the easiest way to get overseas, sounded like a rewarding job, and appeared well within my abilities. After Mike returned, full of stories and pictures of Afghanistan, he walked me down to the Afghan Desk and introduced me to Todd Wilson, a retired U.S. Army colonel and West Point graduate working for State. I told Todd I wanted to work in the worst place, from a security perspective, they needed someone and Mike spoke well of my qualifications. Once a decision had been made, Todd sent me an e-mail a few days later saying he needed someone in a province called Uruzgan where we had a PRT in their capital, Tarin Kowt.

Todd then put me in touch with the current state adviser, a man named Frank Light. Frank was a senior foreign service officer who had completed a previous tour in Afghanistan with the Peace Corps and a stint in Jalalabad Province and he was finishing up a three-month tour as the first DOS adviser in Uruzgan. Frank was, as I came to appreciate, always upbeat and positive, and he now focused on helping set up a colleague for success. He wrote me on November 13, 2004:

Dan—

A future welcome to Tarin Kot! You got me on my way home, so this will be a short one. I'll send more when I am home. Living conditions that had been the hardest of any PRT (at least any that had a State rep) will soon get far better as the PRT moves to its new site, probably in the next week or two. By the time you get there construction should be just about done. Official opening tentatively set for Dec. 8. As the first State rep there, I was in country for just 90 days (the max my family allowed), repeating what I did a year ago in the then PRT-to-be in Jalalabad. Great experience in both places. You will have an USAID rep—Kerry Greene. Green and Greene. Just so it's not green on green [this means Afghan on Afghan violence]. In addition to the PRT, the 2-5 battalion of the 25th ID (infantry division) is headquartered right next door to your new location. Like the PRT, they have been very helpful. When I catch my breath, I will try to forward you messages that are still on my system. In Tarin Kot I left you a hard copy of my reporting plus a CD of a farewell Powerpoint and an 18-page description of local officials. A new issue will be possible cutoff of QIP (quick impact project) aid moneys and possible cutoff of CERP (commander's emergency relief program) for police support. Your work will definitely be cut out for you. That's what makes it so much fun. Please keep sending the questions. I'm glad to respond. Best regards, Frank.

You couldn't ask for a warmer or better introduction to the province and the work. Frank wrote me again on November 16:

Dan—
As I noted, living conditions will change considerably when the PRT moves to its own site later this month. We have been living in tents. The new site will have hard-walled barracks with rooms in them. You will probably share a room with the USAID rep. Possibly you might get your own room. Internet/email was out quite a bit while I was there, sometimes for days at a time. Even when it [was] up, it was slooooow. State/USAID will put in our own system soon; certainly it should be in before you arrive. Commo should be more reliable, and the Net should be much faster.

While I was there we had no running water, no hot water. You will have both at the new site. Almost everybody did their laundry by hand in plastic buckets; Kerry and I lived it up and sent our laundry with an interpreter into town for $5 a load. Quality was not the best.

The best thing of all about the new site (just a kilometer away) is you will be out of the dust. The dust was really bad. You and your equipment never got clean.

I stayed there the whole time except when arriving and departing. The new PRT air service greatly facilitates travel. I left Tarin Kot on that. A C-12, it took me directly back to Kabul, after stops in Farah, Herat, and

Bagram. PRT commanders conference happen about 3 times a year and give a good excuse to go to Kabul and Bagram. If you sign up for a year, you know [sic] get those nice two R&Rs/consultations in the States.

You should be supplied with a vest, helmet, Thuraya [satellite phone], cell phone (which I never used), laptop, printer, memory stick, and digital camera. I brought my own laptop too for own stuff and for downloading personal photos. I also brought my own camera and videocam.

Security is an issue. Greatest danger is IED, then RPGs, then small arms, then stray 107 rockets. That said, I was never shot at this time, and IEDs are a working hazard Coalition Forces do what they can to mitigate. During the time I was there two 25th ID guys were killed and four were wounded seriously enough that they are now in Walter Reed or Trippler. No American from the PRT was hurt, though two Afghans members in a PRT convoy were injured by an IED. The soldiers (PRT and 2-5) will take very good care of you as they did of me. They're smart; they're good. And 99% of the people are friendly. They will deal with you if for no other reason because you represent a rich and powerful country. And most of them like us. In my view, it is important we keep the numbers of US personnel down to keep that positive image. The 2-5 is doing that by spreading itself thin but not too thin. Then the PRT fills in some of the gaps. All the best, Frank.

Frank's e-mails mentioned dust, violence, death, friendly people, great colleagues, and a lot of meaningful work; you couldn't ask for anything more. I couldn't believe my luck—I would have a chance to work in this province of Afghanistan, away from D.C. and its bureaucracy and the often-petty agendas. Before I began my tour, I had one last hurdle to overcome: I had to secure the approval of my immediate supervisor.

Following the president's reelection, I approached my boss telling him about my desire to serve in Afghanistan for a six-month stint. Instead of getting the heartfelt support I expected, the first thing he said was, "How is this in my self-interest?" Momentarily stunned, I responded that Secretary Powell had asked for volunteers and that I was sure he would get credit for helping out. He went on to lecture me about missing out on an opportunity to move up in the arms control world and possibly getting a job on Capitol Hill where I could rewrite the nation's export laws. He also wondered why I wanted to

be, as he put it, "some Lawrence of Arabia." Following this painful experience, he finally agreed to let his subordinate decide my fate. Thankfully, his
subordinate was fully supportive, but I had found my boss's attitude par for
the course for too many people in D.C. who focused narrowly on their personal power and not the greater mission. It was a tragedy to see such a short-
sighted view in such a senior leader, but Afghanistan beckoned and I was on
my way to see it.

2   AFGHANISTAN

To enable one country to appreciate what another people really thinks and
desires is both the most difficult and the most vital task which confronts us.
    —John Bagot Glubb, *Britain and the Arabs: A Study of Fifty Years, 1908–1958*[1]

As our white up-armored van pulled out of Kabul International Airport
(KIA) toward the long stretch of road leading to the U.S. Embassy in late
January 2005, the full reality of what I had signed up for rushed in. A multistory photo of Tajik leader Ahmad Shah Masoud, who had been killed by
Al Qaeda on September 9, 2001, dominated the front of the control tower,
and as our vehicle pulled away, we passed a Soviet MiG fighter jet tilted skyward on a pedestal, a silent reminder of the Soviet-Afghan War. Along the 2.5
km road to the embassy, I could see the Afghans going about their business
on the street, frequenting the numerous shops that lined the route, and the
full grittiness of urban Kabul pressed in with its trash piles, damaged buildings, and traffic congestion on full display. The stores were a collection of
small food kiosks, auto shops, pharmacies, eateries, and women's clothing
stores. We passed Maihan Gym, with its larger-than-life pictures of two
bodybuilders above the front; the Sabawoon Steel Works; Hashmatullah
Blacksmith; and the Duanyai Learning Center, where, later in the year, I
would see pupils milling about its front doors, waiting for school to begin.

11

A mix of Afghans walked the street, some in Western clothing, others in turbans and *shalwar kamis* (traditional Afghan male clothing), and several wore some combination of both. The women were also dressed in a variety of clothing styles, including the ubiquitous blue *burka* along with more modern, conservatively cut outfits. I noticed a small pack of girls wearing white head scarves and black dresses with multicolored school bags dangling off their backs, their innocent wanderings a stark contrast to the shabbiness of the buildings, shops, and vehicles. Our convoy lurched around the traffic and whipped past the Masoud Traffic Circle, a giant reddish obelisk memorial to the great Tajik leader, at a fast clip, finally ending at the closed-off street that split the U.S. Embassy's grounds. A thick gate was rolled back and our vehicles drove into the courtyard where a few Marines were standing guard behind a makeshift wood-and-sandbag outpost. The grounds were covered in slush and snow and the Kabul air, full of wood smoke, smog, and dust, permeated our nostrils as we stepped out of our enclosed vehicle. The old U.S. Embassy loomed over us and on each of its corners, sandbagged observation posts looked out. As I grabbed my two sea-bags and backpacks and moved to in-processing, I thought to myself, "This is exactly what I want." I also felt that my background had prepared me well for this experience, whatever it chose to throw at me.

After I stashed my bags, I started to get my bearings around the embassy's compound. The main embassy was a squat, two-story building with marble steps and was covered in white stones, now faded from Kabul's dust and pollution. A large metallic U.S. crest sat atop the main arched entrance, and two Hesco wire baskets filled with dirt flanked the walkway into the building, adding a nice tactical edge to the diplomatic setting. The main foyer was covered in black marble, and Marine guards stood behind a protective booth. Following the 1979 killing of U.S. ambassador Adolph Dubs and the Soviet invasion later that year, the U.S. government had had no official diplomatic representation in Afghanistan; the chargé d'affaires resided outside of the country from 1979 to 2002. The embassy had largely remained abandoned since 1989 following the departure of Soviet troops and when fighting surged between various mujahedeen factions around Kabul. From that point until 2001, the building and compound had been largely unoccupied, ably maintained by local staff who eked out a living as Kabul was slowly destroyed. Although the building had been effectively abandoned, no Taliban had ever set foot inside it or on the grounds of the embassy in general. As I walked around the corridors, the building felt shabby chic (without the chic) and smelled like an old, mothballed battleship. But it had character and a reliable sturdiness that had obviously stood the challenges of the past few decades. Every so often, I'd see reminders of a bygone era. In one room I noticed a photo of Secretary of State George Schulz; in another, a picture of former vice president Spiro Agnew; and, along a hallway, a formal portrait of President Nixon. I eventually came across a slightly off-center pencil drawing of Ambassador Dubs hanging off a nail in the basement, his smile beaming from a better time. The embassy definitely felt like a wartime diplomatic post, which set the mood for my deployment and felt strangely comfortable.

I finally settled into a shipping-container apartment or "hooch" that was quite nice in light of where we were. It had its own shower and bathroom, a couple of beds, desk and chairs, and a television set. It was certainly more than I had expected. I also had a roommate, another DOS Political Officer on his way to the PRT in Gardez, Paktia on the border with Pakistan. His name was Tim Timmons, a retired U.S. Army major who had recently done a tour in Wasit Province, Iraq, in a similar position.[2] He was tall and athletic with a brown beard, and had a strong, leadership presence. He was cooling his heels after having come back from leave and was waiting for the snow to be cleared from the roads leading to his province. He had already made two attempts to get there in the last several days but had had no luck. After retiring from the military, Tim had joined the Foreign Service and did a year punching passports in Islamabad before heading to Iraq for a year. He was definitely not your typical Department of State officer and I admired his background and dedication. Tim was scheduled to be in Afghanistan for a year and he heartily encouraged me to work for a year as well. Based on the few stories he shared and the nature of the work, I definitely entertained the thought.

I eventually made my way around the embassy, meeting officials from the consular section, the political section, and the United States Agency for International Development (USAID). I eventually sat down with George White, who was the head of the PRT Section at the embassy and my boss. George bore a striking resemblance to Gustav "Gust" Avrakotos from *Charlie Wilson's War* by George Crile, with a little bit of Albert Einstein thrown in for good measure. He and I had shared a flight to Afghanistan and he was more than keen to make sure I was taken care of and well prepared. George issued me a blue bulletproof vest, a black helmet, a satellite phone, and a Tough Book computer. He also went over his general expectations of what I needed to report on and some tips on how to work with the military, which he provided to me in a draft "PRT Handbook." Since George had once been a magazine editor, he gave me some great advice on writing tight, cogent reports from the field, focused on informing policymakers in Washington, D.C. I was keen to do my best and hoped to meet his high expectations.

A lot of the staff at the compound referred to the PRTers, as we were collectively known, as "pretty much loners who appear to be well-adjusted." I would say that described me quite accurately, as it did the few PRTers who were hanging around the embassy waiting for a flight or convoy. Besides Tim, there was Jim Hunter, who was working in Asadabad and was a reservist in the Virginia National Guard. Jim had done ten years of service in hardship posts in Africa. He also had the unusual distinction of having been in a firefight, which gave him some street cred with the military and an unusual aura among State officers. Gene Del Bianco, who had been working in Zabul Province in the south, was a lieutenant colonel in the U.S. Army Reserves and had survived an improvised explosive device (IED) that had hit the vehicle in front of his car. These were "men's men" and were examples I wanted to emulate. Some of their tips and guidance were all too useful to me. They once had a spirited debate over the best place to sit in a Humvee in order to survive an IED strike, and counseled me on where to go in a firefight and what I needed to do to help out our military colleagues. I took a lot of mental notes and hoped I would perform to standard if called on.

The compound across from the embassy—or CAFE side—as it was called, was where most everyone lived. It was a collection of hooches and a chow hall and the offices there were a series of interlocking shipping containers modified into "modern" workspaces. Besides State and USAID, the Afghan Reconstruction Group was there as well, a Pentagon-funded outfit of private sector advisers working with the central ministries of Afghanistan. The group was led by Martin Hoffman, who had once served as the U.S. Secretary of the Army during the Ford administration and was a close confidant of Secretary of Defense Rumsfeld. While I thought the idea of the Afghan Reconstruction Group was good, the organization was universally loathed by many of the embassy personnel, who either saw it as a "Rumsfeld thing" or objected to its charter, which they viewed as being in competition with their work. As always, the bureaucratic battles of D.C. had found a place to play out overseas. Over the next few days as my body adjusted to the 9.5-hour time zone change, I worked with George to figure out how I could get to Tarin Kowt. George had e-mailed the PRT commander, a Lt. Col. William LaFontaine, and had put me in touch with him. He was very supportive of my coming out and said an office and hooch were all ready for me. The great challenge of leaving Kabul was the snow, which had fallen in huge amounts that month. After several abortive attempts to fly out of KIA, George managed to arrange a ride for me to Bagram Air Field, a forty-five-minute drive north of Kabul.

As our convoy left Kabul, small smokestacks jutted out from the collection of adobe homes and ramshackle dwellings. Their billowing smoke indicated an active home brick factory feeding the construction boom in the city. Once we had left the outskirts of Kabul, the snow-white Shomali Plain opened up with the black road slinking its way across the gentle hills. Every so often we would see an abandoned home with its roof missing and windows and doors gone. Each one of them had a neon orange "X" spray-painted on it indicating, as I soon learned, that it had been cleared of landmines.

We eventually came to the sprawling Bagram base and I was deposited into transient housing near the flight line. The base had served as a major lifeline for Soviet troops in the 1980s—they had used a nearby highway from Tajikistan to deliver supplies to the base and Kabul. The road went very close to Ahmad Shah Masoud's home in the Panjshir Valley, and road traffic had frequently been a target for his men to attack. However, there was also talk that Masoud had colluded with the Soviets to protect the overland route in return for money and materiel support. Regardless, the small military city that was Bagram was a sight to behold. It was one of the few places where the military had to return salutes and it had a giant Post Exchange (PX) as well as a number of offices and headquarters staffs. The presence of a Pizza Hut and Burger King also added to the surreal out-of-country atmosphere that military bases can create. Much of the runway was still the original Soviet construction with rectangular metal plates laid down to form a flat surface. I eventually got on a list for a C-17 flight to Kandahar and cooled my heels in the passenger lounge. Construction had begun for a

United Services Organization (USO) center named after Pat Tillman, the famous NFL player who had joined the service and was killed by friendly fire in 2004. I admired his devotion to his country as well as his conscious choice to avoid the spotlight while he served. While I felt a USO lounge didn't seem to be the most appropriate way to honor him, I was glad the effort had been made. A few days later, I departed for Kandahar and landed at the airport on February 13, in the middle of the night.

Kandahar City is the center of gravity in southern Afghanistan and was the spiritual headquarters of the Taliban movement when it formed in the early 1990s. Taliban leader Mullah Omar famously took the Prophet Muhammad's cloak from a shrine in the city, becoming the "Commander of the Faithful," and led the Taliban movement to victories across the country. In the 1980s, Kandahar Air Field (KAF) was the central supply hub for the Soviets in the south but now it was a jumble of trashed Soviet planes and Hinds, helicopters made famous by the movies *Rambo III* and *Red Dawn*, shoved aside and forgotten. Unlike Bagram, KAF felt more like a war zone and, with the fighting going on in the south, its reverberations were felt directly at KAF every day. I had hoped to fly out the next day, but a commanders conference was being planned and Lt. Colonel LaFontaine; his executive officer, Maj. John Dayton; and their USAID adviser, Kerry Greene, were on their way from Tarin Kowt to attend the conference and stop by the Post Exchange. A slight rain came down as I found a hooch to crash in and the talcum powder dust of KAF became an unmanageable muck that stuck to my boots and sucked my feet into the mud. I fell asleep that evening knowing I was closer to my final destination.

The next morning, the bright sun stood in stark contrast to the chilly temperature. I zipped my fleece higher to keep the breeze out and leaped between islands of crushed rock and long trails of mud en route to the showers. The airfield was a collection of makeshift wooden huts and field tents with a couple of chow halls, and the familiar smell of KBR bacon, eggs, sausages, and pancakes beckoned me. The main flight line had the only "permanent" buildings at KAF. A giant PX, like a small Walmart, anchored a shopping area, and the ubiquitous Burger King, Pizza Hut, and Green Beans Coffee surrounded a covered boardwalk. Two small, circular huts that looked like Smurf homes anchored the square, offering tourist trinkets and fake tomahawks. They sat next to several smaller stores containing a dry cleaner and tailor.

The main airport, which had existed for several decades since the United States built it in the 1950s, was a stone's throw from the PX, and it looked eerily similar to the desert dwellings in the original *Star Wars* with its bright yellow pastel dominating the subdued building. Its large, gaping arches looked like the tops of church organ pipes. As I walked around the base, I eventually arrived at "The Taliban's Last Stand," a large, gaping hole in the room of a building where the insurgents had resisted the U.S. takeover in 2001. It now had a large flagpole jutting out its center; the carbon scorch marks of the bomb that had struck it framed the silver pole's ascent to the sky. With a few dollars at the PX, you too could have your flag run up the pole and a certificate printed for posterity. It was an otherworldly tourist attraction and its name proved only too wrong just a year later. Over the next few days I stopped by the various military offices, munched on some pizza, and visited the local bazaar.

On February 18, I attended the Regional Command–South Commanders Conference led by Maj. General Olson and Colonel Pedersen; the latter was commander of the southern area of operations. All of the PRT commanders, maneuver commanders, and interagency staff from the State Department and USAID were there to get briefs on the situation, to share best practices, and to do some shopping at the PX. I quickly met my PRT commander, Lt. Colonel LaFontaine, Major Dayton, and USAID representative Kerry Greene. I also got a chance to finally meet Lt. Col. Terry Sellers who was in charge of the Twenty-fifth Infantry Battalion headquartered at Forward Operating Base (FOB) Ripley in Tarin Kowt, the provincial capital of Uruzgan Province.

In general, many in the group were quite optimistic about what had been accomplished since the current unit rotated in, and much of the conversation focused on reconstruction and development. General Olson stressed the need to separate the guerrillas from the population, which seemed sensible, and said the key was to view security and development as linked. A happy population that views its future in a hopeful manner is less likely to support the Taliban or any other forces opposed to the Afghan National Government. He also emphasized the need to focus on enabling Afghan institutions and transitioning them to independence. He stated that while the Taliban was still a concern, he was confident U.S. forces had sufficiently decimated their middle-level commanders and isolated their top-level leaders so that they were not a viable large-scale threat. General Olson also stated that the Taliban were unable to mount coordinated, broad-scale operations in the South. Each PRT and maneuver unit commander delivered a briefing to the group about security operations, development projects, and views on provincial and district leaders. They used matrixes to convey the information, color-coded green, yellow, and red to indicate different levels of security, governance, and cooperation, among a bunch of other subjects. The meeting greatly improved my understanding of the whole southern area and as it broke up, I was anxious to talk with Lt. Colonels LaFontaine and Sellers, Major Dayton, and Kerry.

Lt. Colonel LaFontaine stood at an impressive six feet, eight inches and was a Green Beret who had served in Special Forces for sixteen years before transferring to the civil affairs community in 1997. He was incredibly relaxed and extremely happy to meet me, and said he was looking forward to getting me out to Tarin Kowt. He spoke glowingly of his close relationship with my predecessor, Frank Light, saying, "I learned a lot from that man." His executive officer, Major Dayton, was a gregarious, jovial, and easy-going reservist who, in his civilian life, worked in the concrete business. He had a thin mustache, wore wire-rimmed glasses, and had a ready smile. Lt. Colonel Sellers was a sharp commander originally from Waterloo, Iowa, and was in charge of providing security in the province. Of medium height, he was a West Point graduate and always seemed to have the green U.S. Army notebook in his hand. He was tough and focused and seemed to get along well with LaFontaine. Kerry was my comrade-in-arms in the land of the military and my USAID counterpart. He sported a thick brown beard and a full mane of hair. With his sunglasses on and his six-foot, two-inch presence, he looked suspiciously like an intelligence agent. But Kerry was a laid-back southern California surfer who had followed the waves to Indonesia, where he lived with his wife and son after having converted to Islam to marry her. I would learn later that Kerry owned a bar called "The Green Room," so named after the space that is created when a wave is perfectly formed, and had an extraordinary ability to watch a surfing video and tell you exactly what country the wave had been filmed in. He also bore an uncanny resemblance to "the Dude" in the movie *The Big Lebowski*, both in his appearance and in his mannerisms. All of these men looked like great partners, and I was looking forward to getting to know them better. After the conference we went our separate ways for the day but pledged to meet for dinner that evening. In the next day or two we'd depart for Uruzgan, but in the meantime they wanted to do some serious shopping at the Post Exchange, frequent the selection of fast food joints, and unwind a bit. I looked forward to our trip and the challenges of Uruzgan.

3 URUZGAN:
THE HEART OF ASIA

This is first a political war, second a psychological war, and third a military war.
—Lt. Gen. Lewis Walt, USMC, on Vietnam (February 1967)

As our cargo plane approached Uruzgan and the great desert sea of browns and khakis interspersed with brief mountain peaks and gnarled hills passed beneath us, the plane began a quick and tortuous dive, circling sharply to the left. Because I was on the left side of the plane I didn't initially see Tarin Kowt to my right as we approached Forward Operating Base Ripley from the south. However, as the plane began to dive and fly in increasingly tighter circles in a downward spiral, I briefly caught furtive glances of the provincial capital: a flash of green on one rotation, a bit of a white façade of some building on another, and a quick bit of blue from the river before we landed with a thud on the dusty landing strip of Ripley. As we taxied to the vehicles awaiting us, I looked out of the circular window and could make out the Hesco walls of the forward operating base, surrounded by a carpet of crushed rock; this would be my new home for the next several months. A few trucks were driving around, khaki dust trails billowing up behind them and the temperature was cool. The refreshing change of altitude and general lack of people at the base invigorated me after having been cooped up in the plane with all of our gear and suffering through being too close to the flag pole at Regional Command–South.

As our Humvees bumped along the flight line, they kicked up the ever-present talcum-powder desert of Afghanistan, and the squat, cylindrical two-story guardhouses that anchored each corner of the Tarin Kowt Provincial Reconstruction Team appeared overhead. A six-foot-deep antivehicle ditch surrounded the base's walls, and the land twenty to thirty feet immediately beyond it was covered in interlocking concertina wire to delay a foot assault. Within the ten-acre base were several one-story buildings in an L-shape, the longest side running parallel to the longer part of the rectangular perimeter that faced the town of Tarin Kowt. The trucks dropped me off at a white, one-story adobe building with high ceilings. After stowing my gear and securing a cot, I made my way over to Lt. Colonel LaFontaine's office, noticing a concrete mortar bunker to my right and that crushed rock had replaced the baby powder dust of the road. The doors to the tactical operations center (TOC) were red-painted sheet metal with a small latch, and the building was constructed of brick, mortar, and adobe, also painted white.

The TOC was the nerve center of the base and had offices for the commander, his executive officer, the force protection leadership, Military Police, my USAID colleague, and me. As I walked into Lt. Colonel LaFontaine's office, he was working on his computer. After we renewed our acquaintance, he said, "Let's go," and quickly grabbed his cover (hat) to give me the grand tour of his command. We had all of the amenities we needed at the base: a gym, a maintenance bay, a proper chow hall, and a latrine with the best hot showers you could ask for, along with actual flushing toilets and laundry machines. All these facilities were beyond my wildest expectations, and I had the good fortune of working with the men who had built it and who took special pride in the place. They certainly welcomed its comforts after having lived for six months at a far simpler base where babywipes, cold chow, colder showers, and the relentless dust were a part of life. A helicopter landing pad was located in the center of the PRT, surrounded by green sandbags that defined its outer limits. A new barracks had recently been finished and another was under construction. All chow was brought in via overland shipping containers and water for our showers was drawn from the water table by large pumps and heated in a 150-gallon water heater. The PRT was situated at the southwest corner of FOB Ripley, and even though it was within the general perimeter, we were largely responsible for securing our own section of the base. The corner towers were manned around the clock and guards watched the two entry control points to the small base, one of which faced Tarin Kowt and the other, directly opposite from it, the flight line.

THE TARIN KOWT PROVINCIAL RECONSTRUCTION TEAM

If the forces have to be adapted to their new missions, it is just as important that the minds of the leaders and men—and this includes the civilian as well as the military—be adapted to the special demands of counterinsurgency warfare. Reflexes and decisions that would be considered appropriate for the soldier in conventional warfare and for the civil servant in normal times are not necessarily the right ones in counterinsurgency situations.
　　　　　　　　　—David Galula, *Counterinsurgency Warfare: Theory and Practice*[1]

The Tarin Kowt Provincial Reconstruction Team had been established in the summer of 2004 and was part of a general effort by the U.S. government and the government of Afghanistan to assist local officials throughout the country and to improve the living conditions of the Afghan population. Forming the heart of the PRT were civil-military units typically comprising a U.S. Army or Marine Corps civil-affairs team that was trained to fight but also educated in the nuances of working with indigenous populations. The team was charged with providing relief for short-term disasters and constructing basic infrastructure such as wells, schools, clinics, and roads. Each team had a pot of cash called the Commander's Emergency Relief Program (CERP) and each PRT commander had the discretion to spend up to $25,000 on a specific project; higher totals were sent up the chain for approval. This central element of the PRT was supplemented by civilian officials from the U.S. government's interagency such as a USAID development adviser who, in addition to providing advice and expertise, had access to millions of dollars of reconstruction and development money. The other interagency civilian attached to the civil-affairs team was a political adviser from the U.S. Department of State, which was what I would be. These advisers would usually be Foreign Service Officers (FSOs) who were trained diplomats and could provide political advice to the PRT commander and work with local officials to facilitate the Afghanistan government's goals. Because the State Department was having such a hard time recruiting FSOs to serve in Afghanistan, they turned to civil servants, such as myself, to fill the gap.

Our security was provided by the Iowa National Guard, who were charged with guarding the base and escorting our convoys around the province, and they were supplemented by our own Afghan Security Force (ASF) which consisted of about forty-five men led by a local Populzai tribesman named Farooq. The ASF lived on the base with us in a set of barracks we had constructed for them that formed the bottom of the PRT's "L" layout and were separated from us by an internal wall, although they were very much a part of our life. Farooq was of medium height and slender build and had black hair and a remarkable beard, somewhat like Captain Nemo's in the movie *The League of Extraordinary Gentlemen*, and he wore a nondescript, dark-brown shalwar kamis. During the time of the Taliban, he had been thrown in jail twice because his mustache had been too long. When Karzai motorcycled from Quetta, Pakistan, to Tarin Kowt in 2001, he met up with Farooq and another man named Haji Ibrahim to begin the Pashtun uprising in the south. As I learned about his background, it became very clear to me that Farooq was a man of significant influence in the province. By simply being our security chief, he had gained a certain amount of prestige with the population. In addition to the $6,000 we paid him monthly to rent his trucks and his $800 monthly salary, he was also a wealthy man in his own right; one indication of this was the fact he had two wives and a fiancée. Farooq used to be one of the governor's militia commanders and was originally tasked to work with U.S. Special Forces in the western district of Deh Rawud (still an area of significant Taliban activity), but he eventually parlayed that job into his current position. He and the governor apparently have issues with each other now that he is his own man and the governor is not getting his cut of our base's largesse. Among Farooq's many skills is his ability, for a small fee, to acquire a weapon of your choice.

Even though the State Department prohibited me from carrying a weapon in the field, in an effort to keep us within the Geneva Conventions as noncombatants and because of liability concerns, it was also generally acknowledged at the embassy that what happened in the provinces stayed in the provinces just as long as you used your best judgment. Soon after I arrived, Lt. Colonel LaFontaine asked me about my views on carrying a weapon, which I stated I supported wholeheartedly. He then handed me an AK-47 that had been left behind by a former UN employee and we quickly went through a basic functions check. LaFontaine then told me that if I wanted to buy my own weapon in the future, the going rate for an AK would be several hundred dollars. My colleague, Kerry, typically used the assault rifle Lt. Colonel LaFontaine had shown me, and he insisted that he only brought it with him on overland trips and never to meetings. I was certainly keen to maintain my own personal protection and decided to acquire a weapon of some sort. I felt I'd rather be alive and ask for forgiveness than dead.

As I slowly integrated myself into the life of the PRT, attending the morning battle update briefs (BUBs) and the nightly staff meetings with the Twenty-fifth Infantry at FOB Ripley, I became better acquainted with my colleagues at the PRT. One of the more interesting and colorful characters was a staff sergeant named Marvin Kraemer who was the head of the Military Police and our main adviser to Provincial Police chief Rozi Khan. Kraemer was thirty-three, half Cajun, and originally hailed from southern Louisiana where he could trace his family's history back over three hundred years. His face was gaunt, a Romanesque nose dominating an otherwise undistinguished face, and his head was clean-shaven. He was the latest in a long line of Kraemers to come from the town of Kraemer, so named after a relative who had opened the first post office there, and who, by having done so, got to name the town when the government cartographer came through the area. Because of his French-Cajun accent, whenever he said "bullshit" (for instance, when he was losing in a game of cards), it sounded more like "buuuullshit." A skull tattoo was on his left arm, replete with a Confederate flag handkerchief and rebel-style gray cover. Kraemer considered himself an amateur genealogist and often talked about his love of Southern history and his numerous ancestors who had fought for and against the Confederacy. After he retired from the military, he planned to go home to Kraemer and either teach Louisiana history in the local schools or work in the stockroom at Walmart. He wanted nothing to do with the military after he got out, but he enjoyed his job as a member of the Military Police and had a unique ability to work with the local Afghans; his aptitude and human touch were widely respected. When the Afghan police chief survived an improvised explosive attack, for example, Kraemer hosted a lunch for him at our base, telling him that we were happy he was alive and that we valued his friendship. This touched the police chief greatly and did much to help our work with him. Even though we were just a few years apart in age, I felt there was much I could learn from Kraemer.

The leader of the U.S. Army Civil Affairs Team (CAT-A), which formed the core of our base, was Capt. Doug Dillon. He was a reservist from Maryland and a schoolteacher in civilian life. Captain Dillon was very friendly from the get-go and enthusiastic about having me on the PRT's upcoming missions. Through sustained interactions with the Afghan people while constructing community projects and as the "labor boss" of the ASF, he seemed to have a special connection to the local population. Doug was also in his thirties and had an unflappable manner that made people feel at ease around him. Even though he was the officer in charge of the CAT-A, he and his men, Sgt. 1st Class David Henry, Pfc. Jacob Sotak, Sgt. Jermaine Dillard, Sgt. Ryan Brown, and Staff Sgt. Travis Blundell, got along extremely well and were very tight. Master Sgt. Will Williams filled out the civil affairs crew. The CAT-A worked with the local population on small-scale projects and partnered with the government and community to address the immediate effects of combat operations. While this was a key element of their activities, they mostly focused on constructing schools, clinics, irrigation canals, wells, and other small-to-medium improvements in the villages around Uruzgan, as well as facilitating the distribution of humanitarian assistance such as portable radios, foodstuffs, blankets, and basic medical and veterinary care.

Our interpreters were one of the most important elements of the PRT and served as our cultural advisers, institutional memory, sounding boards, and friends. All of them had been hired in 2004 when the PRT had been established, and over the course of hundreds of missions they had become integral parts of the PRT's operations. While several worked with us over the next year, three stand out for particular mention. The dean of the interpreter pool was Said Abdullah who was in his early forties. He was of medium height, sported a thick black beard, and had a flawless set of pearl-white teeth that showed often because he smiled constantly. The soldiers referred to him as a tactical "terp" (interpreter) because he often brought an AK-47 on trips and always carried an ammunition belt. We were never too sure of his background, but we liked to think he had been trained by some intelligence agency because he was quite capable with a weapon and had a significant amount of first-aid training.

The second interpreter was lovingly referred to as "Doc." When I met him, he was walking around the base with crutches, both of his legs in exoskeletons. He was soft-spoken, very respectful, and had the ubiquitous beard but was of shorter stature. Doc's legs had been broken by an IED that had destroyed a suburban truck we used on the PRT's first overland mission to the eastern district of Khas Uruzgan. Both he and the Afghan Security Force guard who was with him were severely injured but had survived. Lacking long-term medical care at military facilities, we continued to treat him at the PRT. Doc was noted for his intelligence and kindly ways.

The last interpreter would become the most important for me personally. His name was Mohibullah, although he usually went by Mohib, and he was about twenty-one years old. Mohib was bearded and dressed like most traditional Pashtuns in a shalwar kamis. While I never saw him wear a turban, he would often don a skullcap, the most common head covering for Afghans. He came from the Mohammedzai tribe, which was known for its scholarly bent and government service, and while Mohib had been born in Afghanistan, he had grown up in Pakistan as part of the Afghan Diaspora that had fled the country during the fighting against the Soviets in the 1980s. He not only spoke Pashto, but Dari, English, and Urdu. What was most interesting to me was that Mohib's uncle was the deputy governor of the province, which meant he had more influence in the community than his age would suggest. I also figured he could potentially be a source of information for the local government on our activites, so I had to proceed carefully with our relationship.

THE POLITICAL ADVISER IN THE FIELD

A week after his initial meeting with Wilson, when his assignment had been confirmed and he had finished his processing, Vann went to the embassy for a political briefing on the province. The political section could not find its sparse file on Hau Nghia, and he left.
    —Neil Sheehan, *A Bright Shining Lie: John Paul Vann and America in Vietnam*[2]

Now that I was settled in at the PRT, Lt. Colonel LaFontaine wanted to take me to meet with Governor Jan Mohammed Khan and his assembled provincial government, a meeting which he hoped would take place in the next few days when the governor returned from a trip. I was quite anxious about this, but I studied the notes and personality profile Frank Light had left behind and sketched out a few remarks and questions I wanted to ask. Frank's files indicated that the governor was a strong ally of President Karzai (they both came from the same tribe) and was a former mujahedeen who was blind in one eye and illiterate. He sounded like a fascinating character but also fierce and commanding. I looked forward to meeting him. Since the trip was scheduled a few days away, I took stock of how the PRT operated, what role I should play, and how exactly we were going to further reconstruction, development, and good governance. My USAID colleague, Kerry, was in charge of large infrastructure projects, and the CAT-A was doing smaller scale projects up to building schools. The PRT commander certainly worked closely with the governor but didn't have a lot of time to personally engage with the other provincial officials, some of whom were infrequently mentored by members of the CAT-A. My only mandate was, as quoted in the FY05 Mission Program Plan U.S. Mission to Afghanistan, to "work with the Afghan government and our international partners to help establish security and accelerate the country's political and economic reconstruction." Absent any training or additional guidance from the State Department, I decided to figure out what that meant on my own. I started by reading Frank's twenty-page "Who's Who" of the province and updating it as a way of getting my head wrapped around the personalities and politics of the area. After thumbing through the dust-covered pages he had left on my desk and beginning to develop a sense of the province and its leaders, I considered myself to be very fortunate to have followed such a qualified diplomat.

Frank had clearly picked up on the friction between the governor and Provincial Police chief Rozi Khan. Both of them were former mujahedeen commanders and respectively led the local Populzai and Barakzai tribes. One of Frank's chief concerns was that both men constantly haggled over "lost" pay, and Rozi Khan was always complaining to us that Kabul was not sending him pay, bullets, uniforms, and so on from the capital and the Ministry of the Interior. Frank had also begun to visit with the various provincial directors who led the central ministry departments in Uruzgan, such as the directors of agriculture, public works, reconstruction and rural development, and several others. Thankfully, Frank had taken photos of several of these men, and so I decided one of the best ways of improving governance was to fill out his useful biographies and do a rudimentary evaluation of the men's individual abilities and the capacity of their offices. I also wanted to continue Frank's practice of embedding with the civil affairs team and getting out to see the province.

My days were filled with getting to know everyone, scoping out the local political scene as best I could, and adapting to the new challenge of the assignment. At the same time, I was coming to love the natural scenery of the province. The constant breeze of the valley kept the midday heat at bay, and dust devils lazily sauntered across the desert floor, breaking up as they encountered our Hesco wall. As the sun set it was crowned by the mountain range, its glow making the different sedimentary layers of the hills look like extended rays of the sun. The temperature plunged as night fell; with the windows blackened out at the PRT and no lights downtown, the moon and the stars burst forth from the sky like diamonds on purple velvet. I could easily see between three to four times as many stars in the sky as I could in Washington, D.C., and it was common to see a meteorite streak across the firmament. I began to sit outside at night after each long day, leaning against the mortar shelter to take in the smell of the desert sand, the coolness of the breeze, and the serenity of the black and purple sky. I was reminded of what King Faisal of Iraq had once said when asked his favorite moment of life: he most liked riding on a camel in the quiet of the night crossing a desert with the faint glow of the moon as his only companion (recorded by British officer John Bagot Glubb, who served in Iraq from 1920 to 1929 and would eventually be commander of the Arab Legion in Jordan until 1956).

Since the governor's return had now been delayed, I decided to go on the next PRT mission I could in order to see the province and its residents. On February 24, Jeff Sanders, the representative of the United States Department of Agriculture (USDA) at Regional Command–South, arrived from Kandahar Air Field to help the PRT with his unique expertise in soil and water conservation. His arrival gave me my opportunity. Jeff was in his late forties and six feet tall, a solidly built former 101st Airborne "Screaming Eagle" from Tennessee who clearly had stayed in shape over the years. He had a great personality, a strong presence, and a slight Southern twang. After Jeff had dumped his gear in my room and introduced himself, he and I went to the convoy briefing, looking forward to our first mission outside the wire. We left in the early morning with a group of Farooq's men in our up-armored

Humvees. I was in the second Humvee; Farooq's men both led and followed our convoy. The goal was to visit several villages and find areas to create ponds for them by building check dams to capture water from the mountains after the heavier than usual snowfall and rain.

After leaving the main road and driving overland for a while, we dipped into a dry riverbed (*wadi*) that functioned as our informal highway. As we drove to a nearby village, the soldiers commented on how green everything was—a sea of fuzzy grass had burst from the khaki soil following the recent rains. As we left Tarin Kowt proper, a mob of children ran up to the convoy and either gave us a thumbs-up, made a victory sign, a surf's-up sign, a long-horn sign, or, occasionally, gave us the bird. We were apparently the most exciting thing to come to town that day. Most of the buildings we saw were made of adobe and the fields radiated out from the main river, ending where water could no longer be coaxed from its natural path. Where the green fields stopped, the desert began. As we left town it became more mountainous and we began to see small caves carved into the rocks. We'd come across small cemeteries as well, usually piles of rocks in a rectangular pattern with a larger rock arranged at the head. Many cemeteries had green, white, red, and black flags that, as I learned later, symbolized the way in which the person had died. Black meant the person had died on jihad; green, that he was a martyr; red, that he had died violently; and white, that he had been with the Taliban.

As the sun came through the clouds, vibrant patterns were created on the mountainsides that formed the edges of the Tarin Kowt bowl surrounding the capital. The majestic peaks were a nice shade of purple and darker brown and their jagged surfaces stood in marked contrast to the muted khaki colors of the flatter areas. As our team conducted assessments of the villages, we noticed large holes about twenty feet across that had been dug directly to the water table. They looked remarkably like the holes Luke Skywalker was going to be dropped into by Jabba the Hutt in *Star Wars*. One of the ASF picked his way down twenty feet to the bottom of one to catch a glow stick one of our team had dropped in at another hole farther up. After a few minutes, it floated past, confirming our theory that they were connected. Each village had done everything it could to capture water from the river and to channel it to their fields. As we stopped in each village, Jeff would survey different spots where small check dams could be built to create a pond for irrigation. Each village turned out as we arrived, but what was most notable was the absence of women. During the whole six-hour trip, we only saw two women, both of whom were in full burkas. We saw a number of little girls but none past twelve or thirteen years of age. Overall, everyone seemed quite friendly toward us, and the children were fearless in approaching our convoy. In one village, a little girl was heard yelling in Pashto, "The Americans are here, the Americans are here," and a pack of children came spilling out of the alleyways looking for presents. This was pretty much the pattern for the day, stopping at a town every so often, making an assessment for possible pond projects, and meeting the Afghan people.

A few days later, we went on another mission to scout out potential dam locations. We again used the various dry streambeds as roads and got to put our new Humvee, only 135 miles on the odometer, through its paces. Not too far out of town we located an area that seemed to be promising for a dam and a pond. As we pulled up, an Afghan work crew was digging drainage ditches along the road. Jeff and I, with Captain Dillon, wandered up the rock-strewn hills and Jeff used a hand level to survey the water line of the future dam. In many places, the local Afghan population had created small ditches to guide the water to their plots. Because this area had had a drought for the last seven years, local farmers had carved small riverbeds out of historically larger ones. Near our stopping point were three caves that Farooq said were used as schools. Each was hewn out of the living rock and, per standing army procedures, we clambered up to them to investigate. Just beyond the three-foot entrance, a large room about fifteen feet deep by six feet tall by eight feet wide opened up. You could tell that at some point it had been used as a holding pen for livestock because the smell of dung was strong along with stale straw. Two or three small alcoves were carved in one cave for some sort of illumination (probably candles) to aid the students.

En route to our next location, one of the ASF's trucks lost its wheel completely. All three of its bolts (yes, only three) popped off and the whole wheel just spun away. The Afghans were on it, and while we waited we noticed a group of Kuchi tents; these are Afghanistan's nomads who usually move between Afghanistan and Pakistan as the seasons change. It was becoming very clear to me how precarious life was here, and how the people did their best to scratch out a basic existence. Theirs was an elemental life, shorn of its niceties, in harmony and in tension with what nature provided.

With the truck fixed, the team made it to our next destination and had some discussions with village elders about school construction, placement, and enrollment figures. When asked how many students were in the area, one villager told us eighty. This didn't seem to square with the population numbers we saw, and when we pressed a little more, he conceded that girls were not included in the count. At this, Sergeant Henry and Captain Dillon said that girls must attend the school and that this was a directive from the minister of education himself in Kabul. The villager didn't have much of a response to this, so we figured there were probably at least eighty girls in the area as well. After we left, we made our way to lunch at the home of Sultan, who was our deputy commander of the Afghan Security Force and Farooq's brother.

Like most Afghan homes, Sultan's was surrounded by a tall mud wall that made it feel more like a compound than a home. His residence sat at the top of a twenty-foot cliff overlooking an expansive riverbed easily fifty yards across. Once we parked our vehicles, leaving two gunners outside for protection, we were shown into Sultan's guest room, which was a large rectangular room festooned with colorful posters of various Pakistani cities. The posters covered the walls from the bottom to the top. On the ground was a plastic mat, and a series of pillows and cushion seats were arranged along the edge of the room. After we had seated ourselves, a man came in with a pitcher of warm water and a basin to wash our hands. Then a yellow towel was circulated so that we could dry our hands. Next, a purple cloth was introduced, and two men rolled it the full length of the room after they had neatly placed their shoes at the door. Wrapped inside it was bread that roughly corresponded to where each of us was sitting. After removing his shoes, our server and, at times, our host, tiptoed on the cloth and introduced plate upon plate of food. In addition to the bread we had large bowls of rice, bowls of fries and meat (probably lamb), cups of sliced apples and oranges, nuts in honey, some sort of milk treat, and the traditional drink of the Afghan people, Pepsi, along with some orange drink. Following this we drank tea and got down to work.

Sergeant Henry and Captain Dillon discussed through our interpreter our commitments to build a well and a ten-room school for the village. We also stressed to the local elders that it would take a long time to complete all of the projects we'd like to do and that patience was the key. The elders seemed satisfied by our commitment to stay the course and appeared to be happy at the prospects of getting a school and a well. Following this discussion and more tea, we went across the street to survey the area for the school. The elders said that the community had about 180 students (boys and girls) and that they would be willing to have girls attend school. Sultan was donating the land for the school and we discussed the size of the building. On our way home we drove over some rocks that had been lined up across the road at largely perpendicular angles to it. When I asked what they were, Captain Dillon said they were property lines. Without wood for signposts or fences and since barbed wire was a rarity, the stones seemed to be a commonsense response to an obvious need.

My first exposure to the Pashtuns showed them to be a hardy and resourceful people who made the best of the limited circumstances they found themselves in. Their hospitality was impressive, especially in light of the obvious poverty of the area and their meager possessions. As we drove around Tarin Kowt, it became evident that the natural environment clearly dominated the lives of the people. Every family was doing its utmost to squeeze water from the countryside, to capture one more foot of arable land, and to find some way of making money. It was an elemental existence that seemed more forthright and honest, where the central drivers of life were family, tribe, and community. The friendliness I experienced from the few Pashtuns I had met and their clear willingness to work with us were encouraging. Having avoided any glaring cultural faux pas, I looked forward to a deeply rewarding tour in service to a welcoming people. I planned to write up our mission and continue my studies of Afghan culture and the personalities of the province in anticipation of meeting my first Afghan government officials.

HEARTLAND OF THE TALIBAN

Guerilla warfare depends chiefly for its success on the support of the people of the country. Guerillas cannot have regular lines of communication, and are obliged to resort to the villagers for food and shelter and for their intelligence as to the movements of Government forces.
    —John Bagot Glubb, *The Story of the Arab Legion*[3]

Frank's files gave me a wonderful overview of the town of Tarin Kowt and its surrounding districts. As much as he and I needed to focus on the political personalities of the area, we were both drawn to the geography of the land, the culture of the people, and the rich tapestry of humanity that made up Afghan village life. Though Uruzgan Province was located in the center of the country, it was considered one of Afghanistan's five southern provinces. It is bordered by Kandahar, Helmand, and Zabul provinces in the south and west, Ghazni to the east, and Dai Kundi to the north, and is approximately 250 miles southwest of Kabul.[4] The fourth-smallest province in Afghanistan, it stretches "about 130 miles north to south and 95 miles east to west" and has approximately 205,000 residents.[5] The Helmand River cuts through the western portion of the province and small rivulets feed into it from the surrounding valleys. Uruzgan's provincial capital, Tarin Kowt, is 76 miles north of the ring road that connects Kandahar City in the south to the eastern provinces and, eventually, to the nation's capital of Kabul. Tarin Kowt is approximately 4,400 feet above sea level and located in the center of the province in the district of Tarin Kowt.

Like much of Afghanistan, the geography of Uruzgan is one of its most singular features and challenges. Situated at the bottom of the "Tarin Kowt bowl," the provincial capital is surrounded by a mountain range and population that ekes out an existence by cultivating small plots of land along the Tarin Kowt River. The rest of the area is a barren desert covered by fine silt with small, undulating hills punctuating the countryside. As you move north, the province becomes significantly more mountainous with peaks reaching upward of 7,000 to 8,000 feet. Added to the dominant dark- and light-brown colors of the sandy southern part of the province are a collection of light-green, red, and black-tinctured rocks as the countryside rises to the mountains. Vegetation is a little more numerous as the hot climate of the south gives way to the cooler climes and more frequent precipitation of the north, but villages still cling to the verdant sides of the streams, and the population is sparse. During the summer, temperatures often rise to about 120 degrees Fahrenheit in the "bowl" and dust devils traverse the area rising to several hundred yards in height. In the north, snow falls so thickly in some places that entire valleys are shut off from the world for months on end, and an isolated road that connects a valley is covered with upward of ten to twenty feet of snow in some places. Many villages actually stockpile food in the expectation that they will not receive supplies for approximately three months.

The infrastructure of the province is almost as bleak as the geography—the only paved road is the Tarin Kowt–Kandahar Road, which is being built by U.S. Army engineers. Most roads seem to be dry riverbeds and the rudimentary paths that do exist are often simply improved goat trails in some places. Residents apparently get whatever power they have from generators, or they use propane tanks. There is one radio station in the whole province, and it is at the governor's compound. Besides a few wealthy families, very few residents have a satellite dish or access to television. Radios and word of mouth are the only way people learn about anything. Most students study in a handful of schools and many take instruction under trees or tarps from a local village resident or mullah who is literate. Also, no public sanitation or sewage system exists. The health system, if it could be called that, consisted of one hospital and a few clinics operated by a nongovernmental organization.

The local economy is predominantly agrarian with many small businesses providing basic services to local farmers. Farmers grow a variety of produce such as wheat, almonds, melons, eggplants, and tomatoes, and most villages have a small vegetable and fruit market. The agricultural sector constitutes about 85 percent of the local economy and most of the nonagricultural sector is devoted to serving the needs of the farming economy. Farmers typically flood their fields for irrigation and plant trees to shore up the ditches they've constructed to funnel water to outlying crops. Afghans raise a unique type of sheep for food called a fat-tailed sheep. The sheep have a flab of blubber on their butt that flops around as they graze along the countryside; this fat is typically used for cooking. (The U.S. soldiers refer to the sheep as "J.Lo" sheep after entertainer Jennifer Lopez.) Some of the wealthier farmers have horses, and camels are quite common but are mostly seen among the nomadic Kuchi tribesmen that frequent the area.

Besides farming, there are a variety of small businesses such as auto shops, pharmacies, gas stations, general stores, and construction companies. A vibrant transportation sector includes jingle trucks (highly decorated delivery vehicles), taxis, and fuel trucks. This constitutes probably 10 percent of the economy, and the remaining 5 percent is taken up by government expenditure. Most commerce flows along two southern roads, one through the Delanor Pass in the Nesh District of Kandahar Province, the second through the Shah Wali Kot District of Kandahar where the Tarin Kowt–Kandahar Road runs. In addition, a large portion of trade takes place along the Helmand River and in the western portion of Uruzgan toward Helmand Province. Uruzgan Province is also a major source of poppy crops, and a large portion of the local economy is fueled by their pernicious effects.

The people of Uruzgan Province are ethnically Pashtun and Sunni Muslim and are loosely organized along tribal lines. The Pashtuns are divided into the tribal confederations of the Durrani and the Gilzai, and most tribes in Uruzgan come from the Durrani. The three dominant tribes in the area, the Populzai, the Barakzai, and the Achikzai, are Durrani and are generally distributed in certain geographically coherent areas. The Populzai tend to congregate to the south of Tarin Kowt, spreading out to the east and west of the province and spilling over into northern Kandahar; the Barakzai are located to the north of Tarin Kowt, fanning out to the west and east of the district as you move north; and the Achikzai are east and north of Tarin Kowt and abut the eastern border of the province. Two of the smallest Durrani tribes in the area are the Mohammedzai and the Alkozai, who tend to live in the village of Tarin Kowt.

The Gilzai branch of the Pashtuns live mostly in the western portion of the province, and many of the senior leaders of the Taliban, reputedly including Taliban founder Mullah Omar, come from this area. In the northern part of the province, along its eastern edge, is a sizable Hazara population.

The Hazara are Shiite, and the community that lives in Uruzgan is a remnant of the majority-Hazara Dai Kundi Province that was carved out of Uruzgan in early 2004. The Hazara resemble Mongolians and are the implacable foes of the Taliban, which is a predominantly Pashtun movement.

Also present in Uruzgan are the nomadic Kuchi and their camel caravans, sometimes numbering about twenty camels, which we often saw traversing the deserts en route to grazing areas for their livestock.

The Pashtun men in Uruzgan closely follow the rules and expectations of the Pashtun code of behavior called *pashtunwali*. Most Pashtuns will offer hospitality to a stranger who requests it, which usually includes *chai* (tea), some bread and meat, and a bed for the night. This generosity, called *melmastia*, is even provided to the host's enemies. Afghans also practice a form of revenge and justice called *badal*. Any transgression and any slight is paid in kind by the aggrieved party. It was not uncommon, for example, for these grievances to be nursed for several years until the right moment for justice presented itself. Conversely, the third aspect of the code, called *nanawati*, is a complete and humble admission of guilt, asking for forgiveness from the wronged party. The code's final principle is called *zan*, *zar*, and *zameen*, which is a defense of women and family, treasure, and property. U.S. and

Coalition Forces try to improve women's rights where we can, but the male members of our forces were always very conscious to not interact with the local Afghan women, any misconstrued gesture or comment could cause us significant problems and, quite possibly, endanger our lives.[6]

4   A PROVINCIAL AFFAIR
(Tarin Kowt—Spring 2005)

In military civic action, remember that friendship is earned, not bought.

—Edward Geary Lansdale, *In the Midst of Wars: An American's Mission to Southeast Asia*[1]

As our Humvees bounced along the dirt road en route to the governor's compound, I began to get a better sense of what the town of Tarin Kowt actually looked like as opposed to the jumble of adobe walls and buildings I had seen from furtive glances over the FOB's walls. Our convoy briefly dipped into a dry riverbed and then made its way to the dirt road that formed one of the two main arteries of the town. A large section of the road had been blocked off behind us and was in the process of being paved, cutting a pitch-black ribbon into the khaki countryside. The low, one-story buildings on either side of the road were made from a mix of adobe, wood, and concrete. On my right, the stores seemed to be some sort of auto mechanics area with cars in various states of disassembly; periodically a gas station would whiz by as well. I also noticed an Afghan man leading his flock of black-and-white fat-tailed sheep to some unknown location. We slowed down at one point as we came upon a checkpoint and one of the soldiers told me that the impressive-looking building on our right was Matullah's compound; he was the governor's main militia commander and leader of the Afghan Highway

Police. After passing this important landmark, the road quickly led to the center of town where a two-story tower set in a large traffic circle greeted us, and the surrounding shops had now increased in size to two stories. As we whipped around the circle, I could briefly see the other main road of the capital trailing off into the Afghan countryside, similarly flanked by simple storefronts.

The governor's compound was about half a mile from the traffic circle, and as we arrived I could make out a large white arch signaling the entrance to his headquarters, which were surrounded by a low adobe wall. Written on the white arch was a phrase in Pashto I later learned meant "God is great." As we drove toward the governor's office, two Afghan guards in gray police uniforms with AK-47s slung over their shoulders eyed us lazily. Our convoy parked around a two-story concrete building that functioned as a sort of bank for the province and a makeshift barracks for the governor's militia. It was located twenty feet away from a Soviet BMP, an amphibious tracked infantry fighting vehicle that the front gate guards apparently slept on during the afternoon. As I dismounted, I could see the inner gate of the governor's compound with its red-, black-, and green-colored metal shining in the sun. Two of his guards were sheltering themselves in the shade of a nearby tree close to the compound's second wall. As we walked toward the governor's compound, the sound of our boots on the crushed rock filled the silence, and we passed through this final gate before entering the inner oasis of the provincial government's seat of power.

Rose bushes lined the gravel-laden path and two outside verandas greeted us on either side of the trail as we approached the governor's offices, festooned with Afghan flags and pictures of President Karzai. Concertina wire was coiled around the extensive foliage and several Afghan men sat on the outside verandas waiting for an audience. Gray smoke rose lazily from behind a wall to the right, which I assumed was where food was being prepared. We shed our helmets and body armor as we entered the governor's office; it was perched on a small cliff overlooking the Tarin Kowt River. A dark-green carpet lined the large room and deep, plush seats were arrayed against the walls; the governor's desk was in the corner. Pictures of President Karzai hung from the wall, as did a ceremonial shovel painted in the colors of the Afghan national flag and several antipoppy posters. A large window ended the room, and through it we could make out the river's meandering path, cutting a wide swath through the fields that had been cultivated around it. A ridge of brown mountains loomed in the distance.

As we entered his office, Governor Jan Mohammed Khan sat with his provincial government assembled around him. All the men wore turbans and had beards of varying lengths and colors going from black to brown to gray. Their gaunt faces stared back at us, and their tan skin and muted colors blended together as I crossed the room to find a seat. One man stood out from the rest: he was clean shaven except for a mustache, and his bald head was uncovered. He sat across from the governor and even though he was dressed in traditional Afghan garb, he seemed distinctly more modern to me; perhaps it was the photographer's vest he wore. As I soon learned, the gentleman I was seated next to was one of President Karzai's seven brothers named Qayum Karzai.

Major Dayton introduced me to Governor Jan Mohammed Khan and told him that I was Frank Light's replacement and would be serving as political adviser to the PRT commander. The governor nodded in response as he reached for some candies in a bowl on the table in front of him. He wore a gray-and-black turban and had a salt-and-pepper beard and a weathered, deeply lined face. He exuded an air of strong confidence, and his blind eye was a milky gray. After quick pleasantries were exchanged, Major Dayton and the governor reviewed some ongoing plans to distribute food and other supplies to certain outlying districts that were snowed in. They also talked about a recent Taliban threat against a local mullah who regularly spoke on the radio in favor of the government. They also discussed a meeting scheduled for the following day that would consist of tribal elders from all around the province. Mr. Karzai was apparently visiting Uruzgan from the States to help set up and convene this meeting of elders through his nongovernmental organization (NGO) Afghans for Civil Society.

Major Dayton asked me if I wanted to say anything and I briefly mentioned that I was glad to be in Uruzgan and looked forward to working with the governor and his government. I thought a short-and-sweet statement was sufficient, but Major Dayton asked me in a whisper whether this was all I was going to say. I hadn't thought much beyond these brief words but I quickly mumbled something that I can't remember. To be frank, the room full of Afghans was somewhat intimidating and I made a mental note to write down some talking points the next time I spoke to them. As we stood to leave, Mr. Karzai introduced himself to me in perfect English and invited me to attend the inaugural Provincial Shura meeting the next day. I thanked him for the invitation and said I looked forward to this momentous event. As we pulled out of the compound, a slight drizzle came down and the dust from our vehicles dissipated as we made our way back to base. My first introduction to Uruzgan's government had gone moderately well, but I would have to prepare myself better if I hoped to have the impact I wanted.

THE PROVINCIAL SHURA

When you break bread with people and share their troubles and joys, the barriers of language, of politics and of religion soon vanish. I liked them and they liked me, that was all that mattered.

> —Julien Bryan, as quoted by John Bagot Glubb, *Britain and the Arabs: A Study of Fifty Years, 1908 to 1958*[2]

At Mr. Karzai's invitation, we went to the governor's office to witness a remarkable event in Uruzgan's history. For the first time since the rise to power of the Taliban in the early 1990s, Uruzgan Province convened a provincial shura of tribal elders. Rooted in Pashtun tradition, the shura, or *jirga*, as it was sometimes called, is a deliberative body comprising elders either of villages at the district level or of districts at the provincial level. The shura met on the second floor of the governor's compound and Lt. Colonel Sellers, Major Dayton, and I attended for the United States. This political event was clearly significant and fired my own ideas of how we could work together to help the province. A bright blue banner hung from the wall behind Mr. Karzai and in both English and Pashto read, "Uruzgan Shura for Peace and Development." The observers of the event were seated to the side and the elders were arrayed in chairs in front of Mr. Karzai and his staff. The goal was to elect a president, two vice presidents, and a clerk as well as to finalize the membership of the shura. There were about twenty-five voting shura members (although they seemed to have several advisers) and about forty observers. The whole meeting was videotaped and audiotaped; our plan was to play the proceedings on our one provincial radio station. Mr. Karzai opened the meeting stressing that the shura was a responsibility and not a privilege and that the people of Afghanistan were giving them the responsibility. He also said that the Afghan government and Coalition Forces could not do every-thing and that we must have the participation of the people. He mentioned that the two goals of the shura were development and ending oppression, and that the shura would assist in the stabilization process. The governor made a few comments as well and stressed that the central and local gov-ernment would benefit greatly from the shura.

After opening remarks, members of Mr. Karzai's nongovernmental or-ganization explained the voting procedures. People interested in running could nominate themselves, but they had to be seconded by another shura member. Two candidates ran for the position of president: Mullah Mawlawi Hamdullah and Dr. Abdul Baki, both from Tarin Kowt. Mullah Hamdullah, who was short in stature and had a black beard and blacker turban, stood up and stated that god had ordered all creatures to learn and that was why he had selected the book as his symbol for this election. He also said that the book represented the Koran and that the Koran was against cruelty and for justice. Dr. Baki, who was taller, dressed in muted colors, and had a long face with a gray beard, stressed that he had fought against the Soviets and the Taliban, but now the future of Uruzgan was in education. For this reason he had chosen the pen as his symbol. He said that he knew whose hands were shady, good, or bad and that this knowledge would make him a good leader. After these brief stump speeches, the shura elected Mullah Hamdullah by a vote of nineteen to six by secret ballot. Mullah Hamdullah delivered a brief speech stating that the Karzai government supported the best interests of the Afghan people and that it was the duty of the shura to support it. He also stressed that the shura was for everybody and that all of the community needed to be involved.

After the voting had taken place, the delegates from the district of Chora arrived. One of their members wanted to run for president and a lot of furtive talking took place; then the Chora delegates left the room to consult with Qayum Karzai. The delegates expressed their concern over being perceived as stopping the shura and asked if they could vote for one of the two candi-dates and perhaps field a vice-presidential candidate. This unwillingness to rock the boat is, as Mr. Karzai later told me, a characteristic of Afghans, who always endeavor to seek consensus, negotiation, and accommodation. Once they had returned to the shura, they voted and we had lunch. We briefly left the meeting room while tables and chairs were brought in for our meal and took in the breathtaking sight of the valley below with its neatly tilled fields and meandering river. As we reentered the area, a long table following the length of the whole room greeted us, and when we sat down a servant came around with a jug of water to wash our hands and a bowl to catch the runoff. A communal towel was eventually produced as well and passed around the room. A sumptuous feast was quickly brought in on glass plates by the governor's staff. Fresh lamb kabobs, fried fish, oranges, onions, and a spicy meat wrapped in dough were served, as well as the ubiquitous Pepsi and orange drink.

After our brief respite, the shura reconvened, absent about thirty observers, and then proceeded to elect five vice presidents (one for each district in the province). The reason there were five vice presidents was that, in addition to having one representative for each district, the president also wanted a deputy who would be able to stay in Tarin Kowt most of the year. The delegates seemed to balk at this idea initially but eventually decided on five. Karzai and Hamdullah implored Dr. Baki to become a vice president in order to maintain harmony among the participants. After this election, a clerk was selected, although the first person chosen declined the responsibility, and by acclamation a second man was elected who agreed to take on these duties. After this final election, we were invited to sit in front of the shura, introduce ourselves, and talk about what we did. I spoke of how important it was for the shura to be successful because democracy was the answer to terrorism and that Lt. Colonel Sellers and I understood it quite personally because we had both been at the Pentagon on 9/11. One person asked who controlled the construction of the Tarin Kowt–Kandahar road (both the PRTs of Uruzgan and Kandahar did); a second asked why his district, Gizab, hadn't had any development projects (weather, and the fact that the district didn't fall under the Tarin Kowt PRT until recently). A third question was what the PRT and the FOB were going to do to help farmers who got rid of their opium because of the governor's policies against drugs (answer: seeds, fertilizer, tractors, and increased market access through the road). After these questions were answered, we left for FOB Ripley in our armored convoy. I was amazed at how well organized and serious the shura had been and how refreshingly authentic it appeared. It was so different from the politics of Washington, D.C., and the participants seemed to be genuinely focused on helping their community. I felt very honored to have witnessed this special event and was determined to do what I could to ensure the shura's success.

THE PROVINCIAL POLICE CHIEF

I believe that he who has less in life should have more in law.
—Philippine president Ramon Magsaysay

Having briefly met Governor Jan Mohammed Khan and seen the beginning of a viable shura for Uruzgan's residents, I was anxious to meet the other key personality of the province whom Frank had highlighted in his reporting: Provincial Police chief Rozi Khan. The PRT organized a trip for me and our two new police advisers to meet the police chief at his headquarters in downtown Tarin Kowt. The two advisers, Art Smith and Travis Nelson, were police officers in the United States on contract to help build our local department by providing advice, assistance, and mentoring. Art was the police chief of Hagerstown in Maryland and was an energetic personality with a university degree in math who was keen to get out around the province. Travis was a former sheriff of a county in Texas, the first Republican elected to that position in the county's history, and had all the charm and grace of a Southern gentleman. Travis was an easygoing chain-smoker and brought a lot of wisdom to the PRT. His accent would often lilt across the tactical operations center and he frequently hyphenated multisyllabic words like "Mah-tullah" and "mos-quito." On March 11, we departed the PRT with Staff Sergeant Kraemer to visit Chief Rozi Khan and his staff. This was my first trip to his office and I looked forward to meeting this political opponent of the governor.

The police compound is probably a hundred yards away from the governor's sprawling complex and overlooks the main river that goes through Tarin Kowt. Between the police station and the governor's place was a mosque, a girls' school that the PRT had built, and several other provincial government buildings. In terms of facilities, the police station was pretty impressive by Afghan standards. It consisted of three buildings, one of which was two stories tall, and all of them were made of concrete with the usual wall surrounding the compound. We arrived in back with three Humvees and force protection. Several police were milling about the courtyard (although you wouldn't know they were police because they weren't wearing their uniforms) and we entered through a small back door. One building served as a mess hall of some sort; the other, an office for various staff; and the third, which was the two-story building, was the headquarters for the police chief, his communications director, and their intelligence guy, among others. Colonel Hotak, who was our ministry of interior representative at the PRT, accompanied us as well. There were two destroyed police trucks in the courtyard. The first had had its wheels taken off, was on blocks, and was missing its whole front area. The second vehicle, lying low against the wall, was missing its bed and wheels and was resting on its bottom. Both had been destroyed by improvised explosive device attacks. The first vehicle had had the police chief in it and no one had been hurt; the second had had six people killed in it, five sitting in the bed of the truck and one passenger in the rear seating area. This vehicle had been carrying the police chief of Khas Uruzgan District Haji Ibrahim. He had been one of the first Afghans to meet with Karzai in 2001. There was also a rudimentary spring in the courtyard that fed a circular concrete pool the men drank from and used for cleaning. It was right across from where the infamous marijuana bush was growing when U.S. forces first arrived, which had subsequently been taken down.

After taking a few snapshots and some general introductions, we settled down into a room on the second floor. After a few minutes Rozi Khan appeared and we started talking business. Like most Afghans, Rozi was slight of stature and, like most powerful Afghans, had a bit of a paunch. He was about five feet, nine inches tall, and his graying beard was dyed a dark brown. Rozi Khan was the local leader of the Barakzai tribe that congregated north of Tarin Kowt, but since he was the Provincial Police chief his responsibilities extended throughout the province. He was a contemporary of Jan Mohammed Khan and didn't fear him. Art and Travis started to ask questions about how many police there were, the proportion of officers to regular police, and about the organizational structure of the station. I was mostly interested in understanding how the budget process worked and what Rozi Khan's relationship was with the governor; I also wanted to follow up on rumors I'd heard about the governor taking money from the police budget. We mostly stayed with nice questions at the beginning, taking a break to go to the roof and scout out a site for a training academy, but after we had an impromptu lunch of chicken, bread, and Pepsi, we began asking the more difficult questions.

As we spoke, Chief Rozi took slow drags off his cigarette and a yellow pall filled the room from the sun shining through the curtains. He told us that all of the province's money that came from Kabul went directly to the governor to be distributed among the various directorates. The police department got roughly 5 million Afghani a month for the whole province and, according to Chief Rozi, 750,000 of that was taken by the governor for his personal use. In addition, the Afghan Highway Police, which was headed up by the governor's old Afghan Militia Force commander Matullah, was encroaching on the turf of Rozi Khan's police. Chief Rozi pretty much saw this as a deliberate strategy by the governor because he had tried at least three times to get Rozi fired and was generally suspected of having planted the two IEDs that had destroyed the police vehicles in the front courtyard. Chief Rozi had survived his attack but six Afghan police were killed in the second vehicle, which he said was targeted because an ally of his, Haji Ibrahim, had been riding in it. I asked Rozi about his background and tried to get a better sense of him as a person. He apparently had a strong reputation as a Taliban fighter and took pride in living a simple life as compared with the governor (who reportedly has four lavish homes), and he leads the Barakzai tribe while the governor leads the local Populzai tribe. He seemed intelligent, but his seven years of formal education were going to prove difficult to overcome if we hoped to professionalize the police. The Afghan Highway Police continued to encroach onto the ANP's turf, most recently by building a checkpoint in the city, and had been monopolizing the training slots we had at the Regional Training Center in Kandahar. The tensions were so high between the ANP and the Afghan Highway Police that the ANP rarely ventured outside their compound and dared not wear their uniforms for fear of being shot at by the highway police.

The next day I sat down at the PRT with Chief Rozi Khan's deputy, a man named Haji Nabi. While the appellation of "Haji" usually refers to a Muslim who has completed the Haj to Mecca in Saudi Arabia, in Mr. Nabi's case it more accurately represented the level of education he had completed. Unlike Chief Rozi, who was effectively illiterate, Deputy Police Chief Nabi was a formally trained officer who had completed high school and spent a year at a police training academy in St. Petersburg, Russia, during the 1980s. When he arrived at the PRT, he was wearing his gray police uniform and was carrying a folder and notebook. He wore thick glasses and had a gray beard and he carried himself with a certain air of professionalism. Nabi was in his early fifties and was a member of the Achikzai tribe. He seemed so different from the police chief—educated, trained, and apparently serious about being a police officer. We met at the PRTs Civil-Military Operations Center (CMOC), which is a part of the PRT where we meet with community representatives for official business or with locals who need some assistance or redress for damages caused by our operations. It is usually run by the civil affairs team and is a major element of our efforts to work with the local community.

Major Dayton, Mr. Smith, Mr. Nelson, Afghan ministry of interior representative Colonel Hotak, and I met with Lt. Colonel Nabi. Our goal in meeting with him was to continue our education about how the justice system worked in the province and to ferret out the tensions between the Afghan National Police and the Afghan Highway Police. Deputy Police Chief Nabi was very happy to meet with us and told us that his happiest day was when the Taliban had fled and he could take his police uniform out from his family's trunk and wear it once again in public. He told us that for all serious crimes such as murder, rape, or theft, the case goes to the governor who, after throwing the case out if the person was a supporter of his or from his tribe, would then decide the person's guilt. The governor occasionally kicked cases over to the province's judge, but since the governor controlled the judges' salaries, the result was usually known. The Afghan National Police handled most minor crimes, but if the parties involved were linked to the governor in some way, they didn't really do anything about it. We also spoke to Nabi about the possibility of opening a training center of some sort in the province to improve the professionalism of the police. He said this would be an excellent idea since most of the police force was illiterate, including the police chief. Nabi also said he would be interested in serving as an instructor and volunteered to let us use several of the rooms at the police station to begin the training. This was certainly very encouraging news. Lt. Colonel Nabi went on to say that because of the tensions between the governor's men and Rozi Khan's men, most of the ANP did not wear their uniforms for fear of being shot. As he told us this, I got the strong sense that Nabi was very frustrated with the overall situation as well as with the shortcomings of his predominantly illiterate and uneducated police force.

It was becoming increasingly clear to me that a lot of tension existed between not only the police chief and the governor, but also between their respective militias. There was even a sense of fear in town. I wasn't yet sure what was true and what were attempts to influence my own thinking in a prejudicial way, but I was certain that I needed to expand my meetings beyond the two key figures of Jan Mohammed Khan and Rozi Khan in order to get a better sense of what was going on. I was hopeful that most of these tensions were being overblown, but if personal diplomacy from the PRT with the main players proved fruitless, the creation of the Provincial Shura might provide a way to address some of these problems. I definitely needed to tread carefully but I wanted to figure out how the Government of Afghanistan in Kabul or, conceivably, Qayum Karzai in his capacity as a tribal elder, might play a role.

My work was definitely cut out for me in figuring out the politics of the province, and now that the shura was standing up, I was sure that much of my time would be spent in Tarin Kowt. However, I was hoping to step away from "pure" politics and see how our development projects were coming along. On March 31, Captain Dillon and Master Sgt. Williams and I took a trip downtown to visit the Malalai Girls School. The United States Agency for International Development had originally built the school, but because it didn't have a wall around it, a must-have in the land of the Pashtuns, no one attended it. Captain Dillon and the civil affairs team had come to the rescue and, with the construction of the wall, dozens of girls started to show up. This was so heartening that we quickly deepened our involvement with the school and purchased more school desks, backpacks, and chairs. The governor even chipped in and purchased school uniforms for all of the girls, who eventually numbered around 150. We occasionally saw small packs of girls walking to school with their white head coverings and black dresses and small multicolored backpacks dangling off their backs. Their innocence and clear appreciation at having a school helped relieve the pressures of working in Afghanistan. The school was well attended because it sat between the governor's compound and the police station. Parents felt confident that their children would be protected.

Arriving at the school in the early morning, we heard the chatter of girls as we walked toward the building. Our mission that day was to deliver a four-by-five-foot wooden board to the principal; it displayed pictures of positive female role models that we hoped the children would emulate—

Condoleezza Rice, Sandra Day O'Connor, Halle Barry, a female astronaut, and many other successful women. We set up a little stand in the front of the school and showed the pictures to the headmaster and other department of education officials. As we approached the school, we could see little girls walking in with the backpacks we had given them the previous week. Each backpack had an Afghan and an American flag on it with a white dove of peace connecting them. When we went through the gate to the school, you could hear the girls reciting their lesson plans in unison. After showing the administrators the photos we took, each class of girls came up to the photos and Said Abdullah explained to them who the women were. I also went into two classes and took photos as the girls sat at their desks. There were probably about eighty girls at school that day. With the start of school, word had spread around the villages and more and more girls wanted to attend; however, many lived too far away to walk or for their parents to drive them. A few days after the school year began, the governor asked us if we would purchase two used school buses to drive around town and pick up more girls to go to school. We thought this was an excellent idea and once they were purchased, we would occasionally see the buses bumping along, the chatter of little girls radiating out. When they would see us they would wave their little hands at us. Small victories like this made all the hard work worth it.

Deputy Governor Haji Aziz Khan came to the PRT in late March to seek our urgent assistance with flood relief in the western part of the province. Due to heavier than usual snows, the province was now reaping the "benefit" of this precipitation through extensive flooding in the Helmand River Valley. It had been so dry for so long that many Afghan families had literally moved into the dry riverbeds and extended their cultivated land there because it was so fertile for crops. Apparently, the provincial government owns some land that was flooded (and was charging rent to local farmers to use it) and Mr. Aziz Khan wanted us to pay the government for the revenue it had lost from the destroyed land and crops and to do what we could to redirect the river somehow because most of the population lived off the crops they grew and any loss of land was pretty catastrophic. Instead of carving a ditch in the middle of a field to allow a portion of the river to flow through it, many of the local Afghans wanted us to build a wall to completely stop its flow. They viewed the loss of land from construction of a canal more of an issue than continuing to push for an idea that wouldn't work. We told the deputy governor that we could not replace lost farmland and that we weren't going to reimburse the government for lost rental income. He told us that a local nomad had lost between forty to fifty sheep, several camels, a horse, and some additional animals and wanted some relief from the PRT. We told him that while we could not replace every lost animal, home, or piece of land, we could offer some short-term relief such as foodstuffs, tents, and blankets, and we could use our helicopters to move residents who were stranded. This was the plan we eventually agreed to and Lt. Colonels Sellers and LaFontaine worked together to coordinate assistance. Once the waters had receded, many local Afghans thanked us for our help. It became clear once again that the lives of the residents of Uruzgan were dominated by the elements.

The Taliban have struck. On March 23, we got word at the PRT that a local mullah who had been speaking on the radio in favor of the government had been gunned down by three assailants as he rode his motorcycle home through Tarin Kowt. Some of the witnesses said that, after hearing gunshots, they saw him take a tumble from the bike and then saw a member of the Taliban rush up to him and shoot him in the head. The mullah had provided the only programming on the province's sole radio station at the governor's compound. Prior to USAID purchasing the radio in 2004, the province's residents had no local radio programming at all. The effect of this killing will not be good. I hope they haven't permanently silenced our little radio station.

Ever since the formation of the Provincial Shura in early March, I had hoped to meet with its newly elected head, Mullah Hamdullah. Although I had attended a few one-day shuras he had convened, I was hoping to formally sit down with him to get his perspective on local politics and to see how the PRT could help. On April 20, he visited the PRT and brought with him shura members from the districts of Khas Uruzgan in eastern Uruzgan and Gizab, a district in Dai Kundi Province to the north. Hamdullah told me he was originally from Kandahar and that he had served as a mullah for twenty-six years, principally in the western Uruzgan district of Deh Rawud but currently in the district of Tarin Kowt. He said he was literate, could read a fair amount, and had some background in science. Though not formally educated, he had attended a *madrassa*, an Islamic school of religious instruction, and during the time of the Taliban had been a judge. He was a member of the Barakzai tribe and a good friend of Governor Jan Mohammed Khan even though he came from a different tribe. When they were both younger, they had fought together against the Soviets in about twenty-three battles; as proof of his fighting prowess, he had a deep indentation in his forehead that he later claimed was from a Russian bullet. I asked him whether the bullet was still in his head, and he cracked a wide, toothy grin and shook his head saying he wasn't sure if it was or not. He said he had been knocked out in the battle and when he had come to he was all bandaged up. Only in Afghanistan, I thought to myself.

After we talked a bit about his background, we reviewed his plans for the Provincial Shura, which was scheduled to begin that Friday. The shura was going to invite the directors of agriculture, health, reconstruction and rural development, and public works; Hamdullah also wanted a member of the PRT and Special Forces to attend. He was also very interested in having a representative from the United Nations Assistance Mission to Afghanistan (UNAMA) there because of the upcoming registration of candidates for the provincial assembly and the Wolesi Jirga (the lower house of the national assembly), which was scheduled to begin on April 30. Hamdullah's initial thought was for these different outside guests, including myself, to sit in on one day of the meetings, but when I asked him if I could attend all three days, he demurred. After switching topics I asked him again, promising to sit quietly and take notes. He eventually agreed. Thus, I was the only American there for three days, copiously taking notes, and trying not to get noticed. I also prompted him to invite Rozi Khan and Matullah to the shura as well, and he agreed to do that. Once our business was out of the way, he had a few favors to ask of me.

Hamdullah wanted a pistol for himself and the five vice presidents of the shura for protection, along with documentation allowing them to own them. He also wanted us to buy him a truck, pay for the food and fuel of the provincial and local shuras, and address the distribution of humanitarian assistance. Specifically, he was concerned that wealthy people in Tarin Kowt were getting too much humanitarian assistance and no one in the outlying districts or the poor were receiving any. (Side note: because we require a signature of the governor or deputy governor before we consider giving out assistance, this, predictably, led to only people in Tarin Kowt getting help and, again predictably, they were friends of the governor.) While not critical of the governor, the shura president wanted to make sure his friends received help and (perhaps altruistically) actual poor people from around Uruzgan as well. I told him I would consider his proposals and get back to him after I had a chance to talk with Lt. Colonel LaFontaine. The Afghans were not shy about asking for help that should rightfully be requested from their government. I thought it would take us a while to wean them of us, but I was sympathetic to their situation.

While the governor and police chief were the two lodestones of the province and Mullah Hamdullah was clearly an influential player, the rest of the provincial government was the center of gravity as far as getting things done in the province was concerned. Frank Light had interviewed a number of the province's directors who were the central government's representatives in the area and were in charge of areas such as health, education, transportation, finance, and public works, to name a few. One directorate that was particularly noteworthy was called the Directorate for Haj and Religious Affairs. It coordinated the annual trips of Afghans to Mecca in Saudi Arabia for the Haj. All of them sounded interesting, and since Frank had done a superb job of at least putting some organization to the local government in his notes, I hoped to improve my knowledge of the local political scene and start to interview these men. I was particularly curious about what exactly they did, how they got their jobs, their assessments of the province and their directorates, and how best we could partner with them to improve the living standards of the people. Since Uruzgan was so poor, I was interested to see what capacity actually existed in their directorates to get something done.

One of the first men I interviewed was the director of finance for the provincial government. We met at 1:00 p.m. at the PRT, and like most adult men in the province, he was dressed traditionally in a turban and gray-and-brown shalwar kamis. His name was Gul Amshah, and he arrived carrying a sheaf of papers, which was encouraging, and seemed serious. He told me that while Kabul authorized the provincial government to spend a certain amount of money, it unfortunately didn't actually send any to the province. This was a curious statement that I obviously needed to look into. Because the local government didn't get any direct money from the central government, they raised revenue through other sources. Amshah told me that the local government assessed a 6 percent tax on bazaar shop owners twice a year, got income from government land that was rented to farmers, had a paper tax on petitions to the governor or police, a transportation tax on jingle trucks, and sundry other taxes that the director couldn't remember. Chief among these taxes was a fee that was charged for people going on the Haj to Saudia Arabia. The director said that all expenditures had to be approved by the governor, which we suspect he uses to hurt his political opponents, skim off the top, and generally not follow through on the central government's policies. While we talked, we reviewed the province's budget figures from a hand-drawn spreadsheet listing various numbers. I asked Amshah if I could copy it and study it further. He agreed and Mohib entertained him while I quickly ran off a copy. This meeting was incredibly interesting to me in terms of coming to grips with how the Afghan state functioned and the kinds of activities that the local community participated in.

I next met with the deputy director of justice who was definitely a unique character. His name was Taj Muhammed, and he seemed dour from the outset. He was a diminutive man who wore a gray-patterned turban and a brown wrap to protect him from the cold. Right off the bat you could tell he didn't want to be at the PRT, let alone talking to me. His arms and legs were crossed, he didn't touch the food or water I offered him, and he also had a scowl on his face. As we started to talk, it became clear why Taj Muhammed was so uncomfortable. He had served as either the director of justice for Uruzgan during the last two years of the Taliban or had worked in their ministry in some capacity. He was very reluctant to share information about the directorate and often referred me to the director of justice for the information I wanted. Of course, that was the person I actually wanted to talk to, but the deputy had shown up instead. Moreover, Taj Muhammed had only been with the directorate for a brief while and claimed not to know that much. Like Hamdullah, he had also studied at a madrassa. These schools had been the breeding grounds for much of the Taliban. The meeting was definitely interesting, and I eventually got the name of the correct director of justice, but it was helpful to realize that not everyone wanted us here.

Once we had finished, I then met with the director of reconstruction and rural development who had accompanied the deputy director of justice. I'd seen him a few times around town, the first being at the Provincial Shura elections, and, as always, he was his usual jovial self. Engineer Mohammed

Hashim had a thick brown beard, a stocky build, and wore a dark-brown shalwar kamis with a black vest. Unusual among the directors, he actually had training in the area he was responsible for and seemed knowledgeable about his responsibilities. Hashim had graduated from the Kabul Engineering Institute and had picked up quite a bit of English by studying it on his own. He had mostly been involved in dealing with the myriad natural disasters we'd recently experienced, but his usual job was to help rural communities with small-scale projects such as water pump construction, irrigation, and flood mitigation. Hashim had been part of the snow-clearing operation we had undertaken to open up the district of Khas Uruzgan earlier in the year and had played an important role in helping flood victims in Deh Rawud district. He usually provided labor, tents, shovels, wheelbarrows, and some engineering advice. In addition to his disaster relief duties, he also assisted in the placement of wells throughout the province. He asked for the typical things such as a wall around his headquarters, several trucks, and various office supplies such as a printer. Interestingly, much like Deputy Police Chief Nabi, Hashim was a former communist and received training from them to become an engineer.

I eventually met with about ten more directors of various stripes over the course of the next several months. What became very clear to me was that even though many of the men were well meaning and some had some training in their fields, they were either undermanned with too much work or overmanned with little to do. Most tended to be the former. With rare exceptions, directorate operations were based in Tarin Kowt and hardly ever extended into the surrounding districts. While some directorates lacked basic equipment such as vehicles, office supplies, power, and, in the case of the Directorate of Information and Culture, a building, the greatest challenge continued to be one of human capital. The directorates were either led by well-intentioned but ineffective illiterates or by trained professionals who possessed limited management experience. Below the level of director and deputy director, few employees could actually be considered educated. Lacking literate workers with even a modicum of training, the directorates had a limited effect on Uruzgan Province, which exacerbated the governance challenge. I certainly had my work cut out for me.

After repeated requests from the Provincial Shura, Governor Jan Mohammed Khan finally provided a building for them to meet at their regular monthly meeting. The structure had originally belonged to a member of the Taliban, but in the mad rush to flee from Coalition Forces in 2001 much of their property had ended up in the possession of the governor and his supporters. The one-story building had high ceilings, a wide-open meeting room, and was situated just fifty yards away from Matullah's checkpoint. Its walls were a light blue and the carpet was khaki brown. I had already sat in on a few one-day shuras so I was looking forward to this longer three-day session. On April 22, the Provincial Shura convened its first full session in Tarin Kowt since tribal meetings had been outlawed by Mullah Omar in 1994. Unlike the previous meetings, however, Qayum Karzai and his organization were not present in order for the newly elected leaders to take more responsibility for their affairs. The PRT quickly spun up a mission for me, and Mohib and I settled in to a back row of white plastic chairs to watch how Mullah Hamdullah ran the proceedings. All the tribal elders from each of Uruzgan's five districts were seated in the front rows in similar plastic chairs, and they wore the traditional shalwar kamis and turbans and had long beards of varying shades of gray.

Each day's session was organized around a set of preselected topics, and representatives of each district were given an opportunity to address the issues. Subjects ranged from concerns about security, how best to handle the remaining flood damage, law-and-order issues, the provincial health infrastructure, and the proper relationship between Coalition Forces and the Government of Afghanistan, among other subjects. These discussions comprised the first two days, and the third day was set aside for presentations from the directors of several Afghan directorates in Uruzgan, the PRT, and representatives from the ANA and UNAMA. Deputy Governor Haji Aziz Khan was there to represent the governor. At my encouragement, Ali Mohammed, the sole radio reporter for Tarin Kowt's radio station, attended as well and covered the proceedings. I provided him with a radio, batteries, and tape cassettes to help with his job and to better connect the shura to the people. Mohib would usually grab one of the PRT's trucks and give him a ride to the shura. Ali Mohammed walked with a pronounced limp—he had been shot five times by the Soviets when he tried to cross into Afghanistan after having visited Pakistan, and one of the bullets pierced the top of his foot, leaving a gnarly scar.

Mullah Hamdullah opened with a prayer, lifting his hands, palms up, to around his midchest region, and the elders stood and prayed with him. I stood as well to show my respect. Once the prayer was over, Hamdullah made a brief speech about how the shura would be run and pointed to five rules he had posted on the wall. I neglected to translate all of them, but they said that only people who were recognized by the president could speak and that topics had to be of public interest; private concerns could be addressed after the meeting. I quietly sat in the back jotting down notes as Mohib whispered his translations into my ear. A recurring theme was the proper relationship between and responsibilities of the coalition, the provincial reconstruction team, and the government of Afghanistan in Uruzgan. Concern was expressed that, all too often, district leaders and the police were collecting illegal taxes and fees from the local population that were being used for personal gain and not for the community's benefit. After some brief deliberation, the shura decided that it would ask the governor to send a letter to all district leaders and police telling them not to steal from the people.

While the PRT was exhorted to do more in Uruzgan, especially in the outlying districts, shura members also expressed disappointment that provincial directors were not doing more and that their leaders were often lazy. Some shura members took the view that since Afghanistan had its own leaders, they shouldn't expect the coalition and the provincial reconstruction team to do everything. In line with this belief, Afghans needed to take responsibility for the lack of performance of the provincial directors. There was some concern that the coalition was detaining the wrong people and relying on inaccurate information from unreliable sources in their search for the Taliban. Moreover, the shura felt that the CF were often assuming the role of the police in Uruzgan and that "normal" crimes should be handled by the appropriate local law enforcement officers. Shura members also agreed that the Provincial Police needed to go on more regular patrols in the province and stop stealing from the local population. Further, they asserted that, through better roads and bridges, security would be enhanced and security forces would be better able to travel around Uruzgan to fight the Taliban. The meeting was impressive in its ordinariness, and the relatively mundane nature of the subjects sounded remarkably like any small town city council discussing matters of public interest.

The next day discussions revolved around similar themes and issues. In the interim I had conferred with Lt. Colonel LaFontaine and Kerry, as well as a representative of the Special Forces, about the discussions of the previous two days. The third and final day included briefs from several of the province's directors. I brought the whole wagon train of representatives from the PRT to respond to questions from the shura's members. I suggested that Lt. Colonel LaFontaine ask for questions after his presentation because I wanted to inculcate the practice of asking community leaders about issues of public concern, and the Afghans usually remained relatively silent when local officials spoke in front of them. Looming over the group, Lt. Colonel LaFontaine made his presentation while an assistant of Ali Mohammed's stretched his arm straight up over his head to make sure he recorded every word. Our police adviser, Travis Nelson, worked the crowd like the ol' sheriff he was, speaking politely to the Afghans in a soft Southern drawl. The Special Forces officer responded to complaints that the coalition had been detaining the wrong people. He said that they had a very deliberate process of choosing targets and endeavored to make sure they had the right people. He said he would meet with anyone after the meeting who felt someone had been unjustly detained.

The Provincial Shura received briefings from the Uruzgan directors of agriculture, health, reconstruction and rural development, and public works. I was very hopeful this would create some modicum of accountability for local public officials. The directors stressed a number of common themes in their presentations such as the need for more trained personnel in their directorates, the challenges that poor infrastructure posed to their operations, and how, because the province was poor, the directorates were limited in what they could do. The director of agriculture stressed that Uruzgan needed more water and could possibly address this through dam construction, and he said people needed to eat locally grown food and not purchase food from Pakistan. The directors of health, reconstruction and rural development, and public works all requested that the shura contact Kabul in order to get more support for their efforts.

Acting ANA Commander Habib Rahman, the executive officer of the new ANA battalion located at Forward Operating Base Ripley, stressed that his men came from many different provinces in Afghanistan and that they were in Uruzgan to provide peace and security for Afghans by Afghans. He also emphasized that Uruzgan residents should approach them with their problems and that the ANA would make every effort to solve them. The PRT reviewed the process by which we selected and funded local development projects, our procedures for distributing humanitarian assistance, and the current projects we had under way in the province. UNAMA's presentation, conducted by elections trainer Kemal Gafarov, whom I had invited, reviewed the procedures for candidate registration and explained the election process for September's elections. He also distributed candidate registration information for dissemination throughout the province. The shura concluded with a summary statement by Mullah Hamdullah, the shura's president. He stated that the shura would be recommending candidates to UNAMA for consideration and would tell people about the registration process. In addition, he encouraged shura members to continue to talk to the people and to listen to their problems. Mullah Hamdullah also exhorted members of the Taliban to stop fighting because the people of Afghanistan had suffered long enough and he wanted provincial, district, and village leaders to help the people and not to keep aid and money for themselves.

The well-organized and orderly nature of the Provincial Shura's meeting was a strong indication that local governance structures were slowly maturing. In many respects, the gathering was more productive and respectful than many government meetings in the United States. I was strongly encouraged by the fact that the shura had invited several provincial government officials to give presentations on their directorate's activities and that the shura seemed to take its role in improving government performance seriously. Shura members had thoughtful discussions of relevant issues of public concern and were encouraged to address province-wide issues as opposed to narrow district or personal concerns. The meeting did wonders for my estimation of how and whether the Afghans could govern themselves. I was also hopeful that I could work with these men to broaden the number and types of individuals we were working with at the PRT. Of some concern was the fact that the shura members didn't really hold the directors accountable in any meaningful way. However, I welcomed their sharp questioning of our group, which was perfectly reasonable since it was their country after all and we were only visiting.

THE BLOODY TRAFFIC CIRCLE

The counterinsurgent reaches a position of strength when his power is embodied in a political organization issuing from, and firmly supported by, the population.
        —David Galula, *Counterinsurgency Warfare: Theory and Practice*[3]

Many of the soldiers had mentioned how the governor would dump the bodies of the Taliban at the main traffic circle, in part to send a warning to other

Taliban, but also as a collection point for their families if they were local in-surgents; it also served as a reminder to the local population of who was in charge. At first, I almost didn't believe these stories, but they did seem con-sistent with my own rudimentary understanding of Afghan warfare and pol-itics. So when the opportunity to see the traffic circle firsthand came up, I jumped at the chance. On April 11, I attended the official opening of the Tarin Kowt Traffic Circle. It was essentially a two-story tower set up on and sur-rounded by a thirty-foot-wide cement pedestal. The pedestal was painted in white and red stripes, like a candy cane, indicating the direction of traffic, and the main building was painted cyan with reddish-brown trim. When we got there, the Afghan National Army had already secured the area (they were moving onto FOB Ripley as the Twenty-fifth Infantry Division rotated out), and their men were placing Afghan army recruiting posters on the walls of the bazaar as the locals looked on curiously. Bravo Company's Captain Owen was there with his men as well, also pulling security duty. The provincial di-rectors were gathered into a small group near the entrance to the circle (I made sure to shake their hands) and a crowd of about four hundred people were assembled, watched by the Afghan army and the Afghan National Police. I was ushered onto the pedestal along with Lt. Colonels Sellers and LaFontaine, Governor Jan Mohammed Khan, Captain Owen, and the head of the Afghan army for our area. Captain Owen delivered some nice remarks on how the security situation had improved dramatically in Uruzgan Province through the close cooperation of the U.S. military and the Afghan people. He said that the traffic circle represented this cooperation and that the presence of the Afghan army signaled how the Afghan people were now ready to take charge of their security and how much it had actually improved in the area. After Owen's comments, an Afghan army mullah sang prayers to Allah, the Afghan army commander spoke, and then Governor Jan Mohammed Khan delivered a long address. We used a set of portable loudspeakers and public address system contained in an army backpack to communicate to the crowd as the sun shone from the cloudless sky. After the governor finished, he walked down the steps of the pedestal and cut the red ribbon connecting the low fence that surrounded it. After the ceremony, Lt. Colonels Sellers, LaFontaine, and I climbed the cylindrical staircase to the top of the tower to get a better van-tage point of the crowd. The two main roads of Tarin Kowt met at the circle and we could see the assembled crowd begin to disperse. We made our way down to the Humvees, but I saw no hint of blood trails or any suggestion that this key traffic post was the macabre landmark it had become.

After we got back, I met with the director of information and culture. He was in charge of the radio station and had a staff of four. Miraculously, I think that number was about right for his responsibilities. I think most directorates here are definitely overmanned as everyone tries to get in on the gravy train. He had one man who ran the station and did most of the shows, and a second who was some sort of journalist who also assisted the radio station operator. I told him that we would like it very much if both men could attend the provincial shura meetings and, using the tape recorders we had provided them, create some news pieces for the radio station. The station's reach was about 10 kilometers and ran every day of the week, from 6:30 to 10:00 a.m. and from 6:00 to 8:00 p.m. The director also agreed with my idea of placing message boards downtown for the PRT, Coalition Forces, and the provincial government to communicate with the local community. He suggested we place one at the mosque, another at the governor's compound, one at the hospital, and at least one at the traffic circle. It was a very productive meeting.

My primary interpreter Mohib just got engaged. He is marrying one of his first cousins, and she is reportedly quite the catch. The reason I know this is that, per the custom of the area, Mohib had to pay her family to marry her, which in this case was $12,000. Unusual for this area, however, she's completed twelve years of schooling and is eighteen years old. Brides (and women for that matter) are not usually that well educated or married at such an "advanced" age. Her father is apparently wealthy, and the family has two sons who work in Britain. The amount Mohib paid was also considered quite high. The U.S. presence here (that is, our financial presence) has actually lifted the price of brides in the area because of all the money sloshing around the local economy. To indicate his newfound status, Mohib's right pointer finger was dyed orange, as was the palm of his hand. When I asked him about the pending nuptials, he smiled with a big grin and looked down at the floor. Perhaps we'll be invited to the wedding.

I woke up one morning to learn we had been attacked by mortars the previous evening. Only one of the four got close to the base and struck near the main entrance to Forward Operating Base Ripley, but no one was hurt. Several months later, three mortars struck downtown Tarin Kowt. Miraculously, no one was hurt then as well. The locals were outraged at the attack and wondered why we weren't going on more regular patrols (this was mostly because the Twenty-fifth Infantry were departing). One of the Provincial Shura members wondered aloud at a meeting why we hadn't caught the perpetrators since we were able to read what people wrote from space. We assured the man we couldn't do that but I was impressed with how powerful the locals thought we actually were.

The village that Aziz, who is one of our more senior interpreters, lives in was visited by the Taliban last night, who told him to stop working for the Americans. Thankfully, he wasn't there that evening (he often stays at the PRT), but his neighbors conveyed the message. The Taliban also visited Mohib a few months ago and so he stays at the PRT as well.

MEETIN' THE MULLAHS

I believe that a high and unwavering sense of morality should pervade all spheres of governmental activity.
    —Philippine president Ramon Magsaysay

On Thursday, April 14, I attended a meeting of Tarin Kowt mullahs at the governor's compound. We sat on the ground at one of the governor's outdoor pavilions with the mullahs sitting on the edge of the rectangular structure. There were about forty Sunni mullahs there and they were all dressed in the traditional garb of the rural Pashtuns. Governor Jan Mohammed Khan had called the mullahs together to encourage their support of U.S. forces. He said that the American forces were not like the Russians in that they did not attack the Afghan people or molest their wives. He went on to say that the United States was here to help the Afghan people. One mullah suggested that they go out into the other districts of Uruzgan in groups of four or five and talk with the mullahs located there, telling them about the good things the U.S. forces were doing and asking them that if they had problems with the Coalition Forces to tell the governor or tell the mullahs.

The governor had expected a bigger turnout of mullahs (there are 164 on the government payroll and 86 others), but only 40 showed up. He had also tried to recruit a new mullah to talk on the radio station. The last one who had said positive things about the United States and the governor had been killed by the Taliban on his way home on March 23. Predictably, no mullahs volunteered and the original five or six who were willing to talk on the radio backed out as well.

The next day, Lt. Colonel Sellers spoke of how U.S. forces had assisted in rebuilding the central mosque of Tarin Kowt. He said we were not here to rule Afghanistan and that we respected the Afghan people as human beings. Sellers mentioned that another unit was rotating in and that the Afghan National Army would help. He said the United States was mistaken to have left Afghanistan when the Russians departed and that we would not leave again until the work had been done. At this, the governor broke in and talked about a small boy the U.S. forces had helped whom the governor swore was going to die from his injuries. He also said that Lt. Colonel Sellers himself had helped flood victims in Deh Rawud and helped evacuate 270 people using his helicopters. The United States also provided food, blankets, and tents. Lt. Colonel Sellers concluded his comments by paraphrasing an Afghan proverb: a friend is one who helps when his friend is in need or in distress. The governor said this was true and that a friend helps you when you are poor, in prison, or sick. At this, the meeting broke up and a decision was made to have another meeting of the mullahs the following Monday.

Lt. Colonel Sellers and I attended the next meeting of the mullahs at the governor's compound. I noticed Ali Mohammed was there, our sole radio reporter, along with Dost Mohammed who was the director of information and culture and nominally Ali's boss. In addition to the original group of mullahs, the Afghan army mullah was present. He began the proceedings with a prayer and then talked about the fact that every country had an army and that a house was not a house unless it had a wall. He said everyone could join the Afghan army and that the Americans were here to help our country and not destroy it or our religion. Once the mullah had finished, Governor Jan Mohammed Khan wondered aloud why some mullahs hadn't attended the previous day's meeting. He specifically asked why no mullahs had attended from Mirabad village, saying that if they had problems with him, then he would stay home. At this, many of the mullahs implored him to stay. I was impressed by the political theater. The governor stressed that the

Taliban wanted to make Afghanistan like Iraq, and he encouraged the mullahs to talk with the Taliban in their areas and tell them that we wanted to build Afghanistan and not tear it down. He further mentioned that the mullahs didn't need to go to Pakistan to get an education (I believe he was talking about the infamous madrassas that helped fuel the Taliban's rise to power). He said they should get educated here in Afghanistan. Governor Jan Mohammed Khan then stated that the primary purpose of the meeting was to get the mullahs to go out into the other districts, in groups of four or five, talk to the other mullahs, and encourage them to support the Afghan government and Coalition Forces. Some of the mullahs balked at this, not because of the content of the message, but because of safety concerns since the assassination of the radio mullah. The governor continued, saying the Americans had helped rebuild several mosques, provided paint for them, loudspeakers for prayers, and water pumps as well. He said that any person putting a mine in the road or shooting at the Americans would personally be killed by him, even if that person was his brother. Governor Jan Mohammed Khan encouraged the mullahs to talk with the people, adding that Karzai had offered him several jobs in Kabul but he chose to stay here to help the province.

The Taliban have been busy. We got a report at the PRT today that Dr. Abdul Baki, who had run for president of the Provincial Shura and was now a vice president of the group, was ambushed by the Taliban on his way home from praying at the mosque. He and his son had just left the building when four Taliban attacked them with small arms. His son was instantly killed and Dr. Baki was hit once but retreated to the mosque. One of the Taliban went to look for him and was shot and killed by the doctor who had been carrying a pistol. The Taliban are clearly killing locals who are supportive of the government. Of course, others might be taking advantage of the security situation to achieve their own political goals.

As I was typing up my notes from the latest Provincial Shura meeting, the PRT got word that Shaikh Mir Ahmad, who was one of the only Hazara members of the Provincial Shura, had been killed on his way home to Khas Uruzgan. As details came in, it seemed that the Taliban had erected a temporary checkpoint at a traffic circle in the eastern part of the province and had been going through everyone's things looking for evidence of working with the Government of Afghanistan. They found Mir Ahmad's Provincial Shura membership card and took him to a field where they had already put several people they had captured. At sunset, the Taliban shot all of them in the head. Mullah Hamdullah was extremely distressed about the killing—he actually had tears in his eyes—and he spoke of what close friends they had been. It was an especially hard blow since he was one of the only Hazara in the shura, and it was particularly jarring because I had just been transcribing what he had said at the Provincial Shura. Friendships are not unique between Pashtuns and Hazara but the killing is a severe blow to the shura and my continued hopes of bringing all of the communities under its umbrella.

Staff Sgt. Nathan Dirkman replaced Staff Sergeant Kraemer as the head of our Military Police, as Kraemer returned home. Dirkman, like Kraemer, was a professional soldier who took his responsibilities seriously. He was in his mid-twenties, and, perhaps because our ages were closer, we hit it off immediately. Like many military personnel, he had several tattoos, and his clean-shaven head was framed by thin eyeglasses. Dirkman laughed easily and worked well with a variety of a people of different ranks and walks of life. He was recognized as a thoughtful, competent, and hard-working person and had the respect of our PRT commander. Happily married with three young sons, he met his wife at an upscale gentleman's club in the Midwest. He went to the club with some friends and saw her performing on stage. Nathan turned to his buddy and said, "That woman will be my wife." The art of courting an exotic dancer, I soon learned, had to do with how you folded the dollar bill you gave her. He said he folded his into an arrow and wrote his name and number on it and passed it to her. When his future wife finished her set, she came over to his table and they struck up a conversation. Their courtship began and eventually they married; they are now the image of middle-class respectability. His wife would often send her husband small letters signed with the red lipstick impression of her lips.

The Iowa National Guard departed Uruzgan. They had served as our very capable force protection for a year and were replaced by a unit from the Texas National Guard. This unit was led by Capt. Kenneth "Ross" Walker and his executive officer, 1st Lt. Christopher McElrath. The all-white Iowan unit had been replaced by a diverse unit of blacks, Hispanics, and whites, reflecting the greater diversity of Texas. They were incredibly able, and many of their members were police officers in civilian life. I had the honor of helping one of the Hispanic members acquire his citizenship for having served the United States in a war zone. I always wondered why so many other people blessed with having been born in the United States didn't feel the same need to serve their country in war.

We got a report today that the police were holding a man for stealing the burka off a woman. He had apparently been hiding in the rubble of a building next to the police station and as two women in burkas walked by en route to the hospital, he leaped out and grabbed one of their coverings, telling them he would return it if they slept with him. The women started to yell and throw rocks at the man, and the noise and mayhem eventually alerted the police and they arrested him. Both the police chief and the governor agreed that he should be executed because, in addition to this specific incident, he had also committed other similar crimes. It was in this context that Travis traveled down to the police station to talk with Rozi Khan about police training. Because the police chief respected Travis so much, he offered him the privilege of executing the prisoner. But when the police chief offered Travis his Soviet-era pistol to do the deed, Travis's eyes became as wide as saucers and he politely declined the "honor." I'm sure this made an excellent impression on him of Afghan culture.

5   A VISIT TO THE GREEN ZONE
(Chora—Spring 2005)

The purpose in deploying static units is to establish a grid of troops so that the population and the counterinsurgent political teams are reasonably well protected, and so that the troops can participate in civic action at the lowest level.

—David Galula, *Counterinsurgency Warfare: Theory and Practice*[1]

Although I had a lot of work cut out for me in Tarin Kowt, I wanted to make sure I visited Uruzgan's other four districts and got a sense of the concerns of the people. I also wanted to see the vibrant countryside and venture out beyond the provincial politics of Tarin Kowt. On March 17, I went on a mission to the district of Chora, which is to the east of Tarin Kowt on the way to Khas Uruzgan, and got my first chance to truly see the deserts and mountains of Afghanistan. Our goal was to assess the police force of Chora and for me to meet and talk with as many people as I could. As we made our way through Tarin Kowt en route to Chora, you could clearly see the impact of a few weeks of rain on the area. Bright green plots had sprung up everywhere and farmers had begun to plant their crops; quite a contrast with the khaki-colored soil that turned into dust when it dried. On the way, we had to cross what is usually a dry riverbed. However, after the heavy rains it was a frothing torrent of deeply colored red that spilled into our Humvees as we crossed it. We took a left past an Afghan National Police checkpoint and took the main road out of Tarin Kowt. The clouds were thick and gray, threatening us with another needed downpour of rain, and the smell of moisture filled our noses. A way down the road, we stopped and checked out a suspected IED area we had recently learned about; thankfully, no IEDs were found. We proceeded along and broke out into empty country, winding our way through the rocky terrain and flat desert of the area. At different points we saw the Kuchies, the nomadic people much picked on by their fellow Pashtuns. Collections of camels carried their possessions, and they would immobilize the beasts by tying one of their front legs back when the caravans stopped for the night.

We eventually made it to an open area set between two mountain ranges and saw the blue lights of a police vehicle coming toward us at high speeds with two Hiluxes (sturdy pickup trucks) close behind. Lo and behold, we had run into the Chora police chief Haji Ibrahim and his whole department en route to Tarin Kowt. We stopped in the middle of the road with the barren mountains on either side of us and discovered that he had been reassigned by the governor to the western Uruzgan district of Char Chena. We agreed to meet later in the day at the PRT and turned around. As we all headed to Tarin Kowt, one of Ibrahim's trucks overheated and he had to dump a number of his men off. One of their trucks easily had twenty men shoehorned into the back, all looking uncomfortable. As we went to cross the river again at the same place we had crossed before, there were now at least 150 people on the banks milling around and about 20 cars waiting to cross. An impromptu boat had been put together to ferry people across with guide ropes; the current was so fast and deep that this was the only way people could cross. Several jingle trucks were waiting for the water to go down. We made our way through with no problem and got back to the PRT.

Haji Ibrahim arrived shortly thereafter along with Provincial Police chief Rozi Khan to discuss the politics behind the personnel change. Essentially, the person the governor was putting into Chora, and who was currently the police chief of Khas Uruzgan, had been accused of beating people up, taking their money, and doing nothing. Since he was paid by the governor, he was clearly his man, as opposed to being paid by the Provincial Police chief and being under his influence. Haji Ibrahim was an ally of the Provincial Police chief and, in contrast with his replacement, was incredibly effective, honest, and much admired by the local population of Chora. We learned later that Chora's residents were visibly upset upon hearing about his departure. Both Haji Ibrahim and Rozi Khan have survived IED attacks in the past (it is suspected that the governor was behind them), and my general assessment was that Mr. Ibrahim was being sent to his new district to be killed off by the insurgency since it had a lot of Taliban activity. I was sure his effectiveness would create many friends and allies for him there but I worried about his safety and Governor Jan Mohammed Khan's schemes.

On April 25, I went on my second trip to the district of Chora. I had visited the area on April 8 in order to get better acquainted with the layout, but this time I hoped to meet with the district chief and any other officials I could track down. We proceeded the usual way to Chora, going north through Tarin Kowt and the village of Sar Marghab, eventually breaking out of the green zone and going overland in the desert. I really enjoyed the drive to Chora because the mountain ranges formed a bowl around the desert floor, and even though it was completely devoid of life, its variety of khaki and brown colors interspersed with blacks, greens, and reds made it visually arresting. Just as soon as our eyes adapted to the rich tapestry of khaki, the green valley of Chora opened up with its copses of trees, well-tilled farms, and small dwellings extending to either side of the valley. It was, as Maj. Herbert B. Edwardes described a similar valley in his 1848 book, *A Year on the Punjab Frontier in 1848–49*, a "vegetable emerald." It was overwhelming, and you could smell the moisture of the river coursing through the center of town. Afghan farmers tended their small plots of wheat interspersed with almond trees and lazily eyed us as we descended into the village from the ridge. Chora seemed better organized and wealthier than Tarin Kowt and its isolation very calming. We drove down from the plateau and plunged into the village, crossing a rich and fast-moving river, the water accreting in the foot wells of the Humvee, and after passing several farms we turned onto the main road. Like every other Afghan village I had visited, the main square was arranged into an X, and a two-story traffic circle, which had been constructed by the Twenty-fifth Infantry, was located at its center. We drove into the police station, and the Texas National Guard set up a perimeter. Unlike Tarin Kowt's police station, this one was solely made of adobe and was less well maintained by the police chief, although the Twenty-fifth Infantry had done much to improve it by providing shipping containers and some construction assistance.

After having spoken earlier with Haji Ibrahim at the PRT, I was very interested in meeting the new police chief, Zahir Khan. We met with him in a small room at the police station lined with large posters of Pakistan. A small window with a sky-blue frame was at the end of the room and several AK-47s leaned against the wall. We were seated along the edge as was the custom. Chief Zahir called for chai and candies. The new chief then proceeded to complain about not getting paid by Rozi Khan and requested we provide him with vehicles, additional weapons, and other support. When I asked him about reports that things had not gone well when he had been police chief of Khas Uruzgan District, he quickly dismissed these concerns with a flick of his hand. Our police mentors, Art Smith and Travis Nelson, asked him more detailed questions about his men and took notes for their assessment report. After this brief meeting, and with too much chai in my bladder, we hiked up the dusty, main street to talk with the district leader, Yar Mohammed. His compound had more concrete than adobe in it, and a few dozen Afghans milled about in the courtyard, looking menacing with their AK-47s.

Like most district leaders, Yar Mohammed was a long-time friend of the governor's but, unlike him, was a member of the Achikzai tribe, which was predominately located in Chora and Khas Uruzgan districts. He seemed a nice enough fellow, said that things were all great here in Chora, and gave me some good information on the area. I made sure to compliment the mayor of Chora (who was all of twenty-six years old) on what a good job he'd been doing and how helpful he'd been to the PRT. While there, I finally had a chance to meet with the prince of darkness: Afghan Highway Police Commander Matullah. He was ostensibly in charge of the highway police and was, in a former life, head of the governor's militia. Matullah was a nefarious fellow around the province, and people would often come up to us in the villages complaining about his behavior and were always worried about his informants reporting on them. I told him that everyone said I should meet with him (go for flattery, I say) and I apologized for not meeting him earlier (more flattery) and pledged to see him soon. After a series of productive meetings, we made our way out of town. Little did I know that I had witnessed a crime that I would learn more about a few days later. Before we left Chora, however, I made sure to stop and talk with several shop owners just to make sure they were not being shaken down by Zahir Khan and his men. The two shop owners I spoke with assured me they hadn't been hit

Tarin Kowt

To Chora District

Directorate of Rural Rehabilitation and Development

UNAMA

Directorate of Religion

Directorate of Communications

Directorate of Justice

Directorate of Finance

Directorate of Power

Girls' School

Dir. of Education

Governor's Compound

Mosque

Lumber Yard

Provincial Police Station

Bazaar Chief/ Tk Police Station

Mayor

Governor's Residence

Directorate of Agriculture

RESIDENTIAL

MARKET

Traffic Circle

Hospital

Directorate of Irrigation

Women's Clinic

To Matullah's compound

First suicide vest attack

To Kandahar Province

First car bomb

To Provincial Reconstruction Team

To Deh Rawud District

0   500   1000   1500   Feet

Based on an original map by MGI West, October 2006

Kmandla 2011

The damaged west face of the Pentagon on Friday, September 14, 2001.
AP PHOTO/DEPARTMENT OF DEFENSE, TECH. SGT. CEDRIC H. RUDISILL

Author with Uruzgan Province governor Jan Mohammed Khan at the dedication of the Tarin Kowt traffic circle in 2005.

View of an Uruzgan mountain en route to the western district of Deh Rawud in 2005.

Afghan National Police Chief and Barakzai tribal leader Rozi Khan with PRT Commander Lt. Col. William LaFontaine (L) and Staff Sgt. Marvin Kraemer (R) in 2004. Deputy Police Chief Haji Nabi (with glasses) stands behind Rozi Khan. COURTESY OF WILLIAM LAFONTAINE

Tarin Kowt traffic circle where dead "Taliban" bodies were left for collection in 2005.

Provincial Reconstruction Team executive officer Maj. John Dayton (L) speaking with Twenty-fifth Infantry Commander Lt. Col. Terry Sellers (R) in 2005.

Civil affairs Capt. Doug Dillon participates in a ribbon cutting for the opening of Malalai Girls School in Tarin Kowt in 2005. COURTESY OF DOUG DILLON

Girl peeks out from her home in Uruzgan Province capital of Tarin Kowt in 2005.

View of governor's compound from the Tarin Kowt traffic circle in 2005.

Sgt. Nathan Dirkman stands next to the newly constructed Tarin Kowt–Kandahar Highway in 2005.

Provincial Reconstruction Team interpreter Mohib in 2010. COURTESY OF MOHIB

Author with Provincial Shura president Mullah
Mawlawi Hamdullah in 2005.

Achikzai tribal leader Haji Malem
Abdul Khaliq Khan in 2005.

View of river
cutting through
the mountains
separating
Uruzgan and
Dai Kundi
Provinces in
2005.

Disabled Soviet tank south of Tarin Kowt in 2005.

Dead "Taliban" bodies dumped by the Afghan Highway Police at the Tarin Kowt Traffic Circle in 2005. COURTESY OF THE TEXAS NATIONAL GUARD

up for a "donation," nor had anyone else in the bazaar, and I promised them I would stop by the next time I came into town.

As we prepared to depart, a colleague of mine named Steve, who worked with the Central Asian Development Group, introduced me to a village elder in Chora named Haji Malem Abdul Khaliq Khan. Steve told me that he had been working closely with the man on a number of projects in the province and that he was an influential person in the area. I snapped his photo, took down his name, and told him I was honored to meet him and would very much enjoy sitting down with him so that we could know each other better. We spent maybe ten minutes talking as the convoy geared up; I had no inkling that I had just been introduced to one of the most important men in the province who would shatter my understanding of local politics and the histories of the key players. He gave me the first sense that there was widespread opposition to the governor in the province and that conditions were ripe for a revolt.

MEETING THE OPPOSITION

Why does the guerrilla fighter fight? We must come to the inevitable conclusion that the guerrilla fighter is a social reformer, that he takes up arms responding to the angry protest of the people against their oppressors, and that he fights in order to change the social system that keeps all his unarmed brothers in ignominy and misery.

—Ernesto Guevara, *Guerrilla Warfare*[2]

A few days after coming back from Chora, Haji Malem Abdul Khaliq Khan visited me at the PRT with Police Chief Rozi Khan. After exchanging pleasantries, I asked him a little bit about his background and was intrigued that he had been able to bring the police chief with him to the PRT. While he had been a senior at the Tarin Kowt Boys High School in the 1970s, prior to the invasion of the Soviets, Governor Jan Mohammed Khan had been working as a janitor and night watchman there and was there known as "Jano." Like Jan Mohammed, Khaliq eventually became the leader of his tribe, but for whatever reason, perhaps because he had already started in a position of influence and was educated, he lacked the ruthlessness that Jan Mohammed Khan possessed that was required to rise to the top in Afghanistan. Largely for this reason, he was well thought of by most residents in Uruzgan, with wide support not only within the Achikzai tribe but also among the Barakzai, Hazara, and Kuchi. As a mujahedeen commander, he had led a loose coalition of fellow tribesman who had headed their respective village militias. He was five feet, six inches tall and had the cheeks and droopy eyes of a bloodhound, but his physical stature belied the authority he wielded in the community. Born in the village of Chora, he is a member of the Achikzai tribe, who live mostly north/northeast of Tarin Kowt, and he had served as the district chief of Chora before Jan Mohammed Khan fired him.

As I soon learned, the reason there had been so many people in Yar Mohammed's compound in Chora was that Matullah and his men from the highway police were in town to steal from Haji Malem Abdul Khaliq Khan. Matullah had seized twenty-one vehicles from Khaliq (most originally taken from the Taliban following their collapse) and had tried to confiscate a substantial weapons cache that he also had in his possession. Khaliq had refused this request and turned the weapons over to the Afghan National Police in Tarin Kowt and to Chief Rozi Khan who was also his political ally and friend. These weapons were then handed in to the Afghan army battalion located at FOB Ripley. Two days later, a radio broadcast from Kandahar, purportedly from the Afghan army, labeled Khaliq a member of the Taliban, further stating that the weapons that had been turned in by him had actually been seized from him by the Afghan army. This announcement enraged Khaliq and Rozi, and the PRT intervened, setting up a meeting with Afghan army Operations Officer Maj. Noor Agah. Agah stated that the Afghan army had nothing to do with the broadcast and pledged that the Afghan army would remain neutral in the upcoming elections. He agreed to make a broadcast clearing Khaliq of the Taliban moniker, which was subsequently done. Khaliq and Police Chief Rozi Khan strongly suspected that Governor Jan Mohammed was behind the effort to brand Khaliq a member of the Taliban. The politics of the area are complex and if what Khaliq and Rozi said was true, we needed to be on our guard that we didn't accidentally hurt the interests of the people through our support for the governor. However, we also needed to empower the people if we hoped to limit the governor's pernicious behavior.

Our police liaison, Travis Nelson, has decided to curtail his tour. He had originally been assigned to Kabul to mentor senior police leaders but the pollution in the capital badly affected his lungs, so he was sent to Uruzgan for the cleaner air. He was a great guy to be with, and his wealth of experience in policing and, quite frankly, his age helped add a touch of maturity and judgment to our operations that was definitely welcome. He liked Uruzgan enough, but the challenges of working with illiterate Afghan police officials and being shoehorned into a Humvee for several hours a day proved too much for him. We were all sad to see him go. Unfortunately, a day or two after he left we got word that not all had gone well for him at Kabul International Airport. The usual procedure when you land in Kabul is that the airline staff take your bags off the plane and deposit them right on the tarmac next to the plane for you to take to your vehicle. They don't take it to the airport terminal because the luggage carousel doesn't work. Travis's understanding of how airports usually worked didn't encompass this wrinkle. As he patiently waited in the passenger lounge for his bags, the Explosive Ordnance Disposal team was called in to deal with a suspicious package. Little did Travis know that his bags were in the process of being destroyed by the team. Minutes turned to half an hour or so and when he looked out the terminal window at the plane he had arrived in, he noticed his bags had been vaporized. All of his possessions, including gifts and souvenirs, had been destroyed in a millisecond and all he had left were the clothes on his back. We at the PRT could not stop laughing and most of our sides were hurting throughout the day. We didn't laugh because we wished Travis any harm; it's just that none of us had ever heard of anything like that happening before and we could just imagine him pitching a fit with his Texas drawl booming at the airport. Just crazy.

I bumped into LaFontaine at the dining facility one night as we both scrounged for an evening meal. In the shadows of the chow hall, illuminated by the lights of the massive refrigerators, he told me of a local Afghan boy who had been saved by the surgeons up at FOB Ripley. He said the boy was a Kuchi who had been burying an IED in the road in Char Chena District when it had gone off accidentally, causing him to lose both of his legs and one of his arms. It happened close enough to FOB Cobra that the soldiers there were able to save his life and medevac him to FOB Ripley. Our guys up the road saved him, but it was with mixed emotions that I heard the news. The visceral part of me, the part focused on surviving at any cost, had no sympathy for him.

But the other side, the side that had gotten to know the Afghan people, wondered if he had done it to pay for food for his family, or if perhaps the Taliban had threatened his family to force him to do it. Sometimes, there are no good answers.

Life has settled into a nice routine at the PRT. The staff meet two or three times a week and plot out the schedule for the week and the next month and report on our various activities to the group. The force protection guys are great about supporting my missions, and I would say all of us are friends; we have little to none of the friction we've been hearing about at other PRTs. We often unwind in the evenings by playing Command and Conquer Generals or Halo 2, war never being far from our minds. Besides our regular meetings with the Afghans, such as the Provincial Shura meetings, following up with the directors downtown on various projects, and visiting area villages, we also get drop-ins who want to gossip or ask for something. We have hot chow three times a day and though the summer heat can be oppressive, we generally tolerate it pretty well. We try to play volleyball on Fridays, which is also the day we get steak and lobster for dinner, an amazing luxury to have out here. All of us feel like we're moving the ball down the court, but we feel very limited in what we can do because of our size.

A VISIT HOME

For me the antiseptic veneer of my hotel room and coyly curtained British Airways window seat compounded an acute sense of dislocation and alienation. The Marriott's complimentary fruit bowl with its plastic cover "for your protection" quietly enraged me; and the everyday concerns of life outside Iraq seemed impossibly banal. The change in our environment had been abrupt. I no longer knew who I was or where I properly belonged. I temporarily lacked the language to reintegrate myself into "ordinary" existence, perhaps because it seemed difficult then to imagine a life freed from the regular threat of violent injury or death. One saw that it was not only modesty that urged reticence on those asked to speak of their experiences in conflict, but the futility of attempting to describe that onslaught of sensation.

> —Mark Etherington, *Revolt on the Tigris: The Al-Sadr Uprising and the Governing of Iraq*[3]

It was with some trepidation that I went on leave. I was happy to go home but I wasn't sure how I would feel when I got there. Looking back, I probably shouldn't have scheduled two weeks of annual training with the navy and several extra reserve drills during my three weeks home. I never really had a chance to "come down" from the experience. When I left Kabul en route to Dubai, I had a chance to share the ride with Mike Metrinko, who was one of several retired diplomats who had volunteered to work in Afghanistan at a PRT. Mike was in his early sixties, sported a black-and-gray beard, and wore wire-rim glasses. He had closely cropped hair, a sturdy figure, and was a dedicated foodie. I would learn later from reading Mark Bowden's 2006 book, *Guests of the Ayatollah*, that Mike had been a hostage during the Iranian hostage crisis in the 1970s and 1980s and had been in solitary confinement for ten months, repeatedly being beaten by his captors. Mike was a hero in my estimation and I was honored to be his traveling companion and share a little bit of his time. I had never visited Dubai before so I readily accepted his offer to accompany him on a few visits around town. Dubai was a huge change from Afghanistan, and its Arab and Islamic culture helped me adjust to the "real" world even as the multistory office towers and glaring advertisements assaulted my senses. I also appreciated its dry heat and multicultural atmosphere. While we took in the sights, Mike suggested we visit a friend of his who owned a carpet dealership. I thought it was a wonderful suggestion and suspected that any carpet dealer Mike knew was going to be impressive. We were eventually picked up in a Mercedes by the son of the dealer's owner, and he ushered us into his shop in a low-rise shopping center. Although the store had been closed, they opened it for Mike and prepared a private showing of carpets. The owner had recently secured a contract from the president of the United Arab Emirates to provide upward of seven hundred carpets for his new home in London. We spent the afternoon sipping chai and munching on snacks as Mike went through the carpets. He was clearly an expert and I marveled at how much he knew. The whole experience of working and living in the Muslim world was new to me, but it had many charms such as hospitality and the focus on family that I found welcoming. Mike had devoted his life to the people of the region, and it clearly showed in how much they respected him.

For the next few weeks I attended a navy school in Dam Neck, Virginia, and finished up my additional drills for the reserves. After having shaved my beard and donned my uniform, I noticed I had lost about twelve to fifteen pounds. I hadn't seen the face I now saw in the mirror since I was a teenager. It was nice to be around other military personnel for a few weeks, even though many of them hadn't been to Afghanistan. Several were curious about my experiences and I gladly shared the little world of Uruzgan with them. One of them remarked to me that it sounded like I really cared about these people. The sincerity of his remark and the slight surprise in his voice took me aback. He was exactly right; I did care about the residents of Uruzgan and wanted to genuinely help them. I didn't really see them as being too different from ourselves and felt an obligation to give them my best. It was nice to know that my feelings were that apparent.

As I trained in Dam Neck, I began to call around to local thrift stores to see what wedding dresses they had on their clothing racks for Mohib's fiancée. I eventually tracked down a store named Pearl's Thrift Store in Virginia Beach that had fourteen dresses from which to choose. I took a female officer to the store with me to get the right perspective and reviewed Mohib's notes about how long the sleeves could be and how low the neckline could go. After a few minutes of searching and sharing opinions, we settled on two dresses just in case Mohib's fiancée didn't like one. Mohib had originally purchased a theatrical dress online with one of the PRT's female sergeants but his fiancée didn't like it; I was hopeful she would like these two. I also visited an electronics store to pick up a digital video recorder, DVD player, and camera he wanted as well. I rolled the dresses up and put them in my sea bag for the trip back.

Events in Uruzgan continued apace. Art Smith e-mailed me that a candidate for the Provincial Council had been gunned down in Chora on June 24. I wracked my brain trying to remember what his face looked like from the makeshift ballot the United Nations had created. The candidate, Haji Mohammad Wali, and his two guards had been ambushed as he drove home to Tarin Kowt from Chora. There was some controversy, however, because some said he had departed Chora in the district chief's vehicle, which made me think he had been killed accidentally. The district chief was not very popular in Chora and was widely viewed as a crony of the governor's. The governor was adamant that the assassination was the work of the Taliban, but I wasn't too sure. Some alleged that the man had not paid back some debts he owed and had suffered the consequences for his actions. In Uruzgan, life is cheap and death is violent.

As I returned to Uruzgan from home leave, I stopped in Dubai for a day en route to Kabul. I often found traveling through the United Arab Emirates a good way to either transition back to working in the Muslim world or to adjust back to life in the West after living in Afghanistan for an extended period of time. As I took a taxi from my hotel to the airport, I chatted with the taxi driver about the kind of work we were doing in Uruzgan. I mentioned building the girls' school, paving the roads, and constructing wells and dams around the province, and I told him it was very rewarding work. As the taxi approached the departure area, I asked the driver how much he needed and he said he would not charge me. I told him that I felt I must pay him but he refused again, saying he supported the work I was doing in Afghanistan. Nice considerations such as this are not uncommon in the Middle East, and it was gratifying to see our actions in Afghanistan approved of by other Muslims.

6 THE NEW REGIME
(Tarin Kowt—Summer 2005)

*In conventional warfare, the staff of a large military unit is composed
roughly of two main branches—"intelligence/operations" and "logistics."
In counterinsurgency warfare, there is a desperate need for a third branch—
the "political" one—which would have the same weight as the others.*

—David Galula, *Counterinsurgency Warfare: Theory and Practice*[1]

While I was away in the states, the team I had known in Tarin Kowt rotated out. The Texas National Guard guys were still there after replacing the
Iowa National Guard in April, but we had received a new PRT commander
and civil affairs team. All changes have their difficulties, and while I was
happy to return to Afghanistan, it was with some trepidation that I returned
to Tarin Kowt. First Lieutenant McElrath kindly picked me up at the flight
line in Tarin Kowt and I passed him a Pizza Hut pizza I had grabbed at KAF.
As we drove back to the PRT, he gave me his quick impressions of the new
commander. Lt. Col. Robin Fontes was a West Point graduate, former member of the Military Police, and most recently a Foreign Affairs Officer (FAO),
a kind of military diplomat, who had been working in Kabul for Lt. Gen.
Karl Eikenberry. On September 11, 2001, she had been working in Tajikistan
as an FAO, so she already had some experience in Central Asia. Some of the
soldiers were a little worried about having a female commander, but any

concerns they had were soon put to rest. Lt. Colonel Fontes was as much the professional soldier as any lieutenant colonel I had met, and while she predictably clamped down on some of our easygoing ways at the PRT, we weren't surprised by this as every new commander does something similar. The civil affairs team I had started with led by LaFontaine and Dayton also rotated home. They were replaced by a team led by Lt. Col. Douglas Goodfellow from Minnesota, along with Maj. Gustav Waterhouse, Master Sgt. 1st Class Clifford Lo, Staff Sgt. Clint Newman, Sgt. 1st Class Maria Rivera, Spec. 1st Class Robert Whitmire, Pfc. Erik Robinson, and Pfc. Jesus Garcia. What was most difficult to adjust to was that our Afghan Security Force was no longer living on the PRT and had been replaced by the Green Berets.

A few days before I had arrived, a KBR contractor allegedly saw a member of our Afghan Security Force drawing a "map" of the PRT while the Afghan was pulling guard duty in one of the towers. The new PRT commander, Lt. Colonel Fontes, chose not to intervene when the Special Forces commander corralled all the Afghans on the PRT, including the fifty-man ASF and our six interpreters, and PUCed them (person under control, now used as a verb to mean detain). During this process, they kicked and knocked over Doc, our interpreter. Doc's legs were still in hard plastic casts from the IED that had injured him in October. He was one of our longest-serving Afghan employees and was injured while participating in a PRT convoy. Doc's treatment was shameful. Once the men were secured, the Special Forces went through their rooms, found a standard operating procedure (SOP) manual from the Iowa National Guard and lots of paper with writing on it. This "evidence" was apparently enough information for the Green Berets to kick our Afghan Security Force off the PRT; they were eventually allowed to return to collect their belongings and were subsequently fired. Moreover, our interpreters were forced to live in the base of one of the guard towers versus in the barracks with us, and because the Special Forces were skittish about Afghans in general, they were moved shortly to another tower so they wouldn't use the same bathroom as the Green Berets and wouldn't be near their spaces. What an auspicious beginning for the new regime.

Our interpreters were largely the same but we had added a new one named Atifi Baki who had worked at the PRT in Helmand Province. His hair and beard were snow-white, and his build was thin and angular. He was the nicest person to work with and spoke lovingly of the time when the United States had been building the Kajaki Dam in Helmand Province and U.S. engineers and development specialists lived in the province's capital of Lashgar Gah. Atifi said that many Afghans of his generation still called Lashgar Gah "little America." He often patiently explained to me the various ins-and-outs of national Afghan politics and once walked me through each of the key personalities and factional changes of the Communist Party from the 1980s to the early 1990s. He was a fount of information and a warm and generous person. His age gave him a depth of wisdom that was truly an asset for the PRT, and I was glad he was there. After getting settled, I gave my interpreter, Mohib, the two wedding dresses I had purchased for his fiancée. He was very pleased with the selection and was also grateful for the electronics he had wanted.

The temperature now regularly reached about 108 degrees in the shade, and in the sun it spiked to 120. The fighting season had also heated up in the province. Special Forces soldiers began a series of clearing operations and direct action raids in the area, hoping to keep the Taliban off balance. Violence also increased throughout southern Afghanistan. The day after I departed KAF for Uruzgan, several mortars were launched against the base and one amazingly landed on the airstrip, narrowly missing a plane. Luckily, I had already taken off when this had occurred. In addition, a rocket-propelled grenade (RPG) had been fired in Kabul, landing near enough to the U.S. Embassy that people could hear it at 5:00 a.m. when it hit. Uruzgan was still leading the nation in political violence and, to date, we had had one election worker killed, one registered candidate killed, and one polling station shot up. The reminders of war were all around us.

I returned to my usual work routine at the PRT, planning to interview the director of health and talk with the UN about what's been going on in the province and how election preparations were coming along. My compatriot, Kerry Greene, was on leave and would return in the next couple of weeks. In the interim, the "old guard," those of us from the old PRT team, hung out and bemoaned the changes. We converted Sergeant Dirkman and Specialist Robinson's room into a mini-theater using the "one eye" projector, previously used for morning briefings, to watch movies and play video games on the wall. Sergeant Dirkman painted a portion of the wall white so the image was better. We also tended to eat together, although we had been commiserating with the force protection guys and trying to thwart the more harebrained ideas percolating around the PRT. Losing our Afghan Security Force and, potentially, some or all of our interpreters (who asked, by the way, what's the difference between the Americans and the Taliban if both beat them up?) will result in us no longer having the local knowledge and contacts these men had developed. I'm sure Kerry will join me in making this point very clear. The PRT was no longer as fun and, I suspected, would not be as successful as under the leadership of Lt. Colonels LaFontaine and Dayton. I still did my work, trying to discourage bad ideas and nudge people toward good ones. I sometimes wondered if extending my tour was such a great idea.

One of the Green Berets told me a hilarious story of when they first arrived at the PRT. Because very few of the headquarters staff ever got out to the field, the Special Forces brought several of them along to help set up their operations at the PRT. One of the soldiers who worked as a staff officer was walking around the PRT and noticed about a dozen tubes set into the ground at a roughly forty-five-degree angle facing outside the wire. The staff officer remarked that this base was ready to rock and roll if the Taliban tried to attack it with all of those mortar tubes set to go. The Special Forces officer was confused for a moment until he realized the soldier was referring to the piss tubes the soldiers used to relieve themselves. Only in Afghanistan.

The Afghan National Army soldiers are our partners in the fight against the Taliban. While a lot of the U.S. soldiers often got frustrated with how the Afghan army did things, they rarely complained about how they fought. They were fearless—a lifetime of growing up around fighting had inured them to combat. One thing the United States pledged to the Afghan soldiers was that if they died on the field of battle, their families would be assured of getting their bodies. To that end, we had the body of an Afghan soldier in one of our refrigerated shipping containers waiting for a flight home.

A RENEWED FOCUS

That's something the State Department is supposed to handle, but I was the Marine platoon commander, and I had to decide.
        —Nathaniel Fick[2]

Amazed at how much I had decompressed from just a few weeks home and how much energy I had, I threw myself back into work. No longer the new guy, I now felt a special responsibility to get my work done efficiently because my tour would be finishing in a few months. I felt like I had interviewed, poked, prodded, and photographed enough of the province and its people to begin to actively shape the local political environment in a more concerted fashion. Working with the Provincial Shura and slowly helping it develop as an institution, I had also prepared assessments of various leaders and the provincial government. It was clear that the local government was operating under enormous pressure—mostly from the Taliban, but also because it had few resources to work with in terms of money, equipment, and, most importantly, educated people. With the elections coming up in September, there was a new opportunity to incorporate the people into their government. Governor Jan Mohammed Khan, like all governors, had been appointed by the central government and so was indirectly accountable to the people. Moreover, he didn't control the budgets of his own directorates and had limited power to actually run his administration. While he had certainly played a part in getting the heads of the directorates appointed, they were largely autonomous. The general undercurrent of resentment and growing opposition to the governor also provided me with an opportunity to use the newly elected representatives as a lever to prod him to act more responsibly. Even as I was putting these plans together, other voices were demanding Jan Mohammed Khan's removal without understanding the cascading effects of this type of decision. While deciding whether or not the governor should be removed was certainly above my pay grade, I was determined to make sure that if the decision was made, it was at least made based on the most local knowledge and wisdom that could be mustered in a report. I started to draft a cable to the ambassador not only outlining the strategy I felt we should pursue in changing the leadership of Uruzgan, but also recommending a series of other personnel shifts focused on improving the management and leadership of the government. I eventually produced a comprehensive report on the subject and provided it to the ambassador at the end of my tour (see appendix A).

THE GOVERNOR'S MILITIA

Vann shared Porter's ideal of the soldier as the champion of the weak.
—Neil Sheehan, *A Bright Shining Lie: John Paul Vann and America in Vietnam*[3]

After interviewing a number of leaders in the province and getting a chance to observe the area, I felt confident enough to finally meet alone with Jan Mohammed Khan's strong arm in the province, the Afghan Highway Police, and their commander, Matullah. Matullah was tall by Afghan standards, around five feet, ten inches, and he had a lanky frame, dark skin, and a neatly trimmed black beard. Like many residents of Uruzgan, he tended to wear black turbans. He was illiterate like the governor, but in contrast to him Matullah had a generally vacant expression on his face, giving the distinct impression that not everything was well with his mind. However, he knew how to organize men and acquire power and was an indispensible ally to our Special Forces teams. His willingness to go after the Taliban was impressive. Though he had a home in town, he was most often at the checkpoint/barracks/AHP headquarters that sat next to the Tarin Kowt–Kandahar Highway, and he always greeted us as we entered town. It was a low, squat building surrounded by a wall, and its concrete structure indicated that Matullah had a certain amount of wealth. A small guard shack stood just outside the ornate gate and from it a large metal bar restricted traffic into and out of the provincial capital. The whole compound sat next to a small trickle of a river that wound its way through the family compounds surrounding the area and a large water tower we had constructed was just outside the building.

The PRT's force protection dropped me off at the building in the afternoon and hung around outside. The compound had a number of barracks rooms for the Afghan Highway Police, and several Afghans were sitting outside with their AK-47s, chatting in the shadows created by the late afternoon sun. I asked for Matullah and was ushered into a guest room with plush chairs. Mohib sat next to me anxiously waiting for the commander. I had already heard a number of stories around the province that Matullah was a cold-blooded killer and went after not only the Taliban, but also the governor's political opponents. As Mohib and I waited for Matullah, I reviewed my notes and quietly sipped the Pepsi his men had given me. An air conditioner clicked on and the dry arid heat of the room slowly dissipated. Originally appointed commander of the Afghan Highway Police in January 2005, Matullah commanded a sizable force of men who seemed to largely dominate the Tarin Kowt area, and the clear tensions between them and the Afghan National Police demonstrated that their writ was not uncontested. My developing sense was that, like the governor, Matullah was officially "in charge" of the highway police, but was really the leader of a laundered militia that had acquired official backing but was not universally supported throughout the province.

Matullah and one of his men entered the room and Mohib and I rose to greet him. I thanked him for meeting with me and explained that I had long wanted to talk with him to get a better understanding of the highway police and that as the political adviser to the PRT commander I valued his importance to the people of the province. He expressed his interest in answering my questions and gestured to one of his men to get more refreshments. He introduced his associate as Wali Jan, who acted as his consigliere and administrative officer. When I asked Matullah about his background, he told me that he had been born in Uruzgan and was a member of the Populzai tribe. He said he hadn't received much formal schooling because of the various wars that had ravaged Afghanistan. After the Taliban's first incursion into Uruzgan, he had originally fled Afghanistan for Pakistan for about seven months but eventually returned to the province to "stay at home." Matullah remarked that he had been a driver for a brief while for a high-level Taliban official in the province, but beyond that he hadn't collaborated with them in any meaningful way. He also said he was a cousin of the governor and that his duties extended to other matters beyond patrolling the highway.

Matullah stated that most of the highway police were men who had worked for the governor at one point or another and that many had served with Karzai when he had arrived in the province in 2001. Although the senior leadership was heavily Populzai, he said he drew his men from many different tribes in the province and counted at least thirty of his men as relatives. One notable exception to this tribal inclusiveness was that members of the Noorzai tribe were kept out of the unit because they were at odds with the Populzai in the districts of Deh Rawud and Char Chena. He claimed he had about 360 men under his command and that his forces would soon be increasing by 140 following the recent approval in Kabul for additional resources. Matullah stated that the highway police were responsible for protecting the Delanor Pass to the south of the province, which provided the most direct route to Uruzgan from Kandahar, as well as the Tarin Kowt–Kandahar Road that was being constructed by the U.S. Army Corps of Engineers. I knew from speaking to Lt. Colonel LaFontaine that the highway police also had a contract to provide protection to FOB Ripley and it wasn't uncommon for them to exact tolls from jingle truck drivers and taxicabs.

Next to Matullah, who prefered the title colonel and earned about 4,800 Afghani a month, forty of his men worked as majors and captains and collected 4,000 and 3,800 Afghani a month, respectively; a highway policeman, of which there were 320, collected 800 Afghani a month. The highway police had one checkpoint next to their compound in Tarin Kowt, and Matullah wanted four or five more along the Tarin Kowt–Kandahar Road with two vehicles per checkpoint (he currently had six Russian jeeps given to him by the Twenty-fifth Infantry and at least twenty-one vehicles seized in April from Khaliq Khan in Chora). One assumed he would like checkpoints near the Delanor Pass as well. He complained that the salaries for his men were too low and that, because he didn't receive a fuel budget from Kabul, he had to pay for it himself. He claimed to have paid 200,000 Afghani for fuel for his six Russian jeeps, but because they often broke down, he had to pay for parts and supplies as well. Matullah also indicated a desire for radios for his men and for Hilux trucks because they were more fuel-efficient than his Russian jeeps. When asked to by Coalition Forces, Matullah did conduct patrols along the Tarin Kowt–Kandahar Road, staying primarily in Uruzgan Province and around the Delanor Pass, but he didn't do so with any regularity unless prompted. Though head of the highway police, Matullah clearly relied heavily upon the colleague he had brought with him. Even though Wali Jan had been presented to me as an instructor of some sort, teaching Matullah's men how to read and write, he clearly had a firm command of the issues that were important to the highway police and more often than not would answer my questions while Matullah remained silent.

The meeting lasted for about an hour and a half, and while I wasn't yet ready to follow up more forcefully on my suspicions of Matullah's complicity in intimidating the local population and, quite possibly, killing the governor's opponents, I had learned a great deal about him personally and his organization's capabilities. There was no doubt in my mind that Matullah was a force to be reckoned with, and because of his political connections, knack for leadership, and the fact that he had solved many of our local problems such as going after the Taliban, he would be a difficult person to confront directly. In addition, my ability to restrict his worst transgressions was naturally limited because of both Afghan sovereignty and his close support from the Green Berets. However, for a man with few apparent curbs to his power, his level of corruption was pretty moderate. Since other tribes were not without resources, his predatory behavior was limited to his more immediate surroundings. It wasn't a coincidence that many of our problems with the Taliban came from Noorzai tribal areas in the western part of the province. The governor, deputy governor, police chief, shura president, and the highway police all came from Durrani Pashtuns. However, it wasn't yet clear to me whether the overall exclusion of the Noorzai from local government was the cause of their general alignment with the Taliban, or if it was because of a different level of religious fervor.

We received shattering news today at the PRT. With just a couple of weeks to go before the elections, we received a report of a second candidate's assassination. Unlike the previous killing, this candidate was quite influential and well thought of in the province. His name was Atiqullah Khan, and he had run the 2004 presidential election in the province for the United Nations. Many UN workers knew him in Uruzgan and were now scared for their lives. The killing was especially important because he was a well-known opponent of the governor and had bravely spoken out against many of his actions. The method of his killing was familiar to me. Atiqullah Khan was fatally ambushed as he left a mosque where he had delivered a campaign speech. It was the same method the "Taliban" had used against Dr. Abdul Baki earlier in the year and he had also been an outspoken critic of the governor. It's amazing how many of the governor's opponents seem to get killed or have near-death experiences.

7 JOURNEY TO CHENARTU
(Chora—Summer 2005)

And that is why it is so important to understand that guerilla warfare is nothing but a tactical appendage of a far vaster political contest and that, no matter how expertly it is fought by competent and dedicated professionals, it cannot possibly make up for the absence of a political rationale.

—Bernard B. Fall, *Street Without Joy*[1]

No sooner had the Afghan presidential election concluded in 2004 than Lt. Colonel LaFontaine indicated he didn't want to repeat the mistakes of that period where the election effort of the United Nations had struggled in many areas and the PRT had to take up some of its responsibilities. The key challenges in 2004 were "simply" registering voters, identifying polling centers, preparing security for those polling centers, and transporting ballots. As we started to think in March and April of the upcoming September Parliamentary and Provincial Council Elections, the task seemed significantly more complex, even though my colleagues had gained much experience in running elections. Not only did we have to register voters again, but now we had an unknown number of potential candidates interested in running for the Provincial Council and the Wolesi Jirga, or lower house of parliament, and more polling centers were needed to make sure everyone had a chance to vote. We were fortunate in that our UN counterpart, Jared Hays, an American, was easy to work with, and, because we were all in the middle of nowhere, he liked to visit us at the PRT, get some U.S. chow, and use our gym, which helped to further build our friendship with him. My greatest concerns were whether we would actually get any serious candidates to run, whether the Taliban would strike out at the candidates, and, as always, whether Governor Jan Mohammed Khan and Matullah would be up to the task of pulling off the election and resisting the urge to corrupt the results and intimidate candidates.

While Jared and the United Nations were great partners, they were limited in what they could do directly because they had to train an Afghan staff to implement and lead the election effort. In practice, some of our Afghan district coordinators, who were charged with identifying polling centers and managing the logistics of delivering ballot boxes, ballots, and training local staff, wouldn't go to some areas because of security concerns. By early August, about four weeks before the election, we had no polling locations in a village called Chenartu in the southern part of the district of Chora. Lt. Colonel Fontes decided that we needed to take things into our own hands and travel to Chenartu to set up the polling centers and meet with the villagers about local projects. We arranged a fairly substantial convoy because we had to pass by the village of Mirabad, a known Taliban hotbed where the PRT had been attacked in late 2004. Interestingly, one of the possible reasons these villagers had aligned with the Taliban was because the governor's men sometimes went into their village to steal people's property. This was the same village that had declined to send mullah representatives to the governor's compound earlier in the year. Adding to the risk, some portions of the road were natural ambush points, so we brought several Special Forces soldiers with us as well. It was going to be a remarkable trip due to the heightened sense of danger, the necessity of our work, and the meeting with the two brothers who led the area's villagers and were close associates of President Karzai. I was also keen to add another portion of the province to the list of places I had visited.

There was nothing particularly unusual about the village of Chenartu, which was situated at the southern end of the district of Chora and abutted the Deh Chopan mountain range of Zabul Province to the south. Located at the base of several dusty mountain ranges amid a wide and treeless expanse of desert and scrub grass, it straddled the long dirt track that linked Tarin Kowt in the west to the district of Khas Uruzgan in the east. It was one of

many small villages along the road, along with Mirabad, and its people were
content, though quite poor by Uruzgan standards. What made it stand out
were the two brothers who led it, Akhtar Mohammed, who served as the
local police/militia leader, and Malim Faiz Mohammed, who was the leader
of the local shura. As fellow members of the Populzai tribe, they had served
as bodyguards to Hamid Karzai, a position of great respect and honor, when
he arrived in Tarin Kowt in 2001 to lead the southern Pashtun uprising, and
both were involved in the subsequent push into Kandahar. Akhtar appeared
to have a permanent scowl on his face, although he was quick with a smile,
and even though he was diminutive in stature, he had a sinewy authority and
controlled strength common to many Afghan militia leaders. His brother
also carried his authority with confidence, had more rounded features and,
as one would expect from a political leader, was more polished in his de-
meanor. Following their time with Karzai, both men were subsequently appointed to a number of leadership positions in the province, culminating in
their positions as police and district chief, respectively, of Char Chena District.
After they left these posts, they returned to their home village. As Populzai
tribal members, they deferred to the authority of President Karzai and
Governor Jan Mohammed Khan, but they were also ambitious and proud
and sought a larger role for themselves in the province.

We departed the PRT in the early morning to avoid the August heat and
headed east, following a dirt road that loosely followed a meandering river.
I always loved going on the PRT's missions, in part to break up the monot-
ony of FOB life, but also because of the sense of discovery and the slight hint
of danger. I was confident we could handle anything the Taliban threw at
us, but the hidden killer of IEDs, however, always made us wary. Once we
left Tarin Kowt, we test-fired our weapons and checked our radios once
again. As we proceeded, the landscape became much harsher, and the geo-
logical history of the surrounding hills and mountains indicated a turbulent
and violent past. Sedimentary layers that would normally have been hori-
zontal were now vertical, having been wrenched from their initial resting
place by earthquakes. The rough-hewn rocks came in all sorts of sizes and
colors. We passed by a looming stone plateau at one point and then encountered a surging column of shattered rock just sitting in an otherwise
nondescript rolling hill. The colors were also expressive, because in addition
to the usual khakis and browns there were large swaths of reddish sand. The

landscape was amazing, and as we crawled eastward, talcum dust kicked up by our Humvees, the water started to become scarcer. As we approached Mirabad, our shooters became more anxious. We had intercepted some radio chatter indicating the Taliban had seen us, but we didn't have any inkling that they were planning anything. At one point, we crossed the same dry riverbed the PRT had crossed in late 2004 when it had hit an IED. As our Humvee rolled over it, I clenched my muscles in anticipation of a detonation. Thankfully, nothing happened, and we were happy to move down the road, nearer to Chenartu. We eventually reached a natural chokepoint that we would have to return through to get back to Tarin Kowt later in the day. At this, two of the Texas National Guard soldiers broke off up a hill, taking along a sniper rifle and several bottles of water. They were going to set up on a hillside to cover the road so that no IEDs could be emplaced.

About three hours after departing the Provincial Reconstruction Team, we arrived in Chenartu. The village was very poor, even by Afghan standards, and no discernible river or creek went through it. Most of the people seemed as roughly hewn as the landscape; several had holes in their threadbare clothing and were dirtier than many of the Afghans I had seen. Most of the village's water came from wells they had dug and while we later discovered a nearby creek, it was quite a ways from the main town. After we dismounted, we walked down the main road of the village. Small trash piles lined the road, and the adobe buildings were a reddish hue, much like the desert we had passed through. In the far distance, we could see the mountain range separating Uruzgan from Zabul Province to the south. The villagers hovered near the doors to their homes and shops, curious about our presence. As we looked around, I recognized a face from Frank's personality profile. I quickly asked for Said Abdullah and approached the man. The man looked remarkably like Akhtar Mohammed, whom I originally thought it was, but it turned out to be his brother. What a stroke of luck! Since Akhtar was the local militia/police commander, I asked his brother if he was in the village; he said he was and went to get him. Akhtar arrived in a few minutes and he, Lt. Colonel Fontes, and I spoke to him about the upcoming elections. We stated that we needed to identify two polling centers in his village, one for men and one for women. Akhtar himself was a candidate for the Provincial Council and readily pointed out an unoccupied building. The building looked remarkably like the adobe dwellings of Native Americans out West and seemed perfect. We took its coordinates and I photographed the area, taking pictures 360 degrees around the building. We also identified a few areas where helicopters could land to deliver ballots and voting material. Our mission accomplished, we chatted a little bit with Akhtar and promised him we would come out again to work on additional development projects. He mentioned that his village needed a clinic and a school and that the villagers of Mirabad often blocked the road into Tarin Kowt. We promised to look into the issue with the governor and planned for a future trip. On the way back, we picked up our two snipers who looked like small dots on a mountainside, their camoflouge concealing them perfectly, and they quickly rejoined our column. We made our way home, carefully passing by Mirabad, satisfied by another completed mission and one step closer to having a successful election in September.

8 THE THIN BLACK LINE
(Tarin Kowt—Summer 2005)

Frontier areas are always good places for bandits. If they see the police approaching from one side they can always step across the frontier into the other country.

—John Bagot Glubb, *The Story of the Arab Legion*[1]

Uruzgan Province sits on the edge of the Hindu Kush Mountains to the north and the sprawling wasteland of the Margow and Khash deserts that dominate the south. It anchors the Pashtun south, and to its north lie the Hazara-dominated areas of Dai Kundi and Bamiyan Provinces. Besides the Helmand River, which courses through its western edge, the major means of travel to the south are two roads: one through the Delanor Pass and the other east of it. The Delanor Pass is the most direct route, but it takes you through a deep and winding valley that, depending on rain conditions, has a small river that lazily meanders through its reaches. It is a natural chokepoint and the tops of many of its ridges are too high for a determined turret gunner to hit brigands or the Taliban. Because it funnels traffic into this area, it has long been a place for enterprising tribes to exact "protection" tolls from travelers. To remind travelers of this "required" fee, the carcasses of vehicles dot the route, silent reminders of past ambushes and their unlucky victims.

During the 1980s, the Soviets often used this route when they embarked on punitive expeditions from Kandahar against the mujahedeen in Uruzgan. However, they lost so many men in the pass from ambushes that they created a new road to the east that went through large open sections of the desert where the hills and mountains were far away from the road. This new road was the same path the Taliban took to try to retake Uruzgan from Karzai's forces in 2001 and quickly became the major route Coalition Forces used to resupply their men in the province.

In early August, Lt. Colonel Fontes decided that we needed to drive down the Tarin Kowt–Kandahar Highway to figure out how the villages along the route were doing and to scout out any prospective projects for us to complete. We had received reports that the construction of the newly paved road had not allowed for flooding because of the fear that IEDs could be placed in culverts and ditches, so we also wanted to plot out those sites for possible flood mitigation projects. Trying to beat the heat, we left in the early morning and traveled about a half a mile from the PRT to the new highway. The sleek black asphalt cut a thin ribbon through the khaki dust, disappearing into the low hills south of the base. Our convoy of six Humvees and Afghan army vehicles cruised along at speeds I had never seen in Afghanistan, the drivers letting the engines out on the flat road; it was a welcome change from our usual disjointed trips across uneven country. Staff Sgt. Clint Newman, who had done a previous tour in Iraq and was a mature-beyond-his-years twenty-six-year-old, drove my vehicle. Since he was one of our best civil affairs soldiers, he would be busy on the trip.

The first section of the road, which went to FOB Pacemaker, wound through the open valleys of the province, along generally flat terrain, and passed by two villages one of which was fed by a small, natural spring. We frequently stopped along the road wherever the highway went over a dry riverbed or a sizable dip in the terrain. We'd quickly scan for IEDs and then dismount from our vehicles, taking a GPS reading in order to mark the location on a map when we returned. The surrounding hills and mountains were sun-blasted and barren but full of various shades of red, black, green, and khaki. The road was set in an open plain; we had little concern about ambushes and eventually went through a narrower portion where a small village clung to the edge of a mountain atop a long and narrow ridge. Our convoy pulled into the village for our tactical psychological operations team to undertake some polling of the population on various issues of concern to us. Sergeant Newman pulled our Humvee up to a copse of trees, rare in the southern desert, and we soon discovered they were being fed from a small spring leaking from the mountainside. The local villagers had fashioned a series of small canals to direct it to their homes and crops. Said Abdullah, Sergeant Newman, and I went to its source at the base of the mountain and saw it slowly dripping into the large pool that had collected at its bottom. Small bugs swam for cover as we cast a shadow over the water. It was so peaceful and calm, a welcome oasis from the penetrating heat of August. I found a slight incline and sat down, the small creek slowly bubbling along and the blast furnace heat of the summer dissipated because of the trees. Clint gathered a handful of almonds from the nearby trees, hoping to get a little nutrition. The stresses of the war went away for a brief while.

As we continued, we encountered an abandoned checkpoint to the left of our convoy just shy of the province of Kandahar and its northern district of Nesh. It was located atop a small hill commanding the approaches and had a functioning well; it could be manned if it was renovated. The building was roofless and pockmarked with bullet holes, a lonely citadel among the barren hills. A series of white rocks was arranged below it, spelling a word of Pashto that I asked Said Abdullah to translate. He said that it spelled "Allahu Akbar," or "God is Great," and that the checkpoint had been used by a number of groups throughout history to command the approaches into Uruzgan and Kandahar. Kandahar Province began about two kilometers beyond the checkpoint, and its border was marked by two large rock columns on either side of the road. A road leading to the Delanor Pass branched off to the right for about four kilometers into the district of Nesh. The Tarin Kowt–Kandahar Road passed into the Kandahar district of Shah Wali Kot to the left, passing through an additional two to three villages, and on to FOB Pacemaker and the construction battalion building the road. The tar-sealed road ended a few kilometers shy of the Uruzgan-Kandahar border, but the engineers expected it to run to FOB Pacemaker by September 15, 2005.

The thirty-five-kilometer portion of the road from FOB Pacemaker south to FOB Tiger passed by FOB Kodiak and was the least-developed and most dangerous section of the road. This leveled stretch was covered with crushed rock in many areas, but at its middle point fine silt dominated. Unlike the area from Tarin Kowt to FOB Pacemaker, however, the mountains in this section were closer to the road and covered with numerous boulders. Our turret gunners were on their guard as we passed this section. There were about seven villages along the way and many of the walls from their compounds and property lines came right up to the edge of the road. Crops and trees were also more numerous. In one particular section called "IED Alley," we had been told that ambushes on U.S. forces and commercial traffic were quite common. Since May, five improvised explosive devices had either been discovered or detonated in the road. During this trip, the burned remnants of six jingle trucks from a recent ambush were still present, along with their ransacked shipping containers. The road eventually came out of the mountains into an open area leading to FOB Tiger. By mid-September, this section would have crushed rock placed on it and proper drainage constructed alongside. The road construction vehicles of the battalion were rushing along the road, getting more gravel, delivering more water to keep the dust down, and making sure the pickets along the ridgelines, which protected against ambushes, had enough water and food.

After leaving this desert stretch, we passed over a dry riverbed that was at least fifty yards wide and came out of the mountains. It was dusk, and we could see the illumination cast by the lights of FOB Tiger. This was going to be our final destination. As we pulled in, we met up with a civil affairs officer there who took us to visit a police checkpoint he had been constructing, as well as to meet the local Afghan who acted as the police chief of the area. We quickly visited the checkpoint, which was still under construction but recently ransacked. According to the officer, very few contractors were willing to work this far away from Kandahar, and the local police chief had arrested the man who had built the checkpoint because he was unsure of his status. This action had infuriated the civil affairs soldier since it had been made abundantly clear that the contractor had been hired to construct the building. He speculated that the police chief didn't want the checkpoint since he had another one nearby which he preferred. We decided to meet this chief since his headquarters was about a mile or so down the road.

To call the chief's place of work a "police station" was to give it an undeserved compliment. None of his twelve men were in uniform, and their "building" was a compound as large as a football field, strewn with trash and weeds, with a series of small alcoves set into its left side. However, they did have a nice-looking police car and motorcycle likely paid for by us. They were a sorry lot, looking for handouts and causing innumerable frustrations for the civil affairs team. As we pulled away en route to FOB Tiger, one of the men got up from his plastic chair in front of the building and gestured for a truck to pull over with his AK-47, looking "for a donation."

We drove a little way further, the road once again becoming asphalt, and noticed a large blue lake in the distance. In an instant, we decided to drive over to it, take a refreshing dip, and get away from the heat of the day. The Humvees were arranged around us to provide protection, and six of the team ran into the water. As I reached the water's edge, I kept my clothes and boots on and slowly walked in. I wish I could say it was cold or at least a little cool, but it was warm; we didn't care—it was a nice change from the dust and grime and heat. We got back to FOB Tiger in time to grab some chow and a shower. As I got settled in to the large tent that served as a headquarters for the civil affairs officer, a young female soldier entered. I was immediately struck by how young she seemed, or was it that I saw her with older eyes? She was very young and innocent-looking with no wrinkles on her face. The soldier asked the civil affairs major a few questions, and he snapped an answer at her, the tone of which seemed out of proportion to her tentative inquiry. Following their conversation, I deduced she was the public affairs officer for the road and I walked up to her as she was leaving. After introducing myself, I asked her when she expected the road to open and whether plans were in place to have a ceremony of sorts for the occasion. First Lt. Laura Walker said she didn't have a lot of information but had submitted several requests for information up the chain. She gave me an e-mail address when I mentioned that I would like to stay in touch with her in order to coordinate Ambassador Neumann's trip to the eventual opening ceremony.

We departed the next morning, the cool desert air refreshing to our weary bodies. We all wanted to return to the PRT as quickly as we could and were a little worried about security since we were going back the same exact route. As we neared the middle stretch of the road, with hills pressing in, we were especially anxious. We had to stop frequently as construction trucks passed and the thin dust washed like waves against the vehicle. At one point, we had to stop our convoy because the dust had gotten so bad that our view of the vehicle in front of us was obscured. We tried to drive as fast as we could through this stretch but with a BANG we hit something in the road. I was sure we had been hit by an IED of some sort, but we were still moving and everyone checked themselves for injuries and indicated they were all right. We figured it must have been a huge rock and were relieved that we were still in one piece. We broke off the road at one point as huge trucks carrying connexs (shipping containers) rumbled past. The little crabgrass we rode over was crushed by our tires and small pebbles were getting caught in the wheel wells. All of us were wearing bandanas across our faces, the dust lingering in the heart of the Humvee. It soon cleared up as we gunned our engines down the last stretch of the road, passing sixty miles an hour on the black tarmac. We arrived in the afternoon tired, sunburned, and dusty but happy at having completed another mission.

Even though we had been gone only a couple of days, a great tragedy had taken place while we had been on the road. When we got back, we first noticed that all of the Green Berets were gone from the PRT. Their gear was still there and it was unclear what had happened. Some of the soldiers who had stayed behind said that the officer in charge of the Special Forces team had died in a training accident. I don't know how it went down exactly, but he and one of his men were practicing placing breaching charges on doors as part of their training for accessing compounds to find insurgents. Apparently, they had not been wearing the correct protective gear and their placement, both of the charge and themselves, during the explosion was not good because the inevitable debris flying from the blast hurdled toward them. The explosion essentially splintered the wooden door, and large chunks flew toward the officer, lodging in his skull and chest and killing him instantly. Another U.S. soldier was also injured, as was an Afghan army soldier. The team's higher-ups took the whole element out of country for counseling. It's amazing how quickly a life can be taken.

A few days later, I walked into the tactical operations center to work on my computer and catch up on some news. As I was typing away, I overheard Captain Walker from the Texas National Guard tell someone that 1st Lt. Laura Walker had been killed. I couldn't believe what I had heard and asked what had happened. Though information was incomplete, it seemed that her Humvee had hit an IED, instantly killing the driver and injuring a lieutenant colonel with whom she had been traveling. Captain Walker said it sounded as if she had bled to death at FOB Tiger. The force of the explosion had apparently thrust the frame of the vehicle back with such violence that it effectively severed her legs. Because FOB Tiger was a makeshift base without modern medical facilities, the delay in getting her evacuated resulted in her bleeding out from her wounds. I was just struck dumb by the news. I couldn't believe I had just met this officer six days ago and still had her e-mail address and name in my notebook. I walked out of the tactical operations center and collapsed against a mortar shelter. The cool night air felt good against my skin and the nearly full moon illuminated the base as people went about their business, but I was numb from the shock of the news. I couldn't grasp that this young woman, who had seemed like such an innocent, was dead. My last memory of her was seeing her get yelled at by the civil affairs major. Why hadn't I taken her picture so I could send it to her family? It was the second of what would be many violent deaths in my life in the years ahead. The first is the worst because it forever makes you different from your previous life, and the second means you are never going back.

Having benefited from the hospitality of many of the Afghans we had visited, I hit upon the idea of hosting the Afghan leaders we principally worked with for lunch at the PRT. I broached the subject with Lt. Colonel Fontes and she readily agreed. After I scraped together a few hundred dollars, Fontes matched them with some money of her own. When I spoke to Said Abdullah about locating a good cook who could prepare a feast at the PRT for possibly sixty to seventy people, he said he knew of a man downtown and would speak to him. I quickly assembled a list of local officials and printed off a basic invitation. Mohib translated it for me into Pashto and we ran off about seventy copies. I printed off my list of notables and over the next several days proceeded to hand out the invitations. Each of the officials who received an invitation thought the idea of a lunch at the PRT was great.

On the appointed day, the local Afghan cook showed up at the PRT with two or three assistants. One of his men carried a huge kettle filled with rice and another carried a fuel canister to keep things warm. Several other pots were in a nearby vehicle filled with cooked lamb, baked bread, and all sorts of fruits, vegetables, and French fries. Slowly but surely local Afghan officialdom showed up at the gate. Governor Jan Mohammed Khan arrived with his retinue and about thirty additional men. He seemed to be sharing a laugh with someone as he entered, and he carried a small boy in his arms. Close by him was Haji Mohammed Hashim Watanwall, the governor's erstwhile candidate for parliament. After catching up on gossip outside, everyone quickly moved into the chow hall, and very soon our numerous wooden benches were being scooted across the floor as people readied for the feast. The food was brought in on large platters as the warm sun shone down. We distributed soft drinks from our larder and joined in as I made the rounds welcoming the officials I knew and introducing myself to those who were new to me.

The governor sat with Watanwall and between them sat a little boy who was all of two or three years old. I welcomed the governor and asked him who the little boy was, and he said he was his son. I congratulated him on his good fortune and asked if I could take a picture, to which he agreed. Several soldiers had never seen this many Afghans at once and a small number were taken aback that they were in *our* chow hall. Toward the end of the meal, Lt. Colonel Fontes stood up in front of the men and spoke a few words about how we had long appreciated the much-celebrated hospitality of the Afghan people and wanted to reciprocate by having today's meal. She mentioned that together the PRT and the local government had done much to improve the lives of the people and that much work still needed to be done. She then thanked all of them for coming and wished them well and safe travels as they departed home. It was a great event altogether, and I hoped it did some good in furthering our relations with local leaders.

IN THE LAND OF THE HAZARA

To a great part of the world the desert means fear, exhaustion or at best discomfort. For ten years, it replaced for me the relaxation, the happiness and the affection of home.
—John Bagot Glubb, *The Story of the Arab Legion*[2]

Our CH-47 Chinook helicopter left the PRT in the early morning, and as we lifted off, the cool mountain air replaced the heat of the southern desert. The sky was clear and the adobe compounds of the Pashtuns rushed by us as our helicopter climbed higher and higher. The populated areas eventually gave way to the mountain ranges of the Hindu Kush and a bright blue river meandered its way south through jagged and shell-shocked peaks. As the helicopter rose, the sharp whine of the Chinook's engines and the rattling of the blades dulled our senses as occasional backwashes from the exhausts surged into the back door, the familiar smell of fuel and oil was oddly comforting. Small bushes began to appear on the mountain sides, a clear sign we had departed the south, and well-tilled fields arching out from the river beds told us we had entered the cooler climes of the mountains. The dry desert silt of Uruzgan had given way to boulders strewn about the countryside. As we neared Dai Kundi Province's capital of Nili, the rear gunner got up from his perch at the end of the helicopter in preparation for landing and a narrow undulating airstrip presented itself. With a quick thud we landed and rushed out in two columns to either side of the helicopter to form a makeshift perimeter. Just as soon as it had landed, the Chinook took off, blasting us with a sheet of dry pebbles and sand still clinging to the morning's dew. As we wiped off the detritus, the whoop-whoop of the helicopters drifted off and the cool climate of Dai Kundi's mountains settled on us. The quiet of the mountains created a ringing noise in my ears.

The region of Dai Kundi had once been part of Uruzgan until March 28, 2004, when it was split off to form its own province. It was dominated by its mountains and the Hazara people who follow the Shia Muslim faith. Dai Kundi had no paved roads or electricity and its mountains isolated it from most of Afghanistan. Its residents were snowed in for three months out of the year and suffered through three months of flooding once spring arrived. Like Uruzgan, the people hugged the small rivers and creeks of the valleys, eking out a simple existence, and their farms and homes created a "green zone" that quickly dropped off where water could no longer be coaxed to reach their crops and the harsh desert and mountains began. The province was located 350 kilometers southwest of Kabul and created out of eight northern districts taken from Uruzgan Province. It was approximately 8,088 square kilometers and was 160 kilometers away from Uruzgan's provincial capital of Tarin Kowt. Dai Kundi was bordered by Uruzgan and Helmand provinces to the south, Ghazni and Bamiyan to the east, and Ghowr to the north and west. Most of the approximately 380,000 residents in the province were Hazara but Pashtun and Baluch minorities were also present and tended to live in the southern portions of the province.

Dai Kundi's provincial capital of Nili was several thousand feet above sea level and many rivers crisscrossed the province's numerous valleys, including the Helmand River which meandered south, ending at the Iranian border.

The economy was predominantly agricultural and farmers grew wheat, barley, and almonds, among other crops; poppy was rare except in the southern district of Gizab. The Hazara people were descended from the Mongolian soldiers of Genghis Khan, and while of similar stature and body type to Pashtuns, their Asiatic features clearly distinguished them as a different ethnicity from their neighbors. Many of the Hazara fled Afghanistan as the Taliban increased its control across the country. Most went west to Iran where, although their faith was similar to that of the Persians, they were treated as refugees and discriminated against by Iranian government officials. But the Hazara didn't squander their time in Iran and elsewhere, and they continued their education and re-created their communities as best they could. Most Pashtuns' education had been disrupted from constant fighting or from the Taliban's misrule. As I arrived in Dai Kundi for the first time, I was extremely interested in understanding the challenges the Hazara faced and their differences from the Pashtuns, as well as determining whether a PRT would be suitable to build there. It was a trail-blazing trip for the PRT because no U.S. officials had really spent any time there and no reporting cables detailing the life of Dai Kundi's inhabitants had yet been drafted.

With the departure of the helicopters, Sergeant Dirkman set up our communications gear to get in touch with the UN security and logistics team that was putting together the elections for the province. Within about twenty minutes, a convoy of five Russian jeeps approached the flight line. As they pulled directly on to the airstrip, we could make out what appeared to be their police uniforms. One gentleman stood out from the others in green military fatigues; he had black-and-gray hair and a trim beard circling his mouth. We quickly determined that this was the police chief who had brought his men to pick us up and take us to meet the governor. His name was Habibullah Ahmadi and he said he had been contacted by the United Nations team about our arrival. I took the opportunity of asking him a few questions about his force, the challenges he faced, and his assessment of how the Taliban were doing. According to Ahmadi, prior to his present position he had served as the deputy police chief of Gizab District and as a patrolman in Tarin Kowt. He had graduated from the Police Academy of Kabul during Daoud Khan's reign in the 1970s and said that thirty of his officers had also received training. Chief Ahmadi had been appointed to his position five months ago and was originally from Dai Kundi Province. When his men approached him, they always saluted and spoke to him respectfully, and he spoke to them in a confident manner. He was definitely a different character than Rozi Khan.

As we waited for more trucks to arrive for our crew, Chief Ahmadi gave me a quick overview of his forces. His concerns were familiar to me: he needed more men, supplies, vehicles, and other support. In Chief Ahmadi's opinion, the only security concerns he had in the province were in the southern district of Gizab, which was half Pashtun and half Hazara. The chief said there was a training camp for the Taliban there and that they used the area as a base of operations. Though officially in Dai Kundi Province, the police chief and district chief of Gizab District had both been appointed by Uruzgan governor Jan Mohammed Khan on the instructions of President Karzai (although one suspects that they only represent the Pashtun population). The Dai Kundi police chief was reluctant to send his men into the area to secure it because of tensions between the Pashtun and Hazara communities. Both the governor and the police chief wanted us to operate in Gizab to make it more secure. I thought that the division of Gizab into two districts along the Helmand River might address this issue of ethnic tension because the river effectively split the two communities in half.

With the arrival of the additional trucks, we made our way to the governor's compound. All of the soldiers packed themselves into the Hiluxes and Russian jeeps and bumped along the unpaved roads. Many of us felt a sort of euphoria in Dai Kundi. Looking back, I think it had a lot to do with the cool air and the general sense of security we had from being among the Hazara. The stresses of living in the south just drifted away. We arrived at a large adobe compound with thick khaki walls of dried mud. A circular tower was set right into the middle of the front wall and a sky-blue-colored wooden frame surrounded the gateway into the building to its left. A lone, scraggly Afghan flag dangled off a bamboo poll thirty feet in front of the building. The Texas National Guard entered the compound and did a quick security sweep before we entered. The courtyard had small rooms set in among the compound's thick walls and each of their doorframes and windows had the similar sky-blue color of the front gate. The inner yard was about the size of a quarter of a football field. We were then shown into the governor's office, which was set in to the inner wall at the back of the compound. Its walls had been painted an official-looking white, and plush chairs lined its narrow confines. The governor's desk sat at the end of the rectangular office and a low glass table sat between the chairs with small bowls of treats and plastic flowers adding fresh color to the room. A large photo of President Karzai hung from the wall behind the governor's desk.

Soon after we had been seated, the governor appeared, and all rose. Governor Jan Mohammed Akbari was dressed in a light-gray Western suit, which he wore with a white shirt and no tie. He had black hair and was beardless but had a thin black-and-white mustache. The governor went around the room to shake our hands and once he had seated himself at his desk, chai was brought in as well as more bowls of candy treats. Lt. Colonel Fontes explained the purpose of our visit, which was to assess how the election preparations were coming along and to get a better sense of the development needs of the province. She introduced me to the governor, stating that we planned to make additional trips to the province in the coming months, and looked forward to working with the governor and his staff. The governor welcomed these remarks. I asked about his background, how he had been selected for governor, and his thoughts on the challenges he faced.

Governor Akbari said he had been appointed governor in January 2005 and had previously been a member of the Secretariat staff of President Karzai. He said he was originally from Dai Kundi province and that, in addition to twelve years of schooling, he had had university training in Kabul, as well as at the Institute for Foreign Affairs in India. As we spoke he took notes on a small pad on his desk and would occasionally address an employee of his who had poked his head into the room. The governor said that his main priorities were bridges and road construction, especially the Shristan Road to Kabul, more clinics and trained doctors, and extra police officers. He said he had high confidence in the abilities of his directors but, like most provinces in Afghanistan, they lacked operating budgets, equipment, and trained personnel. I asked Governor Akbari about the threats from the Taliban and he responded that most of the Taliban were in the province's southern districts of Gizab and Kijran, and while he did what he could about them, he preferred to keep his largely Hazara police force out of the area so as not to provoke ethnic tensions. The governor told me that he lost more people to a burst appendix than to attacks from the Taliban. I asked him about the elections process and his views on the UN's efforts in the province. He said he had a wonderful relationship with the United Nations and that the people were very excited about the election. As proof, he cited at least 138 declared candidates for the Provincial Council and the Wolesi Jirga. We spoke for about half an hour or so and prepared to visit the UN headquarters.

Once again, we loaded into the Russian jeeps and bounced along the hard-bitten roads. I noticed dozens of campaign posters pasted onto the walls of homes and businesses; their multicolored advertisements stood in sharp contrast with the sand-colored adobe walls. There were also many signs from various nongovernmental organizations around the capital indicating they had been quite busy in the area. In contrast, Uruzgan had one viable Afghan-led NGO that provided basic health care. We turned off what served as the main road into town and started along a stretch of dirt that wound its way upward along a series of boulders and rocks easily ten to fifteen feet high. After about a hundred yards, we arrived at a two-story adobe castle with towers on each of its corners. Set next to it was a large, two-story hill of boulders with a small sky-blue set of sandbags for an outpost topped by a tarp for the guard. The building was right out of the memoirs of the British officers who had served on the frontier in India, such as *Frontier Scouts* by Colonel H. R. C. Pettigrew, who often described the war towers of the Pashtuns. I could see small flecks of straw in the walls and complex geometrical designs snaked up and down its edifice. The plastered mud was as tough as concrete. We dismounted and made our way into the building through sky-blue double doors. As we entered, I saw a small copse of trees and bushes that surrounded the compound's makeshift well at the center of the building. A small bucket with a rope attached dangled off a metal bar that crossed over the wide hole in the earth. The building's interior was roomy with a dozen rooms lining the inner walls. Small windows peered out from the rooms and were held together with rough wooden slats.

Lt. Colonel Fontes, Captain Walker, and I met with the UN team, which comprised two security consultants who were largely running the whole effort. They had a huge map of the province on the wall with its boundaries clearly delineated in black ink and a series of punch pins indicating the locations of numerous polling centers. The map also indicated the province's district boundaries and the main roads or paths into each of the district centers. The two men, who were British ex-pats, described the Hazara as organized and enthusiastic. According to the consultants, there were approximately 146 polling centers housing 441 polling stations, and they planned to add additional stations to the eastern portion of Gizab fairly soon so that the Pashtuns could also vote. They said there had been no election-related violence in the province, although some candidates claimed to have been threatened when visiting Gizab. While the murder of one candidate had been reported in the media in July, it turned out that the story had been inaccurate.

The consultants said they had a very well organized plan for ballot dissemination, polling station setup and distribution, ballot collection and transportation, and ballot counting. While they felt the present number of police was not adequate to provide security on Election Day at all polling centers, local Hazara were being hired to supplement the force. Reiterating the governor's statement, they stated Dai Kundi had 135 candidates running for the Provincial Council and Wolesi Jirga and that there were 93 candidates for the Provincial Council, 6 women competing for three seats, and 87 men competing for 9 seats. In addition, there were 53 candidates competing for the Wolesi Jirga, 5 women competing for 1 seat and 48 men competing for 4 seats. The men also indicated no Kuchi candidates were running for office in the province. All of this information was incredibly heartening and, through our planning for the elections in Uruzgan, we had become acquainted with the logistical and security needs of administering an election, which made these reports all the more encouraging.

As we departed, I took note of the locations of the various government buildings and tried to do a quick survey of potential sites for a PRT. The provincial administration building that I had originally visited was approximately two kilometers from the airstrip in Dai Kundi. The flight line had originally been built by the Soviets and had recently been improved by the United Nations; even with these enhancements, however, the short, uneven runway was not ready for landings. Nili's single radio station was built by USAID and reached about 12,000 people. It had four employees, including a female announcer, and was fully operational. The station was also going to serve as Dai Kundi's counting house on Election Day. There were three clinics in Dai Kundi, including one overlooking the provincial administration building, but they lacked medicine and power. Six doctors worked in the province, two in Nili, two in Khidir, and two in Shristan. Their training wasn't very extensive and they could only perform simple operations. Because of the poor quality of roads, steep terrain, and numerous rivers, many patients died before they received medical attention. Like Uruzgan, most of the population was illiterate and residents could often only write their name. There were approximately five hundred schools, two hundred of which were for girls—but only twenty of them were actually buildings devoted exclusively to learning. The remaining schools were either tents or private dwellings. Governor Akbari stated that none of Dai Kundi's teachers were trained.

It seemed to me that the greatest challenge for a PRT in Dai Kundi would be the logistical problems presented by the province's high mountains and inhospitable winters. Although the UN staff were currently supplied via helicopter, even during the summer they didn't get reliable deliveries because of low visibility in the mountains. Moreover, heavy snows caused operations to almost completely cease, further complicating efforts at resupply. Significant resources would have to be expended to modernize and operate the runway in Nili if any portion of the problem was expected to be addressed. They definitely needed a large storage capacity in case of irregular supply deliveries. It seemed to me that a possible location for a PRT might be the building the UN team occupied. Its security would be strong since it was situated on a hill, had a commanding view of the approaches, and had external walls that were several feet thick. While it was a few kilometers from the air strip, a makeshift landing area for helicopters could be erected just outside its walls.

Even though we had only been on the ground for about five hours, we had collected a lot of valuable information on the operational challenges of Dai Kundi Province. We were confident the election would go off fairly smoothly and that local government officials seemed confident, educated, and dedicated to their work. As we departed from the flight line in the Chinooks, I was sure we could do a lot of good work in the province if we continued our trips and convinced our higher officials to build a PRT. The contrast between Dai Kundi's governor and Jan Mohammed Khan was significant and pronounced. Even though they were a different ethnic group and had different opportunities to continue their education abroad, the Hazara showed me that the status quo in Uruzgan—the governor dominating his political opponents and creating an atmosphere of violence—was just not the Afghan way of doing business. A literate and talented leader who focused on the people could have a positive impact if he was supported correctly. This trip did much to open my eyes to other possibilities in Uruzgan Province and fired my mind with the challenge of how I could realistically check the governor's worst abuses and adjust how we interacted with the local government. A few weeks later, when we returned to Dai Kundi province with Lt. Gen. Karl Eikenberry to make our case for the PRT, my thoughts continually focused on how I could help the people of both provinces.

Our spartan visit to Dai Kundi Province a few weeks earlier had been replaced with the full panoply of a three-star general's visit. Several Chinooks churned outside the PRT's walls and Apache attack helicopters sat poised to lift off. Lt. General Eikenberry, who was about six foot three and, like Lt. Colonel Fontes, a graduate of West Point, spoke fluent Chinese and was close friends with Gen. John Abizaid, the head of Central Command in Tampa, Florida. I had heard a lot of positive things about him and, before we departed for Dai Kundi, he sat through our briefing on the issues, politics, and assorted characters of Uruzgan. Lt. Colonel Fontes was in top form presenting our mission statement, organization, development priorities, and projects. I followed with an overview of the key political figures in the province and had about four PowerPoint slides with various colors indicating the level of corruption, honesty, effectiveness, and other factors describing local officials. In addition, I summarized the capacity of our local directorates. Engrossed by the slides, the general leaned forward, hands clasped between his legs and arms resting on his thighs. He asked me about the charts and the colors and how I had gathered this detailed information on the local political scene. He then said that he had never received a briefing with so much detail on local personalities from anyone at the U.S. Department of State. Heartened by his comment, I was glad to know that my efforts as the political officer to the PRT's commander were appreciated. It was also encouraging to know that a well-meaning and motivated novice could bring a lot to the fight absent the intellectual baggage of bureaucratic processes at the State Department.

We departed for Dai Kundi on September 11, 2005, four years after Al Qaeda's attack on our country. It was a poignant moment for me to be in Afghanistan on that day, working on behalf of my country to prevent these kinds of attacks from ever happening again. Our Chinooks landed on the same runway we had landed on previously and we rode to the governor's compound. Lt. General Eikenberry had also brought along President Karzai's national security adviser, Dr. Rasool, as well as a collection of Hazara political and tribal leaders. Instead of going directly to the governor's office, most of our little retinue walked around its wall to the back while the general and his colleagues met briefly with the governor. As I rounded the compound corner, my eyes were assaulted by an assembly of a thousand people quietly sitting on the small incline, organized into neat rows. To my left were easily two hundred schoolgirls dressed in the national school uniform of Afghanistan, a white head covering and a black dress. They all held silk flowers in their hands and several held up posters and banners of welcome. One little girl in the front held aloft a large poster attached to a pole with a picture of President Karzai on it. Female teachers walked among them making sure they behaved and had something to drink. The rest of the crowd consisted of men of various ages who also held banners and posters of welcome. A large thirty-foot Afghan flag with writing on it was held aloft at the back. A fifty-foot blue tarp lined the back of the governor's compound and a series of plastic chairs in double rows lined the wall. A makeshift cover also made of blue tarp hung over us to keep the sun off. A small table was at the center of the reviewing area and a loudspeaker system had also been set up. As we settled down, the governor and the general appeared. Policemen with AK-47s and machine guns hovered along the roof and skirted the crowd. It was an incredibly impressive display of welcome for Lt. General Eikenberry. A police escort festooned in their best, with white shoe covers and gloves, snapped to attention as soon as the governor and his guests were seated. They departed in an orderly manner, their rifles at attention, as a police officer directed them to the left.

Over the next three hours, the community of Nili made our visiting party feel entirely welcome. Governor Akbari gave a warm speech about the friendship between the United States and Afghanistan and spoke of how honored the people of Dai Kundi were to have the general visiting them. Lt. General Eikenberry delivered some gracious remarks and said the United States was committed to staying in Afghanistan and working with our friends to stop the Taliban and to rebuild the country. As soon as the speeches were over, a collection of high school girls approached the governor, each carrying silk flowers, which made a strong splash of color against their white head coverings. They then proceeded to sing a song of welcome, magnified by the loudspeakers, and their high-pitched voices bounced off the adobe walls. A young man followed this with a ringing speech of welcome and friendship.

Small groups of students also approached the speakers and gave the general bouquets of flowers. Other Afghan officials gave speeches, which were interspersed with additional songs of welcome. Toward the end of the ceremony, a young man emerged from the crowd and approached the table. He had on a dark-blue sweatshirt topped with gray and wore gray pants and sneakers. Many of the people in the crowd smiled as he approached. The young man said something to the governor and quickly bowed to the visitors before stepping on to the blue tarp. For the next twenty minutes, he went through an amazing routine of karate jumps, kicks, and other acrobatic feats. He exhilarated the crowd and they clapped vigorously as he completed each complex routine. It was a remarkable example of athletic ability and was the last thing I expected to see in Afghanistan. This demonstration of martial arts ability was soon followed by a girls' choir singing for our group. With the conclusion of the events, Lt. General Eikenberry gave some final remarks about how touched and impressed we all were with the singing of the students, the speeches, and, most of all, the karate demonstration. For the next few hours, Governor Akbari and Lt. General Eikenberry visited the town of Nili, stopping at the neat, two-story adobe shops to speak with the shop owners, and I hovered toward the back, snapping pictures and trying to listen in to the conversations the general was having with locals.

We arrived back at the Tarin Kowt PRT in the evening. It had been a long but very rewarding day. The whole PRT assembled in the chow hall so that Lt. General Eikenberry could speak to us. As he stood in front of the dining facility, he praised our efforts in Uruzgan and shared with us his observations of Dai Kundi Province. He said he was optimistic that the elections in September would be successful and that the PRT was going to play a crucial role in making sure they came off without a hitch. A few soldiers asked some softball questions and, just as soon as it had started, the meeting was over. While everyone grabbed food and milled about, Lt. General Eikenberry came up to me to introduce me to Dr. Rasool. The general told him that I knew an awful lot about the leaders in the area and that Dr. Rasool could benefit from spending a few minutes with me. Dr. Rasool was kind enough to do so and we talked about Jan Mohammed Khan and Rozi Khan and he stated that they might be replaced. He asked me about my thoughts regarding the possible changes. I was taken aback for a moment by his statement, worried about the potential effects. Although I gave him the best answer I could muster, I felt that their removal could have a destabilizing effect if not properly managed. He thanked me for my views and invited me to stop by his office at the president's palace if I was in Kabul. I said I would definitely do that, and the official party went up to FOB Ripley for the evening.

9 BRINGING DEMOCRACY
   TO THE PASHTUNS
   (Tarin Kowt—Fall 2005)

My duties were simple; I was to encourage the local inhabitants to stand up for themselves.

—Alec Kirkbride, *An Awakening: The Arab Campaign 1917–18*[1]

Governor Jan Mohammed Khan was focused on making the elections in Uruzgan Province a success. He was already on the hook to deliver the vote for his tribe and to bring allies into the Provincial Council and parliament who supported not only his interests but those of President Karzai as well. Moreover, if the election didn't go well, his leadership would be questioned by the international community, and his standing and support in the province would suffer. To that end, he played an active role in supporting the elections, regularly participating in our weekly security and logistics meetings and making sure his Afghan Highway Police cum militia was at our disposal. On the political front, he was actively recruiting his own candidates and, some would suggest, making sure others knew not to run. With these goals in mind, he had sent for his friend Haji Mohammed Hashim Watanwall from Sweden, where he had worked as a schoolteacher following his departure from Kabul after the 1992 mujahedeen victory. Watanwall was polished and modern, and, from his experience as a senior communist official in the 1980s to early 1990s, knew his way around government and power. Rozi Khan and

115

Haji Malem Abdul Khaliq Khan were also busy recruiting friends and allies to run. An encouraging note was that a large number of Gilzai tribesmen, who were more often than not sympathetic to the Taliban for a variety of reasons, were also running. I was worried that their enthusiasm to run a large number of candidates would split the vote, resulting in most of them not getting elected. Because they didn't have a dominant personality in their ranks to organize them politically, I was sure they were going to suffer electorally.

Planning for the September elections began in early May when we initiated a weekly meeting between UN, coalition, and Afghan government officials. These meetings were extremely useful to us because they allowed the PRT to better understand the elections process and helped us identify potential problems where our assets could be effectively used to mitigate them. For example, the United Nations had decided security concerns warranted fewer polling centers in Uruzgan for the election than last year's presidential election. Since this was identified early on, we were able to ensure that adequate air support was found to transport the UN security detail around the province where they reconnoitered polling centers. Along these same lines, we were able to persuade them to increase the number of polling centers from an initial thirty-one, which would have been a reduction of eleven polling centers over 2004, to forty-four, an increase of two. In addition to the use of our assets, the PRT was able to use the relationships we had developed with local provincial leaders and serve as an intermediary between them and the UN team. At one point, the Afghan National Police, ostensibly charged with providing perimeter security at the UN compound in Tarin Kowt, threatened to quit their jobs unless their ministry of interior–negotiated salaries were increased. Using links we had forged with the police's leadership, we were able to successfully stop this attempt at extortion. The PRT also sent representatives to the weekly UN staff meeting in order to develop personal relationships with their employees in case they were removed from the province because of security concerns, which had happened in other provinces.

Once a sufficient number of polling centers had been identified, we focused our efforts on the logistical issues of distributing sensitive and nonsensitive elections items throughout the province. We consistently stressed to the UN staff that they would have to plan as if our assets were unavailable to them in order to distribute and collect sensitive elections items. However, we tried to ensure that a repeat of last year's elections did not take place, wherein UN officials were not able to as effectively administer the election as they had hoped. Initial ideas of having the provincial countinghouse located at FOB Ripley and using our air assets to distribute and collect ballots were curtailed because of our concern at being perceived as too meddlesome in Afghan affairs. In place of FOB Ripley, the UN team utilized the Malalai Girls School in downtown Tarin Kowt as the countinghouse and were able to secure the use of MI-8 helicopters from the Afghan army. We did lend them several shipping containers for ballot storage and a number of Hesco barriers and sandbags to better secure the countinghouse.

Beginning in mid-July, we initiated a second weekly election meeting on security that involved Afghan and Coalition security forces. We initially identified the training and equipment needs of the province's security forces and assessed their force strength and capabilities. The information we collected at these meetings prompted us to request additional AK-47s, uniforms, and radios. Once the needs of the Afghan forces had been addressed, and as polling center locations were identified, we drafted a comprehensive security plan for Election Day. The election security plan was translated into Pashto and distributed to the participants. While most meetings were held at the instigation of the PRT, we also made a special effort to put the onus of security planning onto Afghan security forces with respect to determining the number of men they needed at each polling center, where best to place checkpoints, and where to perform roving security patrols. Deputy Police Chief Haji Nabi, the bespectacled Achikzai, asked if he could lead the elections training for his men at the PRT. We heartily welcomed his presence, and he proceeded to show the men how to operate as professionals, how to wear their uniforms, how to search a vehicle, how to pat people down, and how to use a confident and strong voice when communicating with the population. It was touching to see the men exhibit such pride in wearing their uniforms and getting ready to face the Taliban on this, their national Election Day. Our security planning continued. We classified all the polling centers as "high," "moderate," or "low" risk with respect to security. Once these data were gathered, security forces were adjusted accordingly. During these meetings, we discussed and planned the Elections Operations Center at the police headquarters and manning requirements were assigned. In addition, through the good working relationships established at these meetings, a test of the operations center was performed on September 16 during which we practiced reporting security incidents by radio and communicating them to the relevant officials. Because Uruzgan Province had had a considerable amount of political violence, our security planning had to be spot on.

To increase female voter registration and turnout, I came up with a plan to have a female MEDCAP (medical civil affairs project), which is essentially a free health screening with limited care provided by our soldiers, as a way of having the UN female outreach coordinators talk to the women about the importance of the elections. I was concerned that if I billed it as a female voter education meeting the Taliban would attack it; if I concealed it within a free health screening, however, the subterfuge might protect the women. I bounced the idea off Mohib, who thought it was excellent, but I wanted to speak with Mullah Hamdullah as well to get his views. He also thought it was a good idea and even offered to announce it on the radio station. I recruited as many of our women at the base as I could to run the program, and Lt. Colonel Fontes kindly agreed to head it up downtown. I put together some fliers and had Mohib translate them for me, then copied them on our fax machine. I then went to the girls' school and had the fliers distributed so the girls could take them home to their mothers and sisters. Mullah Hamdullah spoke on the radio about the free health screening and on the appointed day our female soldiers left for the school. I gave my camera to Sergeant Gould so she could snap some photos to commemorate the event. Approximately two to three hundred women came, and the UN staff attended as well. They passed out elections materials and spoke of the need for the women to register and vote in the September elections, because there were two women running for office. When my colleagues returned, they were full of stories of how the women really appreciated the medical assistance and how well the UN staff had done their jobs. I sincerely hoped our efforts helped increase female voter turnout.

With a background in politics, I was curious about how the candidates would campaign and what charges, if any, they would make against their opponents. In general, the elections were pretty sedate, although this may have had something to do with the ever-present threat of the Taliban. However, I tried to imagine how the candidates would have campaigned if they had been in the United States and what kinds of charges they would have leveled against their competitors. Here are a few I came up with:

My opponent is soft on Islam!

My opponent got a college deferment instead of joining the mujahedeen!

My opponent is a former Khan!

My opponent says he is pro-family but he only has two wives!

My opponent engages in pork barrel politics!

The night before the election, I slept on the floor of the police station in downtown Tarin Kowt, which was also our Elections Operations Center, and left early the next morning with our force protection to begin my election observer responsibilities. The plan was for me to visit as many polling centers as I could and then be handed off to different elements of our force protection throughout the day. The first polling center we visited was located in a boys' school we had constructed near Jan Mohammed Khan's village. The morning was cool and the governor's tribesmen were providing protection. Two soldiers accompanied me and one of them held a spare pistol for me and two magazines in case fighting broke out. Technically, I was unarmed, but I didn't want to take any foolhardy risks. The center opened a few minutes late, but voters showed up over the next two hours and the process seemed to work quite smoothly. As each voter presented his identification card, a clerk would mark down his name against a roster and direct him to a voting booth after giving him one yellow ballot for the Provincial Council and a blue one for the Wolesi Jirga. Each voter marked his ballot in a private, makeshift cardboard booth and then dropped the ballot into a slightly opaque plastic bin that had been secured with tamper-proof locks. It was an impressive process and I was immensely proud of how well the Afghan staff were doing. Forty-three other polling centers were operating throughout the province on Election Day, but violence was still a concern.

I visited six polling centers in the District of Tarin Kowt on Election Day. All of them opened late, one by a full hour and a half, but turnout appeared strong. Candidate representatives were present at five of the six polling centers and election staff were keen to demonstrate the transparency of the process to them. At one polling center I noticed candidate representatives instructing voters on how to vote while they were filling out the ballots. I complained to the local UN employee and he yelled at them. Another problem was that, because of the large turnout at this same station, estimated at approximately two hundred individuals, privacy for voters was compromised. Crowd control was another challenge. Although I intervened with the police to exert more control, the UN staff were overwhelmed and had not set up enough polling stations. About twenty or so polling booths were left unassembled. I radioed this in to the operations center at the police headquarters in Tarin Kowt, and the deputy governor later confirmed to me that additional men had been sent in to restore order. Besides the difficulties at one polling center, voting procedures were generally followed at the remaining five centers I visited. I quizzed each polling center manager about how he had run his center and asked him to walk me through each step. Not a single one missed the proper procedures. Voters were generally well behaved and, with the exception of one polling center, the process appeared to run fairly smoothly. The UN staff thought voting had gone quite well and that local staff had performed ably. Once voting was complete, the delicate process of bringing the completed ballots to the countinghouse at the Malalai Girls School took several weeks to complete.

Over the next few weeks, I visited the countinghouse regularly. Security was being provided by the police and the Afghan army, and it was tight. Election observers presented credentials at a tent within the facility and were issued a separate identification card that was worn around their neck. There were six male counting teams and one female team consisting of eight people per team. Each team was led by a counting manager. A sixth male counting team was added so that counting would be completed prior to the beginning of Ramadan. Several candidates or their designated representatives monitored the counting and were generally pleased with the process. Observers were prohibited from talking with ballot counters so that no counter could be accused of having a bias and so that they could complete their counting in a timely fashion. The counters acted professionally and the whole process was run very smoothly. Count managers adjudicated vote disputes ably and were deliberate in their final tallies of votes. Uncounted ballots were stored in a dozen shipping containers located on the compound and, as they were moved from the containers to the countinghouse, a two-man team would take note of the box's number to ensure the integrity of the process. Interim results from each day's counting were posted and candidates and their representatives crowded around the board taking notes and adding up figures with calcula-tors. All count observers were given a brief presentation on the rules of ob-servation and encouraged to share any problems they may have had with the process to the international staff. I asked the UN personnel who was better at counting the ballots, the men or the women, and the staff said unhesitat-ingly that the women were the best. When I wondered aloud as to why this was the case, they responded that none of the local men would go into the women's room out of respect for the women as well as out of concern that a misconstrued gesture or comment might cause serious problems. The male counting teams didn't do as well because, in spite of the UN staff's best efforts, a lot of the observers chatted with them or otherwise distracted them.

Even though the voting process and countinghouse were generally well run and candidates came from each of the province's districts and major tribes, voter turnout in Uruzgan Province was substantially lower than in the 2004 presidential election. Approximately 23 percent of registered voters participated in the 2005 elections compared with the previous year's 39.45 percent. This was the second-lowest figure in the nation. In 2004, 56,777 people had voted during the presidential election; in 2005, 35,363 voters participated in the Wolesi Jirga and 35,388 in the Provincial Council election. Though overall voter turnout was low, the number of female voters increased substantially. During the 2004 presidential election, only 2 percent of registered female voters par-ticipated in the election. This year, approximately 8 percent of registered female voters participated. Although I was disappointed and a little surprised that voter turnout hadn't increased, I was encouraged that female voting had gone up and that at least one female member of parliament had been elected. It was heart-ening to think that my small contribution to increasing female voter turnout might have produced results, however meager they might appear.

A COUNTERWEIGHT TO JAN MOHAMMED KHAN

The most dangerous moment for a bad government is that in which it begins to reform.

—Alexis de Tocqueville, *L'Ancien Régime et la Révolution*

As ballot counting continued and the membership of the Provincial Council and parliament shaped up, I decided that I needed to do whatever I could to check the governor's corrupt ways and prompt him to govern more responsibly. I had witnessed enough of his actions around the province and pieced together what tidbits of information I could collect to determine that many of the governor's political opponents always seemed to have problems with ambushes and IEDs; the governor and his friends had none. Moreover, the governor was always trying to monopolize whatever funds and projects the PRT and the government provided, which had a negative effect on the quality of our projects and the community's perception of our activities. While I continued to hope that we could work with the governor and surreptitiously check his malign influence by adjusting our interactions, I also felt that we needed to foster his opponents, creating opportunities for them to limit the governor's worst behavior.

I started to undertake a series of meetings with key Afghan leaders to sound out what they thought about the idea of the governor being replaced and what they hoped the newly elected Provincial Council could do. On September 22 I met with Mullah Hamdullah to focus on gaining a better understanding of the relationship between Governor Jan Mohammed Khan and Chief Rozi Khan and getting the shura president's views on possible leadership changes in the province. A secondary purpose was to figure out Mullah Hamdullah's thoughts on what role the Provincial Council could play once the election results were announced, since he was a candidate for the council. According to the mullah, who was also an ally of the governor's, the enmity between the governor and the police chief largely stemmed from disputes that had arisen over the division of Taliban property and money as the Taliban fled and the training and goods that were made available under the disarmament process for area militias. These conflicts apparently turned violent and the governor's brother was allegedly killed. Mullah Hamdullah also said that Rozi had briefly served as governor of Uruzgan once the Taliban had fled and that the ascension of Jan Mohammed Khan to that position, essentially replacing him, was another source of conflict.

When I asked him who should replace the governor if he was promoted to some position within the central government, Hamdullah unhesitatingly said that a man named Malem Rahmatullah would likely be the next governor. Rahmatullah was originally from Uruzgan, a member of the Populzai tribe, and was distantly related to the governor. He was educated, well-connected politically, and was on excellent personal terms with Rozi Khan and the governor's chief political opponent, Haji Malem Abdul Khaliq Khan, the Wolesi Jirga candidate. I later learned from Malem Abdul Khaliq that Rahmatullah had been the governor of Uruzgan following the Taliban's collapse and had traveled to Kabul in the hopes of receiving a senior government post. Since early 2002, he had apparently been living in Kabul waiting for his opportunity to serve. According to Hamdullah, several recent conversations with President Karzai, Rahmatullah, and Governor Jan Mohammed Khan had taken place about Rahmatullah's assuming the position of governor in the province once the results of the election were announced.

Interestingly, Hamdullah, who, as an ally of the governor, would not typically be supportive of such a move, was in favor of replacing Colonel Matullah as head of the Afghan Highway Police as well. He felt this was necessary because Matullah stole from local residents, killed people, and was illiterate. The mullah was supportive of elevating Afghan Highway Police Deputy Commander Dil Agha to commander of the same unit. In Hamdullah's opinion, the Provincial Council and the Provincial Shura should coexist, with members having the opportunity to serve in both bodies (there was presently only one shura member who was also running for the Provincial Council). He did not have an opinion of how the Provincial Council should be organized or what role it should play, but did say that the central government would likely provide the members with salaries and staff.

On September 27 at the PRT, I finally met alone with Haji Malem Abdul Khaliq Khan, the Achikzai tribal chief and ardent political opponent of the governor. As leader of the Achikzai tribe, one of the three main tribes in the province, his writ extended throughout the Chora and Khas Uruzgan districts. He was also a candidate for the Wolesi Jirga. Even though Abdul Khaliq and I had already met a few times, he seemed nervous, and I quickly deduced that he probably thought I was somehow aligned with the governor because the PRT worked so closely with him and the local government. After assuring him that the PRT wanted to work with all of the tribes in the province and that I needed his advice on what we should do, I told him that anything he told me would be held in confidence and that he could trust me. He seemed to be reassured by this and began to answer my questions about the history of the province, Jan Mohammed Khan's activities, and how we could do our work better. Our conversation revealed the governor's colorful and sordid past and a history that directly confronted my assumptions about the province. I took notes as he started to talk and Mohib translated.

Abdul Khaliq filled me in on some of the recent history of the province and its key political players and then shifted to his views on the governor. He told me that there was a pervasive sense of disappointment and growing opposition to Governor Jan Mohammed Khan and, by extension, the Government of Afghanistan in Uruzgan Province. Governor Jan Mohammed had made a number of promises upon assuming the position of governor in early 2002, including reducing corruption, improving governance, and helping the economy among others. However, according to Abdul Khaliq, the governor had enriched himself at the expense of the people, consolidated his power by installing district and police chiefs who were not well liked by local residents, and intimidated his opponents. To make his point, Abdul Khaliq mentioned that he always traveled to Tarin Kowt from Chora with a protective detail provided by Police Chief Rozi Khan because he feared being attacked by Jan Mohammed Khan's men. At several points Abdul Khaliq asked why, given the widespread discontent of the population, the governor was still in power after three years. He said local leaders had repeatedly asked the Government of Afghanistan to replace the governor. Abdul Khaliq went on to say that if the governor was not replaced soon after the new government was seated in September, violence would likely break out throughout the province.

In addition, Abdul Khaliq strongly recommended that Chora District Chief Yar Mohammed Khan be replaced because he was a poor leader who often arrested the Taliban and local residents and then released them after receiving a bribe. Moreover, he functioned as a spy for the governor against Abdul Khaliq. In his place, he recommended Haji Mohammed Akbar Khan, who was a Chora District resident, member of the Barakzai tribe, and had completed twelve years of education. Like the tribal chief, he had also fought the Russians, and the Taliban had disarmed him when they consolidated their control over Chora. Even though the PRT generally had a dim view of Chora police chief Zahir Khan, Abdul Khaliq spoke favorably of him and also positively commented on Yachtan police chief and former Chora police chief Haji Ibrahim who had met up with Hamid Karzai in 2001. Interestingly, of the many things he told me, he noted that of all the candidates who were running for office, the only one with a recognizable Taliban past was Mullah Hamdullah, who was serving as the head of the Provincial Shura and running for the Provincial Council. Abdul Khaliq stated that Hamdullah had served as an assistant to the Taliban High Court and had also worked as a Taliban judge.

After we finished, I asked Sergeant Dirkman to see if the governor or any of his allies were at the gate; I didn't want them to see Abdul Khaliq and for his safety to be in jeopardy. Dirkman ran up to the front gate and came back telling me all was clear. As we slowly made our way to the gate, I was asking Khaliq about his family when I noticed the governor striding confidently toward the tactical operations center from the front gate. He hadn't noticed us yet because his left eye was blind, but his assistant saw us and told him about Khaliq. As soon as I had seen the governor, I gestured for Khaliq and his friend to dash behind a low Hesco wall. I then waved to the governor as he and his assistant continued walking. When they were out of sight, I escorted Khaliq out the gate and promised to do what I could to help him. Later in the day, one of our guards mentioned that the governor was asking what Abdul Khaliq, or the "snake," as he called him, was doing at the PRT. Even though I knew Abdul Khaliq had an ax to grind in sharing this information about the governor, many of his observations meshed with my own and corroborated much of what I had been hearing from the people.

Ballot counting took almost two months, and the elections process was almost universally praised by the locals and viewed as fair and complete. The assessments I had done of the candidates prior to the election helped significantly in understanding how the Provincial Council and Wolesi Jirga were shaping up. Haji Malem Abdul Khaliq, the governor's main political opponent, received the highest number of votes in the whole province for parliament, which gave me greater confidence that his observations on politics and the pulse of the people were largely accurate. However, Jan Mohammed Khan was not without resources and was able to get Mohammed Hashim Watanwall, his fellow tribesman and supporter during the mujahedeen period, also elected to parliament. The sole female member of parliament, Sonia Nilofer, had also been elected, more great news. The Provincial Council was also shaping up nicely. Provincial Shura president Mullah Hamdullah was elected, and then chosen by his peers to be the president of the Provincial Council. This was very heartening since I had worked to develop the governance practices of the Provincial Shura in hopes that some or all of them would bleed over to the Provincial Council. Hamdullah's election made sure this would happen. Former tank trap builder and retired schoolteacher Noor Mohammed was elected, giving Rozi Khan an ally on the council as well. Haji Khairo Jan received the greatest number of votes which automatically made him a member of parliament. Khairo Jan's prior experience as mayor of Tarin Kowt would also help. Mohammed Hanif Khan's election gave Haji Malem Abdul Khaliq an ally as well; Hanif Khan would also serve as a temporary member of parliament until district elections took place. Haji Gul and Haji Nazar Mohammed were also elected, and since they were in their early twenties, this gave the council a touch of youth. With the elevation of Haji Khairo Jan and Mohammed Hanif Khan to Parliament, the next two vote-getters automatically moved up. The most interesting one was Atiqullah Khan, who had informed on his brother, Naqibullah, in April, which prompted the Special Forces to detain him and almost prevented him from running for the Provincial Council. We were able to get his brother released in time, but his fellow council members eyed Atiqullah suspiciously. The Provincial Council and the members of parliament were representative of the three main Durrani tribes in the area and contained a mix of members for Jan Mohammed Khan, Rozi Khan, and Haji Malem Abdul Khaliq Kahn's factions and nonaffiliated tribesmen. Although no Gilzai tribesmen had been elected, Mullah Hamdullah wanted them to participate, which was encouraging. I was hopeful for the future.

10 URUZGAN'S BLOODY PAST
(Tarin Kowt—Fall 2005)

Social injustice, bullying by military or police, and corruption must be seen as grave weaknesses in the defense of a country, errors that can lead to its downfall and eventually, as our friends are eliminated, to the downfall of the United States.

> —Edward Geary Lansdale, *In the Midst of Wars: An American's Mission to Southeast Asia*[1]

As I undertook a torrent of interviews with local officials and tried to piece together Uruzgan's past, it became very clear to me that my simplistic understanding of our relationship with the governor had to be revised. He was not simply focused on building the province and making sure all his residents had better lives. He was ruthlessly exploiting the people for his personal gain and that of his family and supporters. The residents of Uruzgan were paying for it, and some of them were dead because of it. In addition, although Uruzgan appeared to be just another rural patch of Afghanistan where time seemed to stand still, it had actually been buffeted by the great political, military, and social forces that had crossed over the country in the last thirty years. While a small province, it had played a crucial role in mujahedeen operations in the south and contributed its fair share of senior communist government officials in Kabul. As the Taliban pushed north in the

1990s, it lent many of its sons to the fight, some of whom would rise to be among its most senior leaders. As my attention to and knowledge of the people increased, my focus broadened from just the governor, police chief, and provincial shura president to include the rich tapestry of Uruzgan's residents whose lives had been so deeply affected by these waves of history that had showed up so frequently onto their shores.

THE SOVIET INVASION

The Soviet invasion of Afghanistan in 1979 transformed Afghanistan, and the province of Uruzgan was deeply affected by the conflict. The war brought to power many of the province's residents, some serving with the communists in Kabul while others resisted, and through the crucible of war crafted enduring reputations and lifelong enmities. Over the course of the ten-year conflict, the Soviets never completely controlled Uruzgan, in part because of the lack of strategic significance of the province, but also because of its isolated terrain and tenacious fighters. Much like the challenges the Soviets faced in the 1980s, U.S. and Coalition Forces also confronted the forbidding geography of the province, which provided fighters with safe havens, especially in the western district of Deh Rawud, from which to fight the Government of Afghanistan and its allies. This district would subsequently serve as the home of Mullah Omar, the founder of the Taliban, and many other senior Taliban leaders. These various factors prevented the Soviets from dominating the province; however, they did attempt to kill the insurgents and suppress the population that supported them through limited operations in the area, such as brief overland incursions and air operations from Kandahar Air Field. Their scorched-earth tactics generated immense hatred among the population, and several of the Afghans I met with recounted tales of capturing and torturing the Soviets and the Afghan communists who often accompanied them. Because they were never able to or chose not to hold the province, the Soviets left a limited footprint in the area. According to the United Nation's Afghanistan Landmine Impact Survey, of all of Afghanistan's provinces, Uruzgan was "the sole impact-free province in the country."[2] That being said, hulks of rusting Soviet armor dot the province's landscape, although many more were hauled away as scrap, and act as reminders of the

Soviet incursions of the 1980s. One Soviet BMP tank actually greets visitors at the governor's compound in Tarin Kowt as a captured prize, and two tanks anchor a riverbed southwest of the capital. One of the most significant battles of Uruzgan took place in the district of Deh Rawud in a Soviet attempt to eliminate a mujahedeen safe haven that served as a logistics hub and staging area for guerrilla operations against the Soviets in the provinces of Helmand and Kandahar to the south.

The community of Uruzgan had been irrevocably changed by the time the Soviets departed in 1989 and the Afghan Communist Government collapsed in 1992. Key leaders whom Hamid Karzai would join in Tarin Kowt in 2001 to lead the uprising of the Pashtuns had cut their teeth fighting the Soviets and were veteran mujahedeen with numerous battles under their belts. Although they were a little older and their wounds still ached as constant reminders of past action, they were keen to turn the Taliban back by 2001. The war years had made these men heroes, and they had a special authority because of these experiences and were widely respected in their communities. Of the few locals who had supported the Soviets, most had fled the country, often ending up in Europe where they reestablished their lives. Many of the minor Communist Party officials returned home to Uruzgan, using family and tribal links to facilitate their safe passage through mujahedeen lines, and settled down into quiet lives. Following the Taliban's departure in 2001, many former communists would return to public life and take up positions of responsibility in the community, often being the best educated and most experienced of all local officials. Of the mujahedeen who remained in Uruzgan during the time of the Taliban, their fighting experience and bravery were crucial to Karzai's success in seizing control of Tarin Kowt. Many of them would be with Karzai when he entered Mullah Omar's home in Kandahar Province as they pushed south to liberate southern Afghanistan.

THE COMMUNISTS (1979–1992)

Even though Uruzgan had few resources, was of limited strategic importance to the Soviets, and had a population that was strongly opposed to the communist occupation, several residents still managed to gain substantial power under the communist regime. A few became national-level figures, while

many others served in the ministries of Kabul or in other leadership positions around the country. Three important men who would eventually run
for the Wolesi Jirga, or the lower house of the National Parliament of
Afghanistan in 2005, were Haji Mohammed Hashim Watanwall, Abdullah
Atifi, and Sher Jan Mazdoryar. While these men had fled the country following the mujahedeen's victory, many of their lesser-known colleagues returned home to their villages in Uruzgan. In an odd twist of history, the fall
of the Taliban brought to power many of the old communists the United
States had struggled against in the 1980s, and because they were often the
most "anti-Taliban" officials in the area, they were useful allies to the U.S.
and Coalition partners. Their lives shed some light on the nature of the conflict in Uruzugan, how the war had transformed the lives of many of its residents, and on the innate survival instincts of the people.

Haji Mohammed Hashim Watanwall was born in Uruzgan in the village of
Touri just outside of Tarin Kowt and is a member of the powerful Populzai
tribe. In his late fifties, he has the figure of a man of comfortable means. He
doesn't sport the typical beard and turban of the Pashtun, usually preferring
a mustache and an uncovered head, although when he ran for Parliament his
campaign photos conspicuously had him wearing a turban. He grew up in an
educated household with a father who was a prominent local mullah, and although he rejected his father's religiosity, he still embraced its fervor.
Watanwall continued his education and graduated from high school, completing his studies in science at Kabul University. He worked briefly for
UNICEF as a supervisor and ultimately became the director of education for
Uruzgan. Later he was made chief of finance in the province of Herat, a key
overland route for goods from Iran and a major source of income for the
communist government. Eventually, however, Watanwall was jailed when his
faction of the Communist Party of Afghanistan, called Khalk, was violently
replaced by a rival group. This faction was led by a man named Amin, who
had been an assistant to Khalk Party head Taraky, who had also been assassinated. Watanwall was fortunate he hadn't been killed while imprisoned. In
1979 the Soviets invaded and released him after killing Amin. Following
Watanwall's release, he joined the Ministry of Public Works, working there
for several years, building homes and government buildings, but was later
jailed again when his faction, this time called the Purcham, was replaced by
one led by Dr. Najibullah. Watanwall stayed in jail until the mujahedeen

freed him; subsequently he fled to Pakistan and then to Sweden, where he became a teacher. Though a committed communist, he used his influence with the Soviets to protect his village from being bombed, which had the effect of creating a safe haven for the local mujahedeen led by his village neighbor and childhood friend, Jan Mohammed Khan. This favor would not be forgotten many years later when Watanwall would be called back from Sweden by then-governor Jan Mohammed Khan to run for parliament.

Abdullah Atifi was born in the village of Chora and is also a member of the Populzai tribe. A diminutive man, he is full of opinions, plans, and grand ideas. A pupil of Watanwall when he was director of education, he graduated first in his high school class and had high hopes of being a lawyer, writer, or historian. However, Watanwall counseled him that the future of Afghanistan needed engineers, not writers, so Atifi trained in Kabul as an engineer. Following the Soviet invasion, he lived in the USSR where he continued his studies in electricity and power generation and learned Russian. Upon his return, Atifi worked at the Ministry of Electricity and Power and eventually became the head of the party shura at the ministry. He was there for only six months when his political faction was kicked out of power and he joined the army, serving for two and a half years. When he left the army, he got a job working at the main prison in Kabul which fell under the Ministry of Interior led by his friend and fellow Uruzgan resident, Sher Jan Mazdoryar. Although down on his luck and half-heartedly putting in time at the prison, Atifi was well connected and "knew many powerful people." Before too long he was made head of the propaganda committee of the central committee and then a member of that body as well. His writing skills were finally being put to use. Atifi was also offered jobs as head of the ministry of interior and deputy to the president, among other positions. Although members of his political faction of the Khalk Party had all been arrested, he was spared that fate and, when Dr. Najibullah assumed power, he made Atifi head of the Communist Central Committee. Before too long, however, other members of the committee were having problems with his leadership, and some felt he was passing information to the opposition. Eventually, it was suggested to Atifi that he go to Paktia Province in the southeastern part of Afghanistan to lead the party committee there. Its location next to the Pakistani border and the training camps of the mujahedeen made this "opportunity" seem very unattractive.

Seeing that his time was running out, Atifi volunteered to take a lesser position at the Ministry of Transportation, now led by his good friend, Sher Jan Mazdoryar. Although it was a minor position, he still had an income and before too long he petitioned the government, received a passport, and then departed for Pakistan and Russia. He settled in Ukraine where he became the founder and editor of two Pashtun newspapers, published a book of poetry, and wrote and published a history of the Pashtun people. While he had been a member of the Communist Party his whole professional life, Atifi had secretly been making trips to Pakistan to visit the exiled King Zahir Shah and his military adviser, General Qatawazi, who provided Atifi political advice and guidance. Once the Taliban left, he returned to his home village of Chora with his wife and took care of the children of his deceased brother, since they had no children of their own. As of 2005, Atifi was a much diminished man, having gone from the highest positions of the government to living in a village with no electricity to run his portable computer. He edits his tome of the Pashtun people surrounded by illiterate peasants and tries to make a living by occasionally doing contract work for the coalition and dabbling in local politics. Atifi ran for the Wolesi Jirga in September 2005, his poster prominently showing his communist-era photo as a senior apparatchik, but didn't get elected. A proud man, he thirsts for a return to the center stage of politics, although recent history in Uruzgan suggests this doesn't seem promising.

Sher Jan Mazdoryar was born in the village of Tarin Kowt and is a member of the Mohammedzai tribe. A balding man with a black mustache, he prefers the dress of a Westerner, and most locals don't even acknowledge his presence. After completing high school he moved to Kabul where he attended the military academy and became a member of the military wing of the Khalk Party. He eventually became a principal supporter of the coup against Mohammed Daoud Khan in 1978 following Daoud's attempt to arrest the leaders of the Communist Party of Afghanistan. Following the coup, he became the minister of the interior and, after the Soviet invasion, the minister of transportation. In both positions he was able to help his friend Atifi. Mazdoryar later became the Communist Government of Afghanistan's ambassador to Hungary and settled down in western Germany following the victory of the mujahedeen. He came back to Uruzgan in 2005 to run for parliament but many residents remembered his role in the ousting of Daoud Khan, a fellow member of the Mohammedzai tribe, and his support for the several military incursions into Uruzgan against his tribal rivals. He never ventured far beyond the government buildings of Tarin Kowt, knowing all too well that the relatives of his victims had long memories and would seek justice. Following his defeat in the September elections, he left Uruzgan and hasn't been seen since. While Watanwall, Atifi, and Mazdoryar were probably the most prominent residents of Uruzgan to work in the communist governments that ruled over Afghanistan, other locals played minor but important roles.

THE MUJAHEDEEN (1979–1992)

Although Uruzgan Province was not a natural place to find sympathy for the Communist Party and the Soviet invasion, it was fertile recruiting ground for the mujahedeen. Local fighters used the province's geography and relative isolation to their advantage as they conducted operations against the Soviets in the south and safely stockpiled supplies in the province's valleys. While the direct impact of Soviet military operations was relatively light in Uruzgan when compared with the rest of the country, it had an enormous impact on the lives of local residents. Many inhabitants rose to positions of great influence during the war, as their bravery, mastery of men, and strategic thinking helped them stand out as great leaders. The bonds these men forged in combat created lifelong friendships and formed the nucleus of the subsequent warlord factions that reigned over Afghanistan once the communist threat dissipated. During this time tribal and personal conflicts were significantly muted but never fully eliminated. As some men rose to power, others were marginalized, fundamentally altering the power dynamics of the tribes. Following the Soviet withdrawal, local strongmen, flush with weapons, turned their ire against each other and preyed on their own populations. This subsequent fighting between local mujahedeen commanders would later create opportunities that the Taliban would exploit when they took over the province in the mid-1990s. While the leadership of local mujahedeen commanders fluctuated considerably depending upon the nature of the threat, the direction of the attack, and on the politics in the province, several rose to prominence and maintained and consolidated their power following the Soviet withdrawal.

When the Soviets invaded Afghanistan, Jan Mohammed, or Jano as he was then called, was employed as a janitor and night watchman at the Tarin Kowt Boys High School. He was originally from the village of Touri outside of Tarin Kowt, and, as mentioned, a member of the Populzai tribe. A diminutive man, he is illiterate and blind in his left eye. Although not formally educated, he is a sophisticated political actor and has the shrewd and cunning nature of a survivor. Jan Mohammed started out as a minor player in the province, but by the end of the war and the subsequent fighting between mujahedeen commanders, he came to dominate the local Populzai tribe. He was grudgingly accepted as their leader while he and his men intimidated other tribes. Over the course of numerous engagements with the Soviets and their Afghan allies in Uruzgan, he gained a reputation as a ruthless fighter who personally tortured and killed captured soldiers, yet he was also a charismatic leader of men and had a devoted following. His fighting prowess would serve him well, eventually allowing him to become the local leader of his tribe, but his duplicity would also earn him many enemies within his own community. During the Taliban period, his influence would be curtailed but his position in the province consolidated. Following the U.S. invasion in 2001, his power would reach its fruition. He was now known locally as Jan Mohammed Khan, having added "Khan" to his name as a mark of his status as a local powerbroker. When Karzai and his Pashtun force pushed south from Uruzgan to Kandahar in 2001, Jan Mohammed Khan was one of two prisoners Karzai asked the Taliban to release to him. Their relationship had been sealed when Jan Mohammed frequently visited Karzai and his family when they had gone into opposition against the Taliban in the late 1990s and moved to Quetta, Pakistan. By this time, Jan Mohammed was making regular trips to the Karzai family compound from Uruzgan and was reportedly with them when Karzai's father, Abdul Ahad Karzai, was assassinated walking home from praying at the local mosque in 1999. The Taliban arrested Jan Mohammed in early 2001 because of their suspicions of his traveling to Pakistan to meet with Karzai, who was now an active opponent of their regime. An excellent account of Jan Mohammed's release is contained in *Karzai: The Failing American Intervention and the Struggle for Afghanistan* by Nick B. Mills; the story of the great push south by Karzai can be read in Eric Blehm's *The Only Thing Worth Dying For: How Eleven Green Berets Forged a New Afghanistan.*

Haji Malem Abdul Khaliq Khan was a senior at the high school Jan Mohammed was working at when the Soviets invaded. A shorter man, he has a full face and dark tan and wields much authority in the community. Born in the village of Chora, he is a member of the Achikzai tribe. Like Jan Mohammed, he became the leader of his tribe, but perhaps because of his nature, or that he had already started in a position of influence and was educated, he lacked the ruthlessness required to rise to the top. Largely for this reason, Khaliq Khan is well thought of by most residents of Uruzgan, garnering wide support among the various tribes. As a mujahedeen commander, he headed a loose coalition of fellow tribesman who led their respective village militias. One of these men, Pai Mohammed, was a subcommander of Malem Khaliq Khan in the southern Uruzgan village of Sarkhome.

Pai Mohammed was born in Tarin Kowt, is a member of the Achikzai tribe, and is a convivial man with a stocky build who dresses in the traditional Afghan garb of the area. His friend, Noor Mohammed, specialized in digging tank traps and would typically erect a wood scaffold with a thatch cover and put mud on it so that it conformed to the countryside. Together with Pai Mohammed and a group of mujahedeen, they attacked a convoy of Soviet tanks en route to Tarin Kowt from Deh Rawud in the mid-1980s. The mujahedeen had built several traps along the edges of a dry riverbed about six kilometers southwest of Tarin Kowt. Snaring the final two tanks in the convoy, they attacked the Russians with rocket-propelled grenades from their hideouts in nearby compounds. As they blew the tank treads off the tanks, the tank commanders radioed ahead that they had become stuck and were under attack. At this point, the convoy stopped, turned their turrets toward the endangered tanks, and opened fire on the mujahedeen, killing several fighters. Pai Mohammed and his men captured the tank drivers and commanders, eventually killing them after they were interrogated.

Noor Mohammed is a member of the Barakzai tribe from the village of Khan Agha and a well-respected mujahedeen fighter who participated in battles in Uruzgan and in Kandahar. A quiet man who upon first impression appears to be quite reserved, he is, in fact, quite expressive and ready with a quick smile. Noor Mohammed subsequently became a schoolteacher and principal and later retired to tend to his farm. He was eventually approached by Barakzai tribal leader Rozi Khan to run for the Provincial Council and was elected by a respectable margin in 2005.

The third major mujahedeen leader to emerge in Uruzgan as one of the key powerbrokers in the province was Rozi Khan. He is the leader of the Barakzai tribe, which congregate north and northeast of Tarin Kowt. A contemporary of Jan Mohammed Khan and Haji Malem Abdul Khaliq Khan, like them he made his reputation as a mujahedeen commander. If Rozi Khan lacks the obvious energy of Jan Mohammed Khan and is not as ruthless, he still plays the Afghan game of survival well through duplicity, allegiance switching, and coalition building. Rozi Khan is a close friend of Haji Malem Abdul Khaliq Khan and is well thought of by local residents. While he is quick to help a friend who is in danger, he is often quite languid when it comes to administration. This initial impression often misleads those who meet him only briefly, as he is able to marshal his tribe to seize power when inclined to do so. While lacking the extensive political contacts of Jan Mohammed Khan, he is nonetheless one of three personalities dominating the local political scene.

Other Uruzgan residents also made their reputation fighting against the Soviets. Haji Khairo Jan, a Populzai resident of Tarin Kowt and future mayor of the provincial capital, provided fighters to several mujahedeen commanders in the area and collected intelligence on Soviet movements into and out of the province. Haji Nimatullah Alkhan, a member of the Mohammedzai tribe from Tarin Kowt, was known for his enthusiasm in shooting rockets at Soviet helicopters. During one engagement, the Soviets were dropping bombs on his village and, according to witnesses, he became enraged and fired rocket after rocket at the helicopter. At one point, he stripped down to his pants and had fellow villagers supply him RPG round after RPG round until he had extinguished his supply. Another local, Mullah Hamdullah, fought alongside Jan Mohammed Khan in at least twenty-three battles and, during one engagement, was struck in the head by an errant bullet. Knocked out cold, he subsequently said you could see his mind through the hole in his skull.

The political landscape of Uruzgan Province had been irrevocably changed during the Soviet occupation and, after Soviet forces withdrew in 1989 and the mujahedeen were victorious against the Afghan Communist Government in 1992, would never return to the same prewar condition. The war had elevated relatively minor figures in the province to positions of power, burnished the reputations of many prominent locals, and provided several of its residents with educational and career opportunities unthought-of in Uruzgan. While the Soviet threat had helped create a temporary unity among the various mujahedeen commanders in the area, traditional areas of dispute along tribal, factional, and personal lines quickly broke up that unanimity of purpose. With the province now flush with weapons, it was not long before conflicts began to break out between the various commanders. While these clashes were ongoing, they did eventually stabilize into a cold war of sorts between the three dominant tribes of the area: the Populzai, the Achikzai, and the Barakzai. Within the village of Tarin Kowt, for example, Jan Mohammed Khan's supporters controlled the southern part of town and Rozi Khan the northern part. Haji Malem Khaliq Khan retreated to his tribal area, and the truce between the three men remained largely stable; however, Malem Khaliq and Rozi Khan were allied against Jan Mohammed Khan.

RISE OF THE TALIBAN (1992–2001)

Prior to the Taliban's entry into Uruzgan in 1994, the province's key leaders agreed to present a common military front against the movement. Among those who agreed to this pact were Jan Mohammed Khan, Rozi Khan, and Haji Malem Abdul Khaliq Khan, among other less well known but influential militia commanders. However, as the Taliban pressed northward from Kandahar through the Delanor Pass in their Toyota "technical" trucks, Jan Mohammed Khan, who was charged with blocking their movement at this natural chokepoint, changed sides and allowed the Taliban to enter the province unmolested. In the ensuing battle that took place over a number of days, Jan Mohammed Khan repeatedly refused to help his ostensible allies, even though they repeatedly begged for his help, allowing the Taliban to eliminate his political opponents and force them to leave the area. Malem Khaliq fled his home village of Chora after several days of fighting where he lost many tribesman and all of his property. After helping Malem Khaliq as much as he could by sending additional men, Rozi Khan retreated to his tribal area, and as the Taliban further consolidated their control of the province, he eventually became a police official. Efforts by local elders led by Mullah Hamdullah to mediate the dispute between the Taliban and Malem Khaliq were quashed by Mullah Omar himself, who outlawed the traditional shura meeting of Afghan leaders to resolve disagreements. This ban would effectively stay in place until 2005.

Although his main opponent was removed from the province, Jan Mohammed Khan did not remain unscathed. In return for his assistance, the Taliban allowed him to remain in the province but he lost his militia, which was disarmed and disestablished. He was allowed one bodyguard and his freedom, just so long as he did not challenge the Taliban's authority. Rozi Khan experienced the same fate. The reason Jan Mohammed was given such treatment was that he was secretly being protected from within the Taliban by a fellow Populzai tribesman and old mujahedeen fighting buddy named Mullah Yar Mohammed. From his position as governor of Helmand Province, Yar Mohammed protected Jan Mohammed Khan and, as Yar Mohammed went on to become governor of Herat Province in the west and later governor of Ghazni Province in the east, Jan Mohammed Khan focused his energies on his family and making money. He eventually served as governor of Uruzgan for at least two years before being jailed by the Taliban in 2001.

Initially, the Taliban were warmly greeted by the residents of Uruzgan. The movement put an end to the incessant fighting between the various mujahedeen factions and provided needed structure and order to the community that had been missing during the years of continuous fighting. Several local residents, such as Aktar Mohammed Osmani and Abdul Ghani Berader, would later rise to senior positions within the movement. Osmani had been involved in the destruction of the Buddha statues in Bamiyan Province in 2001 and had served as the treasurer of the Taliban; Berader was Mullah Omar's deputy and had been deputy minister of defense when the Taliban fled Afghanistan in 2001. Osmani would eventually be captured by Coalition Forces in 2002 but escape through the bribing of local officials. An excellent account of his capture can be read in *Hunting Al-Qaeda*, written anonymously. In early 2010, Mullah Berader was captured in Pakistan. Other locals, such as the prominent mujahedeen commander Haji Khairo Jan, had also been part of this initial community support for the Taliban and was installed as mayor of Tarin Kowt nearly two years into their rule. Like much of the population, he eventually became their ardent opponent and was jailed on at least two occasions. When he was mayor, however, Khairo Jan was quite industrious; he laid out a good portion of present-day Tarin Kowt and did a lot of work to improve the local area. During his tenure, staff members of the United Nations arrived and sought to work with him to build a hospital, a rudimentary sewage system, and provide other improvements to the capital. They pledged to build a hospital for Tarin Kowt if the Taliban weapons stored in the small structure on the property were removed. The Taliban governor, Sardar, refused, and Mayor Khairo Jan told him that if he didn't remove the weapons he would resign. At this, the governor agreed to the request and the hospital was built. However, this and other disputes put a strain on the relationship between the governor and the mayor. Eventually, Sardar objected to the close relationship Khairo Jan had forged with the United Nations and imprisoned him. The next day, all the bazaar shop owners in Tarin Kowt closed their shops in protest. Shocked by this reaction, which was a clear demonstration of power, Sardar hurriedly released Khairo Jan, but at that point he had become a dedicated opponent of the Taliban and resigned as mayor.

Most other mujahedeen and former communists who were approached by the Taliban to serve in different positions in the provincial government declined and stayed at home. Noor Mohammed, the mujahedeen fighter who dug tank traps, was approached to be a school administrator, which had become his profession, but he declined because the Taliban "didn't follow the rules." Former communist Haji Abdul Samad was also approached about a job but declined, feigning illness. Others were not so lucky. Pai Mohammed, the local mujahedeen commander in the village of Sarkhome, was captured by the Taliban in their general crackdown on the supporters of Haji Malem Khaliq Khan, and personally tortured by senior Taliban official Mullah Razag. To this day, Pai Mohammed wears poultices to alleviate the pain. Upon his release from the Taliban, he fled to Herat where he worked with Ismael Khan, the past and future governor of that province. Some mujahedeen, such as Mullah Hamdullah, the Afghan who had been shot in the head during a battle with the Soviets, joined the Taliban to serve as a judge. However, for most of Uruzgan's residents, the time of the Taliban was a period of relative calm, although one that became extremely harsh and dispiriting as the Taliban applied their doctrinaire version of Islam. Largely staying at home to tend to their farms, the network of former mujahedeen were simply biding their time, waiting for a leader to take them out from under the Taliban's ruthless rule.

THE BAD SEED

In Uruzgan, the wheat seeds sent by the Americans to be distributed to the farmers as an alternative to the poppies were sold by government officials rather than distributed to the farmers. There are clear signs that the Taliban did not hesitate to exploit this opportunity.

—Antonio Giustozzi, *Koran, Kalashnikov, and Laptop: The Neo-Taliban Insurgency in Afghanistan*[3]

As I was getting ready to finish my tour, USAID began their Wheat Seed and Fertilizer Distribution Program in Uruzgan as part of a Government of Afghanistan capacity-building exercise and an effort to help farmers forego planting poppy for the winter. Because it was a national-level program, we were effectively cut out of its administration and only really discovered it was happening at all because the governor was complaining about it. The central thrust of the program was to get seed and fertilizer into the hands of the farmers by mid-October and early November so that they could plant an alternative crop to poppy. In practice, this program was an unmitigated disaster that deepened resentment against the local government and embarrassed the PRT even though we had nothing to do with it. Like most USAID programs, the implementing agent was not a savvy U.S. Government civil servant with years of experience undertaking similar programs overseas. Instead, a nongovernmental organization (NGO) was charged with implementing the program nationwide, an organization that, one would hope, had some experience with this type of work. The NGO implemented its programs through local Afghan staff who started their work in the relatively safer north and gradually made their way south and east where the insurgency was greatest. When they first arrived in Uruzgan, NGO staff requested from our illiterate governor a written list of wheat seed recipients. While his group could have put one together, the logistical and security problems of assembling an accurate list were daunting, especially when the NGO showed up three weeks into the planting season. At this point, the governor's complaints made us aware of the program. Because it would have been impossible to assemble the list in the time we had available, we suggested he write as many names as he could on the documentation and organize trucks to bring it out to the districts. When we started asking USAID questions about the program in Kabul, they told us that it was a national-level program and that we should butt out. Kerry couldn't believe this rebuke. As the post-mortems came in over the next few weeks, the NGO claimed victory because it had "distributed" wheat seed to four of Uruzgan's five districts. However, they defined "distribution" as getting the wheat seed to the district chief without determining whether deserving families had received it or not. We later learned that one district chief in the western part of the province had sold all of his wheat seed to the Hazara up north. It was an incredibly depressing episode in American foreign policy, but par for the course for so many of USAID's programs in the field. An ironic twist in this debacle was that the man in charge of USAID in Kabul eventually got promoted. Also galling is the fact that this same person had the audacity to come to our PRT in the summer of 2005 dressed in Afghan clothing to represent his "deep knowledge" of the Afghan people. USAID field staff were great, but the quality of USAID personnel seemed to change the higher you went up the chain. Such is life working with the interagency in Afghanistan.

Just days before I left for Kabul en route home, Haji Khairo Jan came to the PRT to wish me well. He had received the most votes in the province and was going to Kabul to assume his seat in parliament. When I told him we would be able to fly him and Mohammed Hanif Khan to Kabul so they could both attend the opening, he was deeply appreciative. Khairo Jan went on to say that he had only gotten to know me in the last few months but that seeing how a young American could come to Tarin Kowt to help the Afghan people meant a lot to him. He said that I was always respectful to the residents of Uruzgan and worked hard, and as a sign of his thanks wanted to buy me a complete set of Afghan clothing and introduce me to President Karzai to tell him the good work I had been doing. You never know how you are perceived by other people, especially when they are from another culture, but for him to take the time to tell me these things and to offer to introduce me to his country's president, and to be so gracious about it, touched me deeply. The Afghans are a great people and these gestures of kindness are one of the most attractive features of their culture.

While I generally enjoyed visiting Kabul to unwind, catch up on some sleep, and buy some things we couldn't get in Tarin Kowt, it could be trying at times, especially when running into people who had no inkling of what life was like in the provinces. One example of this was a female civilian working in Lt. General Eikenberry's office. When she had first arrived and noticed all of the low wooden crosses in each of the offices of the headquarters staff, she stated she had long heard that people in the military were religious but had never expected to see it to this degree. Of course, the "low wooden crosses" were there to hold the body armor and helmet that all the soldiers wore. This would normally be an amusing story, but her ignorance would later manifest itself in a decidedly less amusing manner. Late in 2005 a U.S. unit got into a firefight with the Taliban on a side of a mountain. The service members were unharmed, but they had killed several insurgents. When the soldiers asked local villagers to bury the men, they refused. Because the soldiers were unable to move from their position, the bodies began to stink badly and, per Geneva Conventions, the men decided to burn the bodies for obvious sanitary and health reasons. The Muslim faith, of course, prohibits the burning of bodies; and if not for an unsympathetic journalist embedded with the soldiers, no one would have learned about this incident. When it came out in the papers and the inevitable hue and cry followed, I overheard the same female staff member instantly judging the soldiers for not knowing Afghan and Muslim culture. Without even attempting to learn the circumstances, she bemoaned the cultural insensitivity of the military. It was a painful reminder of just how large the gulf could be between some civilians and the military, and I was glad most of my work enabled me to avoid people like that.

COMING HOME

The men with the power to set policy showed no interest in Vann's central concept—to behave like a benevolent colonial power and win the war by winning the Vietnamese peasantry through an American-sponsored social revolution.

—Neil Sheehan, *A Bright Shining Lie: John Paul Vann and America in Vietnam*[4]

When I returned home from Afghanistan at the end of November 2005, I didn't fully appreciate how my experience had changed me or how I would react to returning to the states. For several months afterward, I kept my beard and dressed tactically, at least by State Department standards, retaining my boots, gray pants, and rugged outdoor shirt as my standard uniform.

Because I hadn't seen much violence, I didn't feel as if I had changed that much. Although I had been mortared and three or four people I had worked with had died, I didn't think these experiences had affected me deeply. When I finally got home, I was incredibly numb to my surroundings and felt isolated. The low-grade stress that D.C.'s traffic had once created in me seemed just silly now when compared with the stresses of the war. I was also struck by how fixated television programs were on getting rich quick, losing weight, and improving your love life, all concerns that were ridiculous when weighed against the more pressing issues of survival and the desperate living conditions of the Afghans. As emotionally numb as I was when I returned, I slowly, and then quite dramatically, became emotionally oversensitive. I also began to cry when I would watch shows about returning soldiers, and I quickly became fixated on news about Afghanistan. I soon fell into watching online war videos as a way of staying in touch with Afghanistan and maintaining the emotional edge I had grown accustomed to. I had never really had much of a temper, but that also started to manifest itself as my sense of tactical urgency gave way to the bureaucratic attitude of the State Department. As I returned to my life in the bureaucracy, for what it was, I felt deeply alienated from the department and much of its personnel. There was no sense of urgency about the war effort, and the banal worries of bureaucratic minions seemed trite and unimportant. As I shed my tough emotional exterior, I soon fell into a depression and, even though I'd missed my political friends, I found the substance of our conversations tepid, focused so often on acquiring power and maneuvering for position. When I compared this with the selfless examples of leadership I saw in Afghanistan, the contrast was too much. I was no longer the young political appointee who saw the world in black and white and believed in the good leadership of my superiors. The war had changed me and, even though politics had stayed the same, I was now determined to do what I could from the inside, thinking of the men who selflessly served on the frontlines and were the people I had joined public service to help and to work alongside.

As I was making this personal journey, I kept abreast of all things Uruzgan. In February, my friend and colleague Sergeant Newman, who had lived two doors down from my room, was killed by an IED. A few months after that, Lt. Colonel Fontes and Richard "Ruff" Reiter, who had followed my replacement, Raphael Carland, were returning to the PRT after meeting the governor and survived a suicide car bomb, the first of its kind in the province. In addition, the first suicide vest attack took place near the same road and within sight of the PRT and killed several policemen working for Afghan Highway Police chief Matullah. The security situation had clearly begun to shift. Governor Jan Mohammed Khan was finally fired in March of 2006. This welcome news fell on me like a ton of bricks, although I was worried about the effect it would have on local politics. I knew nothing of his replacement, an Uruzgan outsider named Abdul Hakim Monib, but Lt. Colonel Fontes was very encouraged by what she had seen. In an e-mail she said: "After one week (today) the governor change has been great. Monib has taken charge and has vision and is organized. A real breath of fresh air. We are all doing well out here." This was great news and I was hopeful for Uruzgan.

I tried to keep involved in the war in any way I could. I started to write an article about my experiences, made the rounds of the bureaucracy to tell people what I had seen and experienced, and, although they were polite, they didn't seem terribly interested. I also traveled down to Fort Bragg to brief Maj. Wil Griego's Seventh Special Forces unit about the people and politics of the province, which was very rewarding. However, I felt listless and detached from my surroundings; the banalities of the U.S. professional class with all of their strivings and worries just seemed revolting. Particularly jarring was to return from a society enfused with a strong streak of fatalism, where politics was about scarcity and the struggle for survival, to one that was rights-based, where politics was about overabundance and life was about self-fulfillment and not endurance. Fortunately, I was eventually able to leave my position in arms control and ended up in counterterrorism. Earlier, a Hank Crumpton had e-mailed me from the U.S. Department of State in D.C., asking me to stop by his office when I returned. He had recently been appointed coordinator for counterterrorism, a position at the ambassadorial rank. He also wanted a copy of my resume to put me in for a job in the vice president's office. While incredibly flattered to be considered for such an important position, it seemed so far away from FOB Ripley. Although I didn't get the position with Vice President Cheney, I did end up in Crumpton's office. He was a quiet man with a strength that came from his years at the Central Intelligence Agency. He had a faint Southern accent courtesy of his Georgian roots, and he was very generous with his time. We talked about Afghanistan and the characters of Uruzgan Hank had run the CIA's operations in Afghanistan from Washington in 2001 and 2002 and was intimately familiar with Jan Mohammed Khan and several other Afghans from the area. He kindly offered me a job in his operations office. That was great but sitting at a desk all day and reading about the war and not directly participating in it was hard. After six months, the war beckoned again when Dr. David Kilcullen, Ambassador Crumpton's key adviser on counterterrorism, invited me to accompany him to Afghanistan for a research trip. Thankfully, the embassy was asking for me to come back as well to help fill a gap at the PRT in Uruzgan until the Dutch took over the province. I completely welcomed the opportunity to jettison the emotional rollercoaster that had become my homecoming and return to the field.

11   THE WAR RETURNS
(Tarin Kowt—Summer 2006)

By skilfully exploiting local grievances against the government and against local authorities, [the Taliban] successfully mobilised much of the southern population against the government and foreign contingents and forced a collapse of the structure of government in whole provinces.

—Antonio Giustozzi, *Koran, Kalashnikov, and Laptop: The Neo-Taliban Insurgency in Afghanistan*[1]

W hen I stepped off the plane at the dirt airfield next to Forward Operating Base Ripley in June 2006, I had returned to a military encampment girded for war, as opposed to the isolated outpost on the edge of empire that I had left. The sheer activity of the place was in marked contrast to the quiet pace of life just seven months earlier. The Dutch were arriving in force and hurriedly building their spaces at the newly renamed Camp Holland (FOB Ripley), and the Australians were expanding their presence there as well. Many of the Australians were wearing shirts around the base paraphrasing a line from the movie *Dodgeball*, "If you can dodge a bullet, you can dodge a ball." It was great to have them in Uruzgan. The Tenth Mountain Division had also built a temporary base just outside the PRT in support of their ongoing kinetic operations. Since I had left, the PRT had also changed a fair amount, but the main structures were unaffected. All the rooms were now occupied with various medical, air, and logistics personnel, and two new wings had also been added, significantly increasing the occupancy of the place. Besides a small meeting room that had been attached to the tactical operations center, much of my home was the same. Even though I felt like an old Uruzgan "hand," I was new to the people who were there and had to demonstrate once again my credentials to a new team.

The all-army PRT I had learned under had been replaced by a mix of services and nationalities led by a former top gun instructor and naval aviator named CDR Joe Gates. Unfortunately, the easy friendliness and chumminess of my colleagues in 2005 had now been replaced with a command climate that was corrosive. In my previous time in the province, I had had a strong relationship with PRT commanders LaFontaine and Fontes, both of whom included me in all their meetings with Afghan officials and actively sought my advice. In turn, I had reciprocated by doing what I did best, which was gathering information, leading on the political issues, and trying to solve problems. I had good friendships with both of them, and, while they were strong leaders and were always "on," living full time with the soldiers they led, they were always available to shoot the breeze and listen to whatever advice I could give them. The one initial benefit of arriving when I did is that I got to see my friend Kerry Greene depart Uruzgan on the plane that had brought me there. He was leaving after two years of work as the USAID development adviser to the PRT. He was the longest continually serving American in the province and, for me, a great friend who had been part of the original team that had built the PRT. His departure went unnoticed by the PRT's new occupants, which was a shame.

Settling into my old office, I was nostalgic for my old crew, and wasn't entirely looking forward to establishing new relationships with yet another team and having to prove myself to yet another rotation. At this point, the PRT was scheduled to be turned over to the Dutch by August, leaving us about two months to finish up our work, turn over the projects, and shut down U.S. operations in preparation for a move to the eastern province of Nuristan. The team at the PRT had been there for approximately four months and was moving entirely up to the Pakistani border.

Since our commander considered himself an expert on Uruzgan, he was reluctant to "share" his Afghan opportunities with others. He was convinced that the two most competent provincial directors in local government were

Taliban, although they were former communists, and that the previous team didn't have a development plan for the province (it did), and that the governor was a man who needed our strong and largely unquestioned support; one thing you learn about Afghanistan is to never support any official so unconditionally. Commander Gates did not allow anyone to meet with the governor alone, except himself, and because the PRT was still his operation, he was very sensitive to the Dutch and Australians seeking to establish good relationships with the local government outside of his presence. He was always complaining about the Dutch, how they were unprepared, arrogant, and so forth, and he seemed to go out of his way to antagonize them. Instead of viewing me as a colleague and trusted adviser, I think he didn't really know how to use me or how I could benefit the mission. Although I did advise the commander on many of the personalities of the province and shared with him why certain things were taking place, I got the distinct impression he was keen to have as authentic an Afghan experience as possible regardless of what the mission truly required. He seemed to be acting more like a war tourist than a confident commander. Unfortunately, much of his negative attitude permeated the staff and several of them interpreted his disdainful attitude toward the Dutch and Australians as a license to treat them shabbily. While the command climate was embarrassing, I tried my best to assist the commander and help the Dutch get prepared for assuming control of the PRT. The war continued even as these tensions persisted.

When I had previously been in Uruzgan, stand-up fights with the Taliban had taken place mostly in the western part of the province, although occasional skirmishes occurred in some of the more isolated areas. While the assassination of public officials was still a concern, most of the province was still quite safe and the districts of Tarin Kowt, Chora, and Khas Uruzgan were still relatively permissive. However, as the Tenth Mountain Division and U.S. and Australian Special Forces units conducted clearing operations throughout the province, the war intruded into the oasis of the PRT. Uruzgan's residents were fleeing the fighting and moving to the relatively safe provincial capital. When I arrived in the summer of 2006, we had about 1,750 refugee families in the Tarin Kowt area, and Engineer Hashim and the PRT were struggling mightily to provide humanitarian assistance. The PRT had also acquired a new Afghan resident, an old man from Char Chena district. He had been providing information to the Green Berets on the Taliban, and when he was returning home from one of those meetings, the Taliban riddled his body with AK-47 rounds. Miracuously, he was able to make it to the nearby base and his life was saved. Many soldiers had similar stories of Afghans being shot with upward of a dozen bullets or more in their bodies and still living. The man's son had not been so lucky; he had had his throat slit. The old man hung around the base recuperating and we called him "Blue" after the character from the movie *Old School*.

Even with all of these changes, it was nice to see our interpreters again. They provided the only continuity for me in this ever-changing war, yet even their ranks had changed. Mohib was still there as well as Akram, but Said Abdullah had been let go over an alleged bribe-taking incident to help contractors get some of our business; Doc had left as well. We had a new female interpreter who came from Kandahar and had been a neighbor of Karzai's where they had grown up together. She had recently returned from living overseas to help us out. The interpreters were still living in the base of one of our towers and the Special Forces units had slowly increased their presence in the old Afghan Security Force barracks. They had expanded some of the buildings and had painted the names of all of the Green Berets who had been killed in Afghanistan since the start of the war on one of the PRT's walls. Its black lettering stood out against the whitewash. Thankfully, Maj. Wil Griego of the Green Berets was there, and it was great to renew our acquaintance. Wil was a solidly built officer who was in charge of all Special Forces in the province. He was about five feet, eight inches and had the build of a weightlifter; I would learn later that he had participated in Olympic tryouts for weightlifting. Wil was a member of Seventh Special Forces Group, which largely operated in Central and Latin America, but like all U.S. forces, however, he and his men were increasingly working in Afghanistan. With his thick black beard and slightly darker complexion, he bore a striking resemblance to an Afghan, albeit one who worked out a lot. Wil was a great partner to work with and I was glad he was there. He told me that he and his men were incredibly busy and that they hadn't seen anything like these numbers of Taliban before. They were literally fighting several-hundred-man formations that used complex tactics and were attempting to take and hold territory. Wil would eventually lose the most soldiers of any Special Forces commander in the whole country during that rotation.

I often talked with Mohib to get up to speed on what had taken place since I had left. He told me that when it had become official that Jan Mohammed

Khan was being removed as governor, Mullah Hamdullah had gone around town telling people that he had been behind the decision. I was amazed that he had been saying these things so publicly, since Jan Mohammed Khan had no problem silencing people who had said lesser things. Mohib told me that their relationship had reached a point where Hamdullah and the governor were heard arguing in the governor's office about the mullah's comments and Jan Mohammed Khan had pulled a pistol on his old mujahedeen fighting colleague. Another rumor was that when he had been told he was being removed, the governor had asked President Karzai how he was expected to take care of the eighty-seven people he was responsible for in his household with the salary of a "tribal adviser" to the president. There was a lot to catch up on. I was hoping to speak with Mullah Hamdullah, but he was not in town. He had been selected by the State Department to visit the United States under the International Visitors program. Jan Mohammed Khan had already left the province and moved his family to Kandahar, leaving one son and his family to look after the family's sprawling complex southwest of town. I was hoping to meet with Haji Malem Abdul Khaliq Khan but when I arrived I read a curious newspaper article quoting him as saying that U S. troops had fired upon his car as he was fleeing Chora and that his wife had been badly wounded. I couldn't believe the article and as I asked around, some U.S. military units claimed to know nothing of the incident and others speculated it must have been the Special Forces. I was never able to determine what had happened. The ease with which shooting began and the fact that we didn't even know when our local allies were moving, where they lived, and what they looked like didn't augur well for our operations. An interesting development was that Haji Malem Abdul Khaliq Khan was already distancing himself from us, and our erstwhile allies were already playing up their differences with us; the Taliban's presence must have been strong in the area. Rozi Khan was still in the province but he had also been removed from his position as police chief. I know some of the soldiers saw him as being complicit in a car bomb attack earlier in the year, thinking he had let it go through his checkpoints, but I wasn't too sure. Wil told me that he had no evidence that Rozi was involved with the Taliban, yet I realized he was a survivor as well, so I could never be too sure.

To help find out what had happened since I had left, I logged on to the PRT's share drive. As I wandered around its files I noticed the letter Lt. Colonel Fontes had written to Staff Sergeant Newman's mother about his death in February. It was heartrending to read and to still see his presence around the PRT. It was harder still since no one at the PRT even knew who he was, and the memories of his example had already begun to fade. Later on, Commander Gates agreed to name his new base in Nuristan after Clint based on my recommendation.

February 13, 2006

Mrs. XXXXX XXXX
XXX XXXX XXXX
XXXXXX, XXXXXX

Dear Mrs. XXXX,

On behalf of all the soldiers at the Tarin Kowt Provincial Reconstruction Team, I would like to express our sincerest and deepest sympathies for the loss of your son. Clint was a brave, generous, and talented man who had many friends here and was respected by all. Always ready with a smile, a helping hand, and a sympathetic ear, everyone could count on Clint.

From the moment I joined the unit, I knew Clint was one of the best Civil Affairs soldiers in the Army. Because of his selfless commitment and capabilities, he volunteered to take on the hardest jobs with the most independence. He excelled at this mission, exceeding all expectations and succeeding at convincing people to start supporting the Government of Afghanistan, making a significant contribution to our efforts to stabilize the country.

The Afghans mourn for Clint as well. After 30 years of turmoil, they do not expect to see or meet people who genuinely care and put forth the effort to provide them a better future. Numerous Afghan government officials have asked me to pass on their heartfelt condolences and enormous appreciation for the sacrifices Clint and his family made during the entire time of his deployment.

Your son is recognized as a brave and compassionate man and as a hero by all who knew and worked with him here in Afghanistan. Our hearts and prayers go out to you at this most difficult time.

Robin L. Fontes
Lieutenant Colonel,
U. S. Army Commanding

THE NEW GOVERNOR

They also believed wholeheartedly that to disregard the welfare of the
Vietnamese peasantry was to disregard the long-term interest of Americans.
—Neil Sheehan, A Bright Shining Lie: John Paul Vann and America in Vietnam[2]

In March Governor Jan Mohammed Khan was replaced by an Uruzgan outsider, Abdul Hakim Monib, a former senior Taliban official and Gilzai tribal
member who was literate and well educated. He was a confident politician
with a pitch-black beard and hair who wore metal-framed glasses. Governor
Monib was deliberative and calculating and also charismatic. Since he took
office on March 18, he had been confronted by a number of challenges to his
authority, most coming from the former governor and his supporters, but
also from a deteriorating security situation that undermined his position in
the province. Following his return from Kabul on a recent trip on July 13,
Governor Monib seemed to have found a new political confidence that allowed him to move forward on a host of pressing security and governance
issues that were beginning to solidify his position as governor and broaden
his support base. By reaching out to previously marginalized tribes, educated
locals, and disaffected Durrani tribesmen, including the Populzai, the governor was putting together a support base that, I hoped, would strengthen his
position. By focusing on improving governance by removing incompetent
officials and insisting on results from the provincial government, the governor was slowly beginning to sway many locals who simply wanted honest
and effective administration to his side. With time, I hoped that Governor
Monib's plans to create a viable, inclusive, and effective government that
reached all of Uruzgan would become a bulwark of stability against any future Taliban attack.

Although former Uruzgan governor Jan Mohammed Khan had often complained about his weariness at being governor, a position he had held since
January 21, 2002, his subsequent removal came as somewhat of a shock to
him. Over time, his initially welcoming and supportive behavior toward
Governor Monib turned into active opposition. The former governor used
his contacts in Kabul to interfere in the central government's budget and re-
source allocation for Uruzgan, staged "attacks" by the "Taliban" on the
Afghan National Army and then volunteered his security forces as protection,

and he also spread rumors that it was only a matter of time before he was re-turned to power. Jan Mohammed was also quick to say that Governor Monib could not guarantee security in the province, as evidenced by the increase in Taliban activity shortly after his swearing-in, and that only he had the ability to guarantee security in the area. Since much of the provincial administration and all district appointments had been made by Jan Mohammed Khan, Governor Monib was not only confronted by the former governor's opposi-tion but also by a local administration not inclined to his ideas and leadership. Other local political figures challenged Monib's leadership as well.

Shortly after his assumption of office in March, Mullah Hamdullah, the Provincial Council president, openly challenged Monib's political legitimacy because Monib had come from Paktia Province. Hamdullah even attempted to sign government documents that required the governor's signature and to speak on behalf of the governor when he was not entitled to do so. Although these efforts were eventually beaten back, the "democratic legitimacy" gap that Governor Monib suffered from continued. Former Provincial Police chief Rozi Khan was also an initial supporter of Governor Monib, but his own sub-sequent replacement by Monib loyalist General Qasim soured him on the gov-ernor, and several reports implicated his brothers in anticoalition and anti–Afghan government activities. Subsequent Taliban activity in Rozi Khan's tribal area indicated either his complicit support of the Taliban or implicit sup-port suggested by his passivity at confronting them; either one affected Monib's position in the province by contributing to a loss of security in the area.

While Jan Mohammed Khan's Populzai tribal supporters and other local political figures continued to voice their displeasure at Monib's leadership, other residents of Uruzgan were wary of Monib because he was from the Gilzai branch of the Pashtuns; most Uruzgan locals come from the Durrani line. The governor's tribal background was particularly concerning to some because the great bulk of Taliban fighters came from the Gilzai. Other locals felt that Monib was too young and inexperienced for his position and that the increase in fighting in the province following his appointment indicated Monib's support for the insurgents. Various tales circulated in the area of Monib's cavorting with different Taliban leaders and fighters, although no real evidence existed to substantiate them.

Coming from another province with few local allies in Uruzgan and with the continued opposition of several key political and tribal leaders, Monib's tenure began quite precariously, and Uruzgan's residents were counting the days when Jan Mohammed Khan would return. Over the last several weeks, prior to my most recent arrival, and especially since his return from Kabul on July 13, Governor Monib worked aggressively and decisively to broaden his support base, improve governance, and enhance provincial security, efforts that were beginning to bear tangible results. He started to actively reach out to previously marginalized tribes and make allies among the majority Durrani Pashtun by delivering on his promises and practicing good governance. On July 20, for example, he convened a series of meetings with village elders from Mirabad, Drushan, and Sar Marghab to discuss the security situation in their areas and their development needs. What was notable about this meeting was that these elders had never met with former governor Jan Mohammed Khan when he was in power. The main reason was that the former governor regularly victimized the villagers because they were Gilzai. Obviously, the elders felt comfortable talking with Governor Monib, not only because he was an outsider to the tribal conflicts in the area but also because they came from the same tribe. He also reached out to Gilzai tribesmen in the district of Char Chena, mostly populated by the Gilzai subtribe of the Noorzai. To this end, the governor hoped to bring the Noorzai tribal leader Arif Noorzai, who was also a member of parliament, to the area to help select a district chief and to bring the Noorzai closer to the Afghan government. Since 2002, all the district chiefs and most of the police chiefs of Char Chena had come from the Populzai tribe.

Governor Monib also made a point of visiting each district for up to five days at a time to consult with village elders, get a sense of the community's needs, and determine how their district and village leaders were doing. He also used the meetings to gain a better understanding of the local political and tribal situation in order to choose local leaders the communities actually supported. This type of local consultation was often lacking during Jan Mohammed Khan's reign when he usually imposed his political and tribal supporters on an unwilling population. In addition, Governor Monib was planning to hold elections for the position of mayor of Tarin Kowt and wanted to expand this idea to other major villages.

One of the more unfortunate legacies of former governor Jan Mohammed Khan's rule was the lack of structure in local government and the total absence of accountability and results from public officials. Governor Monib made it his express intention to provide this badly needed structure and systematically removed incompetent or corrupt officials while retaining and promoting educated and honest civil servants. In April, Governor Monib fired the illiterate and corrupt director of agriculture and promoted the only trained employee of the directorate to director, Haji Sardar Mohammed. On July 20, he arrested the director of health, Dr. Khan Agha, for selling medical supplies in Tarin Kowt and actively recruited a new director and local doctors, many of whom had been alienated by Dr. Agha, to join the Health Directorate. He then replaced the director of education with a more able administrator and was seeking to find suitable replacements for the directors of communications and public works, both of whom were deemed incompetent. On July 25, Governor Monib replaced the corrupt and inadequate mayor of Tarin Kowt, Mullah Obaidullah, with the director of irrigation, Engineer Kabir. Mullah Obaidullah, a member of the Populzai tribe and longtime friend of Jan Mohammed Khan, was appointed by the former governor in August 2004 and his replacement signaled a shift toward a more honest and effective administration at the local level.

The governor also convened regular weekly meetings of his directors, security officials, and development advisers and expected participants to have reports ready for discussion. Each meeting had an agenda, which was followed, and the proceedings were well run. The governor was adamant that participants bring paper and pen to take notes and aggressively questioned his officials about how many employees they had (padded payrolls were a constant problem), the nature of their work, the resources they had at their disposal, and their plans for the future. Monib also set about reclaiming the stolen public property that many officials took with them after they had been removed. The governor even tasked the PRT to deliver on its promises and gave the PRT commander deadlines for information, resources, and assistance. The administrative coherence Monib gave to local administration and his insistence that people do their jobs were a fresh departure from the wreckage Jan Mohammed Khan had left behind. Things seemed to be looking up in the province.

With the removal of Provincial Police chief Rozi Khan in May, the rudimentary force that had been called the Afghan National Police completely disappeared in the province. Smaller police units in the districts, which were largely beholden to their respective commanders and nominally under the control of

Rozi Khan, melted away as well, as police chiefs were replaced and the threat from the Taliban increased in late spring. Partly because of the security vacuum this created, the Taliban were able to significantly step up their attacks in the province. To counter this threat and to begin the process of creating a professional police force for Uruzgan, Governor Monib undertook a process of recruiting competent police chiefs and officers, training them at the Kandahar Training Center, outfitting them with the right equipment, and constructing checkpoints in key villages and along the Tarin Kowt–Kandahar Road.

While dueling village elders continued to meet in Kabul to convince President Karzai that Monib had to be replaced by Jan Mohammed Khan, the former governor seemed to have already become resigned to the fact that he was not going to return anytime soon. His local militia leader cum Tarin Kowt district police chief, Haji Ali Ahmed, had also evacuated his family after being removed from his position. With the replacement of his last political ally in Tarin Kowt, Tarin Kowt mayor Mullah Obaidullah, on July 25, the former governor had few friends left in official government positions. One concern I had was that Afghan Highway Police Commander Matullah might be a source of instability for Governor Monib, although their on-again, off-again relationship seemed to have stabilized when Matullah expressed support for Monib (mainly through President Karzai's intervention). Moreover, Governor Monib had split the Populzai community through his active political and material support of Chenartu District Chief Malim Faiz Mohammed and Akhtar Mohammed, both of whom were Populzai tribesmen and former bodyguards to President Karzai. While governance finally seemed to be on a positive track, the security situation continued to deteriorate significantly.

RETURN OF THE TALIBAN

He explained that a strategy of pacification and social and economic reform was the only way to succeed. Attrition was "peripheral" to the real struggle. . . . The United States therefore had to employ its troops to shield the populated areas while it pacified by earning "the trust and loyalty of the people.". . . Pacification and social and economic reform were "a design for victory." Attrition was "the route to defeat."

—Neil Sheehan, *A Bright Shining Lie: John Paul Vann and America in Vietnam*[3]

Beginning in the late spring of 2006 and going through the summer, the Tenth Mountain Division, Special Forces, and the Afghan National Army began conducting a series of clearing operations in Uruzgan Province. As they ran their operations in a counterclockwise fashion up through the Chora Valley, they encountered a robust and well-equipped enemy. Several months earlier, the Taliban had begun an offensive the likes of which hadn't been seen since we invaded in 2001. The war I had returned to in June 2006 was not the one I had left. By the end of my tour in November 2005, I had acquired a pretty good sense of the security threats that existed in the province and had developed the personal safety habits that come with living in a war zone: always remember to look ten, twenty, and fifty feet out from your Humvee window before you step out, always scan the ridgeline, keep an eye out for cover, keep your interval, don't panic, be brave, and keep shooting. As always, the Taliban took advantage of natural and man-made features that funneled our convoys into chokepoints to plant improvised explosive devices—at bridges and riverbeds, or where the geography favored an ambush. But they never assaulted our forward operating bases, conducted any real assassination campaigns of government officials or supportive locals, or seriously disrupted the 2005 elections except for torching one polling center and killing two candidates, who most likely died because of local rivalries. Further, we had never had a suicide attack in the province while I was there or dating back to 2001. Over the course of my time in the province, none of the PRT's' convoys had either encountered an IED or suffered as little as a gunshot. Of course, this may have had more to do with the fact that the vast majority of our convoys were in the very secure district of Tarin Kowt and its capital, Chora District to the east and north, and the Kandahar Province district of Nesh to the south, which we handled because it was closer to us than to the Kandahar PRT. In many respects, this may explain our good fortune, but the active patrolling and intelligence-driven raids of the Twenty-fifth Infantry and the U.S. Special Forces had created a security bubble we obviously benefited from.

Our PRT was within the perimeter of FOB Ripley and nestled in the "Tarin Kowt bowl." It was referred to that way because it was a flat valley surrounded by mountain ranges that often caused storm fronts to swirl within its confines and frequent dust devils were created from the constant breeze. FOBs Tycz and Cobra protected our left flank in their respective districts of Deh Rawud and Char Chena and our right flank was protected by FOB Anaconda in Khas Uruzgan District. All of these FOBs had sizable numbers of U.S. infantry and Special Forces soldiers who actively patrolled their areas. What was unique about this force structure in the south was that it was disbursed throughout the province, which resulted in a coalition presence in 80 percent of the province's districts. Helmand and Kandahar Provinces, by contrast, had one FOB each in their respective capitals and no permanent coalition presence in their outlying districts, except for a small Coalition Force's group in Kandahar's Spin Boldak on the Pakistani border and another FOB close to Kandahar airfield. This distinctive force laydown eerily anticipated the future requirements for dealing with an emboldened Taliban by eliminating internal Afghan safe havens through a widely dispersed coalition and Afghan government presence. In many respects, I was very fortunate to have had the security I did because it gave me the relative freedom to do my work. Even though our PRT had not been hit by the Taliban when I was there in 2005, the same could not be said of our infantry and SF colleagues.

Through my work as a political adviser to the Twenty-fifth Infantry and the Special Forces, my conversations with the soldiers, and daily intelligence briefs, I gained a decent understanding of not only their operations but the threats we all faced. By and large, the Taliban never seemed to mass in numbers larger than a few dozen, although larger groups would occasionally be discovered, and they never really got up to the hundreds that we would begin to see during and after 2006. Although IEDs were a constant threat, they were rare, and when utilized, their most vicious form would generally be a single antitank mine. Mortar fire would take place, but during my time there in 2005, we only encountered one indirect fire attack on FOB Ripley and one attack in downtown Tarin Kowt. The other FOBs did experience more of these types of attacks, and in late 2005 they increased quite markedly at FOB Anaconda. The typical ambush often took place in geography that favored the aggressor and there would be some forewarning such as radio chatter. The fight would usually last between twenty to thirty minutes after which the Taliban broke contact to evade the close air support that generally followed their assaults. Ambushes were rare in populated areas. The leadership quality of Taliban commanders varied considerably but was often quite low, and it was not unusual to have Taliban leaders fight among themselves. The fighters we came upon were usually of Pashtun heritage, although they often hailed from Pakistan, and the few locals who joined them most often came from

Gilzai tribes. Attacks were typically small arms fire and rocket-propelled grenades along with IEDs and the occasional recoilless rifle. Most of the fighting took place in Char Chena and Deh Rawud districts to the west, where a combination of tribal support to the Taliban and a lack of security in the surrounding districts of Kijran in Dai Kundi Province and Baghran in Helmand Province made for quite intense fighting there. Most of the rest of the province was relatively permissive. The Taliban never held ground nor did they undertake a comprehensive murder-and-intimidation campaign on the population, other than night letters threatening locals who cooperated with the Afghan government and the United States. The Taliban shadow government, which was the political side of the insurgency, was largely nonexistent and, if it existed in the minds of the Taliban at all, hadn't yet materialized.

This was where things stood when I left the province in November 2005. I had not been shot at, seen a dead person, lost any soldiers I personally knew, been hit by an IED as much as seen one, and hadn't been ambushed. One local Afghan elder I had worked with had been killed by the Taliban, a local doctor, who was also a vice president of the Provincial Shura, had been shot by the Taliban but had survived, and a U.S. soldier assigned to the engineering unit building the Tarin Kowt–Kandahar Highway had died from an IED a few days after I had met her. I felt I had accomplished much during my tour and initiated several projects that my more-than-qualified successor, Raphael Carland, had continued. Little did I know that all of this was going to fundamentally change in 2006.

From the time I had left the province in November 2005 to when I returned in June 2006, the province's security had declined markedly. It became clear very quickly that the Taliban had been planning a significant and large-scale offensive to not only kill CF members but to push them out of the districts and to hold territory, something that had never happened in the province since 2001. When I got off the plane at FOB Ripley in June 2006, I had returned to a war-fighting province. The PRT was now surrounded by military encampments. Operation Mountain Thrust was already under way and Coalition Forces were slowly clearing villages in preparation for the Dutch assumption of control of the province. There was no plan to hold the cleared areas since the soldiers were needed in other parts of the country.

As a fighting force, the Taliban had also changed significantly. The brief and rare firefights of the past were gone, replaced by stand-up battles where the Taliban stayed and closed in on our positions. While the sheer number of Taliban had increased, often showing up in the hundreds, their tactics, techniques, and procedures had also gone through a minor revolution. The Taliban now attacked in populated areas, rather than using geography favorable to them, and hugged the convoys, pushing right up to their sides. In addition, their tenacity had also improved as the quality of their military leadership increased and foreign fighters started to appear on the battlefield. The foreign fighters were of particular concern because they not only brought additional skillsets to the battlefield, such as sniping and advanced explosives expertise, but they also had a rallying effect on the Taliban, who felt more confident confronting our soldiers.

In February 2006 my friend Staff Sgt. Clint Newman and three of his colleagues had been killed by five anti-tank mines in Char Chena district. Later on, Raphael Carland's successor, Ruff Reiter, and PRT Commander Robin Fontes had been hit by the first car bomb in Uruzgan's history. Both survived the assault because not all of the mortars that had been used as explosives had detonated, but the turret gunner suffered burns and was badly shaken by the experience. In addition, the first suicide-vest bomb attack took place next to Matullah's compound as he and his friend, Ahmed Akbar, the Tarin Kowt district police chief, watched a dog fight. While Matullah and Ahmed looked on from the roof of their compound, the bomber had walked up to the forty or fifty men watching the fight. He got snagged in the concertina wire surrounding the compound and, just as Ahmed pointed him out, asking what was happening, the bomber blew himself up, killing roughly two dozen local security forces. In the summer of 2006 fighting surged across the province as the Taliban took advantage of the Twenty-fifth Infantry's departure the previous year and calculated that the incoming Dutch military would be less likely to confront the insurgents because of weaker political support. Also, the Taliban had been studying our tactics in the districts of Deh Rawud and Char Chena and had extensive experience with U.S. Special Forces units over many years of constant fighting. Certain firefights are noteworthy in illustrating the new, and deadly, environment.

The district of Char Chena was unique among Uruzgan's six districts in that it was almost completely populated by members of the Gilzai tribe. The two main Gilzai sub-tribes there were the Noorzai and Hotak, who tended to have greater sympathy for the Taliban from shared tribal affiliation and because of the predatory behavior of the Durrani Pashtun governor. Moreover, the district anchored the northwest corner of the province and served as the only coalition outpost among three provinces in the area (Dai Kundi, Helmand, and Farah). None of the other provinces had a permanent U.S. presence near FOB Cobra, which gave the insurgents ample opportunity to rest, rearm, and redeploy to Char Chena to fight the coalition. Beginning in late 2005 and continuing until the end of 2007, the district was the scene of some of the worst fighting in the country. In one particular SF rotation to the base, approximately 55 percent of the men were casualties, including seven who had been killed.

When the latest units rotated in to Char Chena in 2005, they expected firefights but never anticipated the extent of the fighting they would eventually encounter. Their indigenous security force, which all Special Forces bases have, was led by a more-than-capable Pashtun named Yassim who had an uncanny ability to anticipate ambushes, locate IEDs, and provide the necessary targets Special Forces soldiers crave on a deployment. However, the unit's leadership quickly discovered they had a spy in their midst, who had been reporting their movements in the area, and they set out to stop his operations. After greater phone discipline had been imposed and the informant had been silenced, the Special Forces soldiers greatly expanded their operations, Yassim taking a leading role. Even though they encountered more IEDs and firefights, the SF were generally content because they were doing the job they had been trained to do. However, not long after operational security had been improved, the Green Beret unit started to incur significant casualties.

On one particular convoy, the SF were initially engaged by small arms fire to their left, prompting the turret gunners to swivel to the sound of the fighting. As they did this, a sniper shot the first turret gunner in the head, killing him instantly, and then grazed the second gunner's cheek with another shot. This man, who was well over six feet, four inches, had a gauze pad passed up to him, and he held it in place with his shoulder while he continued to fight. At this point, more insurgents engaged the convoy on the right flank from a higher point in the valley with small arms and rocket-propelled grenades. The Special Forces soldiers dismounted their Humvees and concluded the firefight with the assistance of close air support. Later operations indicated that Taliban snipers had been using ghillie (camo) suits, which not only concealed their firing location, but were a strong indicator of foreign training and/or presence among the Taliban. From 2001 to 2005, the Taliban hadn't really utilized snipers in any operations. After 2005 this changed, and the IED threat in Char Chena also surged. On another mission during this period, the same SF team hit a portion of road where five anti-tank mines had been buried. Staff Sgt. Clint Newman, who had worked at the PRT and was on rotation to FOB Cobra, was driving the third Humvee in a convoy when he stopped his vehicle to inspect a section of the road that two others Humvees had just driven over. Newman had been the Civil Affairs Soldier of the Year and had done a tour in Iraq prior to coming to Afghanistan. He left the vehicle and saw nothing unusual. As he drove forward, a concealed insurgent remotely detonated the five anti-tank mines, launching the vehicle into the air and shattering every bone in the bodies of the four occupants as the force of the explosion ricocheted in the Humvee. This began a series of increasingly lethal engagements culminating in seven U.S. deaths and twenty-two casualties.

It was eventually discovered that Yassim had been the source for the Taliban's information and had been using the Green Berets to eliminate his rivals in the movement. (It belatedly occurred to me that the slaying of the FOB's Hazara guards the previous year had helped set Yassim up to be the new head of security.) Once this conspiracy had been uncovered, a ruse was concocted to lure Yassim to Bagram Air Field for incarceration and interrogation. He had been told that he had been doing a superb job as the commander of the FOB's Afghan Security Force and that the commanding general in Bagram wanted to give him a medal for his bravery. When he arrived in Bagram, he was quickly arrested and interrogated and was later separated from the general prison population because he had started to organize them against the guards.

The intense fighting had surged across the province and, although the usual tactics of ambushes and asymmetric attacks had increased in size and lethality, a new innovation had appeared. Unlike the past, when the Taliban would often break contact after several minutes of fighting, the Taliban had now started to stand and fight. This was happening throughout the south and was a surprise to Coalition Forces. But the biggest innovation was that they had started to mount full-on assaults on our FOBs with the intention of overrunning them. Just prior to my arrival, they had overrun the district center of Chora, only to be kicked out a few weeks later. To be able to recruit, train, deploy, and lead that many men in a coordinated attack spoke to the state of the insurgency. Not only did they have better leaders who were able to inspire men to attack a fixed and well-defended position, but they had the coordination and equipment to do so. This was no longer a ragtag bunch of fighters; the insurgency had grown into a mature movement, a movement I was about to experience firsthand.

12 THE GOOD SAMARITAN
(Chora—Summer 2006)

*This is a political war and it calls for discrimination in killing. The best
weapon for killing would be a knife, but I'm afraid we can't do it that way.
The worst is an airplane. The next worst is artillery. Barring a knife, the best
is a rifle—you know who you're killing.*

> —John Paul Vann, quoted in Neil Sheehan's *A Bright Shining Lie: John Paul
> Vann and America in Vietnam*[1]

As clearing operations continued throughout the summer of 2006, our
PRT commander wanted to go up to the village of Chora to assess the damage from fighting and scout out possible civil affairs projects while hopefully
reducing any grievances the villagers may have had against the coalition due
to the fighting. As we departed, I thought again of the coalition shooting the
wife of Achikzai tribal leader Haji Malem Abdul Khaliq as they fled the fighting in Chora. It was deeply depressing and weighed on me as we departed for
his home district. He had publicly railed against Coalition Forces in the papers, which I could completely understand. The increased violence in the
province was affecting everyone.

In the early morning hours, we sent forward a small element north of
Tarin Kowt to secure a key bridge the main convoy would have to cross to
get to the Chora District Center; it was a chokepoint the enemy could use

against us and was quite familiar to me from previous trips. We had received a report that when this element rolled up to the objective, they had discovered a small hole and some digging tools where the bridge met the riverbank and had seen two men running away into the village. I was in the second and main element of our convoy, which was idling on the edge of town waiting for the go-ahead from the convoy commander.

The sun had started to rise and the villagers were beginning to mill about town as a low mist skirted the nearby mountains. While we waited, we heard a large explosion near the area where the first element had stopped and a narrow column of black-and-gray smoke shot up in the air. We weren't able to see what had taken place but our convoy quickly pushed out to the bridge to meet up with the first element. As radio traffic came in, it seemed that an IED had exploded down the road from the bridge on a path we were planning to take. All of us were naturally wary of our surroundings when we got to the bridge because it was clear that the Taliban had been in the area. We were on a narrow dirt road that was lined with a small adobe wall and set in a large open field. The bridge was in front of us and the road we planned to take snaked off to the right, in the direction of the blast. As we stood there, small children showed up from the nearby houses and one of the soldiers gave a little girl a balloon. Around that time we got a report from the front of the convoy that a taxi had shown up with a local national spread out in the back, covered with blood. After a quick search of the car, they sent it down the road and it stopped near my Humvee. Our medic jumped out of his truck and quickly assessed the man's injuries. The man's right hand was gone and a sizable chunk of his skull was missing and his breathing was infrequent and labored. He was approximately fifty years old, which was unusually old for a member of the Taliban, but we figured he must have been putting a bomb in the road for some sort of payment. After the medic looked over the man's injuries, he shook his head and said he couldn't do anything for him, and the man quietly expired. The driver, whom we suspected was also working for the Taliban, was distraught and clearly agitated so we detained him.

In the interim, an explosive ordnance disposal truck arrived to clear the rest of the route through the village. As it moved forward, an Afghan army truck swung behind it and my Humvee followed. We traveled about one hundred yards and came upon the blast site where the local Afghan had tried to place an IED. The small bridge was only a few feet long and went over a small rivulet the Afghans had created by diverting the river. The blast had created some damage to the concrete structure, and the tree overhead contained shredded scraps from the Afghan man's turban. I found his blood-covered skullcap and pieces of his head in a small patch where he had presumably landed. The PRT's force protection brought the detained Taliban forward and asked him what was ahead and cleared a couple of compounds that were nearby. The man claimed to know nothing and was still clearly distraught at the death of his friend. The explosive ordance disposal truck discovered a pressure plate anti-tank mine about twenty-five yards from where I stood, and the slight bulge of the top of the mine peaked out of the road. The explosive ordnance disposal staff blew it in place and we dismounted from our Humvees, looking for any remaining IEDs as we left the village. Joining the soldiers, I scanned the road for explosives and the area compounds for insurgents. This whole process took so long that by the time we left the village, the slain man's family was hosting a funeral for him on a nearby hill to our left. Once we cleared the village, we made the decision to travel off-road. The trip to Chora usually took about three hours, but we decided to move to the desert, navigating dry riverbeds and providing overwatch on small hills as each Humvee moved forward. Our trip would eventually take about eleven hours to complete.

We finally arrived at the Chora District Center in the early evening and quickly set up our base at the USAID-built district headquarters. It was great to finally see the finished project that Kerry had started in 2005 and which our soldiers referred to as the White Palace. Before we got situated, however, we set up a MEDCAP for the villagers and passed out hand-crank radios so they could listen to our radio station in Tarin Kowt. Although I asked around for several of the Afghans I used to work with, like many residents of Uruzgan, they had fled the fighting. I spoke with the new police chief for a while and, like virtually all of the public officials I spoke with, he complained about not having enough pay and equipment for his men. Wandering through the police station, I saw that several of the police trucks we had provided them in 2005 had been torched and the makeshift guard posts we had helped them build had been destroyed by the Taliban when they seized Chora a few months earlier. Once we had finished screening the villagers for health issues and prescribing medicine and palliatives, we settled into the White Palace for the night.

The whole building was bereft of any office furniture and other amenities, and the Taliban had done whatever they could to destroy the place. All of its windows had been shattered, and the Taliban had blasted a central support pillar with a landmine hoping to bring the whole structure down. The column was severed and several steel rebar splayed out from it like brittle spaghetti. Using a piece of cardboard as a mattress, I set up for the evening, sharing a room with the PRT commander and other soldiers, quickly falling asleep in my clothes with my AK-47 within arms' reach.

After we woke up, we went on a foot patrol in the village to assess damage from the recent fighting and the spring offensive. In the boys' school, we saw that the Taliban had defecated in several of the rooms. Many of the windows had also been blown out, and they had obviously tried to set the building on fire by igniting the wooden beams and thatch that lined the roof. While the structure still stood, the early morning daylight shone through several holes in the ceiling. We walked along the main street and noticed several blood trails at the traffic circle. All of the shops were still closed and we had attracted a small crowd, curious about the Westerners. As we were inspecting the village, we received a report that the local clinic had three "patients" that villagers identified as members of the Taliban. When we got there, we saw three young men laid out on stretchers with many bandages on their arms, legs, and torsos. I was finally face to face with the illusive enemy. I had often seen the effects of their operations but had never seen them in the flesh. These men were dark skinned, wiry, and wore thick black beards, and their clothing was covered in dirt and blood. They claimed to be local farmers, although the police chief insisted he did not know who they were, and they were recovering from a variety of wounds they claimed to have received when they were caught up in the fighting. Their eyes were glazed over and their actions lethargic, perhaps from the painkillers. Their nervousness was apparent as our troops and the Afghan National Army inspected them. As they were brought out of the clinic on stretchers and put into our medical truck, an Afghan army sergeant harangued them about attacking their own countrymen and destroying what little the village had. They mumbled a few things but didn't really say much in return. Once we had secured them, we continued our foot patrol to the end of the village and eventually returned to the palace for lunch. We finally left town around noon.

Leaving the green swath of Chora, we headed back into the desert with our unusually large convoy. The PRT's force protection formed the bulk of our forces but we also had Dutch and Australian soldiers, the Afghan army, the embedded training team, and a mix of soldiers, airmen, and sailors. Our convoy was led by a young Australian infantry captain named Captain Black. We continued our bounding overwatch posture, this tactic involves one element of a military unit providing cover while another one moves forward, and our convoy was divided into three columns, the majority of it in the middle. We had about three Humvees on each side of the main movement and the Humvee I was in led the right flank. As we approached the village of Sar Marghab, an Afghan army soldier overheard radio chatter from the Taliban saying, "The dinner was ready." The Taliban would often use a rudimentary code to communicate between themselves and, while it didn't always mean an ambush was coming, each time we acted as if it were. My Humvee was well behind the main convoy on the right flank when a large explosion erupted in the middle of the road. We assumed it was an IED, and our Humvee driver gunned the truck, leaping over dry wadis and setting up on a desert ridge overlooking the center of the village. Our turret gunner swung his 50-caliber machine gun over to the left and scanned for targets. Radio chatter started to come in with a distinctive Australian accent indicating that it wasn't an IED that had gone off but was a mortar and that the convoy was deeply involved in resisting an ambush.

Just as the situation became clear to us, the turret gunner dove into the Humvee. All of us thought he had been shot, but he said he had just dodged a bullet that whizzed by his head. I quickly removed the straps on the ammunition boxes and passed several up to him. As the turret gunner scanned the valley for targets, the driver and vehicle commander dismounted and met up with the other Humvees to organize a group to clear several nearby compounds. Commander Gates ran up to my Humvee and told me to stay put because if I were killed or injured it would be a huge information operations victory for the Taliban and a bad day for me. Crestfallen, I put my AK-47 away and tried to do what I could. I monitored the radio, translating the Australian's accent for my colleagues, scanned the right side of our Humvee in case there was a flanking effort, and made sure the turret gunner kept drinking water. While all this was happening, I noticed that right after a huge "thwump" in the village, a puff of white smoke came out from behind a

compound to our front. When I pointed this out, my navy colleague speculated that must be where the mortar was firing from. We then called everyone back into the Humvee and our turret gunner aimed his machine gun in
the direction of the compound. A compound framed each side of the road
ahead and, because they hadn't been cleared and we didn't know what was
on the other side of the houses, we moved forward to the edge of the buildings
and fired our 50-cal. toward the mortar's direction. After firing off several
rounds, we repositioned a little farther off the ridgeline so that we weren't
profiled against the sky. Although we weren't sure we had hit anyone, the
mortar did stop firing.

While the other soldiers were clearing the nearby compounds, they had an
excellent view into the village. One of our soldiers saw two Taliban low-
crawling along an adobe wall and he quickly shot and killed them. As we
were handling the right flank, the guys in the village were involved in a very
intense firefight. As they cleared the village we coordinated our positions by
firing flares to make sure we were protecting their flank. The sun was beginning to set, and it was in our eyes. As soon as the fighting had started in
the village, the men had dismounted from their gun trucks and our turret
gunners had engaged the enemy. The Afghan army soldiers were magnificent
and, unlike our soldiers who were moving around and seeking cover as they
fought the Taliban, they were simply walking around the battlefield, firing off
rounds at the enemy in the Afghan way, without a care in the world. As our
team cleared the village, several trucks took fire and another Humvee gave
out and had to be towed out of the area. As intense as the firefight was
against approximately fifty or so Taliban, we miraculously didn't suffer any
casualties. The firefight went on for about two and a half hours, and because
the sun was starting to set we chose to disengage. The Australian Special
Forces showed up and the Dutch arrived in armored personnel carriers to
cover our withdrawal.

Our main convoy fell back and the right and left flanks rallied at a point
outside the village on the road to Chora. We quickly backtracked our route
to a patch of open desert, where we took stock of what had happened and
planned an alternative way home. We had about two hours of daylight left
and although we largely paralleled our original route home, we went down
a different valley. These villages seemed much more welcoming and locals
waved to us as they went about their evening routine. We finally made it

back to the PRT by nightfall. In an initial battle damage assessment, the Australians reported that they had found twenty-eight Taliban bodies. All of us were still juiced on adrenaline, many discovering for the first time that they knew how to handle themselves in a firefight. After the death of several Taliban, the confidence we had in our friends increased as their true measure in combat became apparent. For me, I was glad I had done all I could in my "noncombatant" role. With my AK-47 and extra magazines, I had certainly been willing to pull my own weight, but I was happy to have gotten through this initial physical test of courage. As we settled in for the evening, taking showers and getting some chow, I realized that this was the first sustained firefight the Tarin Kowt PRT had ever been involved in, and I marveled at how much the province had changed since 2005.

The next day we learned more about what had happened the previous two days. The dead "Taliban" who we thought had died emplacing the IED was actually a local villager who had been killed by the Taliban when they detonated the IED by remote control as he was removing it. Apparently, the man had worked on a project at the PRT and supported the positive things the coalition was doing; in fact, he had been removing IEDs for quite some time. When he had started removing them, he told the brother of then–police chief Rozi Khan. The brother had told him to stop and to keep quiet. To reinforce the point, he arrested the man's son and stole all of his money. Undeterred, the villager kept removing the IEDs but didn't tell anyone. All of this had occurred without any of our knowledge. The other "Taliban" had been the man's son. While we were happy that we had comported ourselves well on the mission and the men had fought bravely, some of the soldiers grumbled that the Special Forces had told the PRT commander not to go to that area because it was still full of Taliban. In light of what we had accomplished in Chora, it didn't seem like the benefits really outweighed the risks. As everyone put their experiences on paper for an official account of the battle, the commander appeared eager to make sure his bravery was captured and that the accounts of his Humvee mates accurately reflected their collective actions. It felt as if the whole mission had been really unnecessary, especially in light of the fact that most of our projects had been shut down from the fighting and we were planning to hand over our operations to the Dutch.

THE BESIEGED VILLAGE

"You cannot win militarily," Krulak said. *"You have to win totally, or you are not winning at all."*

—Neil Sheehan, A Bright Shining Lie: John Paul Vann and America in Vietnam[2]

In the late summer of 2006 as the Taliban offensive was surging, milita leader Akhtar Mohammed and his more political brother, Malim Faiz Mohammed, asked for help from the coalition. Slowly but surely the Taliban had been seizing the smaller villages that surrounded their area of Chenartu and tightening their grip on the valley. The insurgents would typically send a message to the village, either directly or by capturing a villager and having him deliver it, that they had surrounded the area and would kill everyone if they did not declare their allegiance to the Taliban, provide fresh recruits, and give them water and food along with intelligence on Coalition Forces. Although many villages wanted to resist the Taliban, they lacked the ability to do so and some actually joined with them, sensing that momentum was on the side of the Islamist movement. This process culminated when the village of Mirabad, partway between Chenartu and Tarin Kowt, imposed a blockade on Chenartu by seizing the only road to the area from the provincial capital. The residents of Mirabad were Gilzai Pashtuns from the Hotak sub-tribe who had a natural sympathy for the Taliban and were constantly in conflict with the villagers of Chenartu. How much of this blockade was attributable to the Taliban or to the usual intertribal tensions we will never know, but the end result was that the village lacked crucial medical supplies, spare parts, and food, and the Taliban were slowly increasing their influence around the area and threatening Karzai's allies. Accordingly, U.S. Special Forces and the Provincial Reconstruction Team joined with the governor and police chief of the province to visit Chenartu to bolster the brothers and their besieged population.

Our Chinook helicopter lifted off from FOB Ripley around two in the morning and followed the path of the thin river that led from Tarin Kowt east to Chenartu. The moon illuminated the area as the helicopter churned forward, and the stars were plentiful, vivid, and full. I was armed with the trusty AK-47 I had procured from an arms cache the previous year and a daypack with extra water and food. I had linked up with a Dutch Special Forces soldier who sat next to me during the trip so that I wouldn't be completely inept during my first nighttime insertion. We had a number of supplies lined up in the heart of the helicopter and, try as I might, I wasn't able to keep my leg from falling asleep as the containers pushed me up against the helicopter's seats. As the helo landed in Chenartu Valley and the dust cloud pushed out from the back, we piled out to set up a perimeter. Unfortunately for me, my right leg was completely useless and felt like jello as I grasped for something to help me limp along to the back of the helicopter. The Dutch soldier came to my rescue at that moment and held/pushed me along for about twenty-five feet past the back of the helicopter where I collapsed on my bag, using it as a rudimentary stand for my AK-47. As the helicopter lifted off and the dust and commotion died down, the cool night rushed in and we gathered ourselves together. The dark hills surrounded us and I could only make out their general form because they began where the stars stopped. Akhtar's trucks slinked out of the village to pick us up and, after exchanging pleasantries with Governor Monib and the police chief, we all tumbled into the backs of the trucks, bumping along the dirt track on the way to his home. Soon after settling in, the governor, police chief, the PRT commander, Special Forces soldier, and I fell fast asleep and were snoring on Akhtar's open-air veranda.

Akhtar's house was like many Pashtun homes, and was surrounded by thick adobe walls with a series of smaller buildings sprinkled throughout the area constructed out of a mix of concrete and adobe. As was the fashion of the Pashtuns, the gate was brightly colored and a small door set within it allowed people to pass through while perfectly framing the DShK machine gun that guarded his house from any possible attack from the precipice overlooking it. After we had awakened and scrounged up some breakfast, Monib and Akhtar met privately and the governor gave him a thick wad of cash to pay for the costs of his militia. He then sat down to have an audience with the people. Akhtar spoke for the group by handing the governor a series of letters he had received from Taliban leaders. The letters initially sought to entice him to their cause, but following his quick response that he would kill them, a burst of communications between them threatening various humiliations and violence along with dark suggestions of how they would violate each other's women. The governor read these letters carefully as he leaned against the wall and he, Akhtar, and Malim discussed the situation. In the interim, several thousand AK-47 rounds had been delivered by the Special Forces who had driven up ahead of us the night before and had neatly stacked the boxes in Akhtar's home. The supplies were greeted with great joy by the villagers and were a clear sign of Akhtar and Malim's standing with the government; however, the real show of support was about to begin.

We reassembled outside Akhtar's house facing down the wide valley away from the village. Some of the Special Forces soldiers popped green smoke to mark the landing area and all of us waited for the show. A large crowd of Afghans and soldiers gathered in quiet anticipation and several locals had brought their motorcycles, trucks, bicycles and, in one man's case, a small commuter shuttle. As we looked skyward, we made out the small form of a cargo plane flying northeast. After it passed our position, it began to drop more than forty pallets of medical supplies, seeds, salt, cooking oil, and farming implements in large boxes. As the parachutes touched down the Afghans surged forward as if they were at an Oklahoma land rush, their vehicles lost in a plume of khaki dust. Once the excitement had settled down, I wandered out with some of the soldiers to inspect the few not-so-successful airdrops where the parachute hadn't opened. Everything was jumbled up and the cooking oil looked like a pool of blood leaking out of the wrecked cardboard containers. Even though the pallet had plummeted at an incredible speed, a fairly substantial portion of the goods was still usable. People were walking back to the village, their arms full of shovels, bags of salt, seeds, and medical supplies, all of them with a smile on their face at their newfound riches.

Once the airdrop finished and the Afghans returned, laden with supplies, we hiked back to Akhtar's home for lunch. After the simple, though generous, meal, we loaded back into his trucks and rode to the village meeting house where Malim convened a shura of the local villagers. It seemed as if every man in the village had been shoehorned into the small room and Governor Monib, Malim, and Commander Gates sat at the front while everyone else sat on the ground. The governor and Malim led the proceedings, and the complaints and discussion revolved around familiar themes. Surprisingly, the villagers and Akhtar said they could handle themselves when it came to security and were not afraid of the Taliban, but they wanted help setting up a clinic and supplying their schools. They were very concerned about access to Tarin Kowt and vociferously complained about Mirabad's blockade of their village: they wanted the government to intervene. I dutifully wrote down these complaints in my notebook for possible use in some reporting cable. The villagers were very appreciative of the aid we had brought them and we promised to do what we could about their health and education concerns. In order to limit the shenanigans of the Mirabad villagers, the Chernatu villagers were quite keen on building a checkpoint on the road to Tarin Kowt. This request dovetailed nicely with our own goal of establishing checkpoints along this particular route. When we returned to Akhtar's house, he, Malim, the governor, and the PRT commander and I walked to Malim's house for a more secluded dinner. While dining on goat, vegetables, and bread, we continued a quiet discussion of local politics and personalities to the low hiss of a gas-powered lantern, refreshed by the cool night air.

Later, in the pitch-black night, we walked back to Akhtar's home and collected our belongings, venturing out into the wide plain to wait for our Chinook helicopters. While we killed time, my Dutch SF friend showed me his night-vision monocle, which cast everything in the now-familiar green glow. Several infrared strobe lights were blinking on the men as they waited; an occasional cough and adjusting of stance broke the silence as we waited for the familiar whoop-whoop of the helicopters. We eventually heard them approach the village and set down about three hundred yards away. However, as we made our way to the helos, it became evident that the distance was probably half a mile or so, with a series of ravines interspersed along our path. Lacking night-vision goggles, I picked my way through the terrain, balancing my AK-47, backpack, helmet, and armor. Many of the gashes required one man to climb partway up the incline and help the guy behind him. A little tired from the unexpected obstacles, we finally made it to the helicopters and, as we lifted off, the village of Chenartu was bathed in moonlight. It was better prepared to fend off an assault by the Taliban and, led by the brothers Mohammed, we left it alone to determine its fate.

13 THE DUTCH TAKE OVER
(Tarin Kowt—2006)

What is desperately needed is a strong, dynamic, ruthless, colonialist-type ambassador with the authority to relieve generals, mission chiefs and every other bastard who does not follow a stated, clear-cut policy which, in itself, at a minimum, involves the U.S. in the hiring and firing of Vietnamese leaders.

—Neil Sheehan, *A Bright Shining Lie John Paul Vann and America in Vietnam*[1]

One of the reasons the embassy had asked me to come back was to help shut down the American-led PRT and assist the Government of the Netherlands in assuming responsibility for the reconstruction, development, and good governance efforts in the province. I was certainly willing to help out the Dutch team, but it was a bittersweet moment for me. As far as I was concerned, this was the United States' war; we had been attacked and we operated as such, each soldier knowing why he was there and doing the best he could to achieve the mission. Even though some Dutch citizens may have been killed or injured in the attacks of September 11, their government and people didn't see the war as directly important to their national security as we clearly did. In addition, having the Dutch take over indicated a limit to U.S. power, a limit that most certainly was from the Iraq War and also represented a less-than-full mobilization of our society to wage this conflict. The

Dutch arrival was not all bad by any means; for once Uruzgan would be a national priority rather than one of many sleepy U.S. outposts in Afghanistan. Unfortunately, because of the importance of the province to the Netherlands, our actions were of keen interest to the political class at The Hague, who parsed and examined every action or decision. Our ability to do what was needed was restricted by the glaring klieg light of politics.

The Netherlands' assumption of control of the Tarin Kowt Provincial Reconstruction Team from the United States, and its transfer from Operation Enduring Freedom to the International Security Assistance Force (ISAF) on August 1, was a process not without its challenges. Some continued for the next several months, but few seemed likely to cause problems in the long-term. Lacking adequate vehicles for missions and with an understrength force protection element that was largely focused on base improvements, the PRT seemed likely to see a drop-off in operations once the Dutch assumed control. While some workaround solutions were possible, such as partnering with the Australians for vehicles, a Dutch solution wasn't likely to be seen for several months. The Dutch Deployment Task Force, ostensibly charged with preparing the main Dutch base in Uruzgan at FOB Ripley and at a smaller base at FOB Tycz in Deh Rawud, was significantly behind in its preparations. The physical facilities of the Tarin Kowt base were not yet ready for the roughly 1,500 Dutch troops that were going to be housed there, and similar challenges existed at FOB Tycz, which was going to house nearly 300 troops. The soldiers were still living in tents left over from the Twenty-fifth Infantry Division's deployment and the bullet-proof and bomb-resistant shipping containers that all Dutch troops were eventually going to live in were not yet constructed—it was unclear whether they were all in country. Chow was rudimentary but adequate, mostly microwave meals, and troops were limited to taking showers in facilities with a total of eighteen showerheads. Only three of the eleven planned rifle platoons were in Uruzgan, partly because there weren't enough facilities to receive them, and their internal perimeter was still under construction, although their exterior perimeter, one that preexisted the Dutch commitment to Uruzgan, was built and manned.

The Dutch had three types of military vehicles for Uruzgan, none of which was realistic or practical for the operating environment. Their basic tactical vehicle was a Mercedes-Benz truck that had no armor, lacked ballistic glass, and had an open top. It did have two machine guns at the ready, in contrast to the single 240 Bravo or the 50-caliber machine guns that the U.S. Humvees were usually armed with, and was faster because of its lack of armor. However, it still made a ready target for insurgents who had become more adept at utilizing improvised explosive devices and car bombs in Uruzgan as of late. The Dutch also had tracked and wheeled armored personnel carriers. The tracked personnel carrier could not be used in Tarin Kowt because it would significantly degrade the newly paved roads. And their use on PRT missions into surrounding villages didn't send the right message to local villagers; there were too many unfortunate echoes of the Soviet occupation if they used them in the province. The second type of armored personnel carrier, the Patria, was a large, six-wheeled vehicle. While it, too, presented problems with respect to its impact on the local population, it was also too large and cumbersome to handle in large swaths of Uruzgan's terrain. One Patria was lost in May when it couldn't navigate itself out of a ravine and had to be destroyed. Dutch commanders were quite aware of the limitations of their vehicles and had ordered twenty-five Nyalas, APCs with four wheels that stood several feet off the ground. Unfortunately, they were not yet in country, although news reports said the Dutch were going to borrow ten from the Canadians. While the Nyalas were much more appropriate for Uruzgan's operating environment, their absence was going to create a significant hindrance to Dutch PRT operations.

The Dutch team was led by Lt. Col. Nico Tak, who came from the armor community of the Dutch military, and his staff had worked for him for over two years. He was going to lead three four-man civil affairs teams, one of which would be based at FOB Tycz in the district of Deh Rawud, and a robust staff element with a political adviser, development adviser, and a tribal/cultural adviser. Unlike the U.S. PRT, the Dutch PRT was not going to have its own organic force protection element and planned to borrow men from the Dutch Battle Group at FOB Ripley. Because the battle group only had three platoons, which were mostly preoccupied with protecting their perimeter and constructing their own physical infrastructure, I felt that Dutch PRT operations were likely going to decline. They had no direct control of force protection assets and their use could be vetoed by the lieutenant colonel who controlled them. In addition, the Dutch task force commander had to approve the request for force protection for a Dutch PRT mission. Instead of the unity of command exercised at the U.S. PRT, there were now two other commanders, complicating Dutch PRT operations significantly and tying up numerous resources in coordination, evaluation of the security threat, and whether a PRT mission merited force protection at all. Another difference from the U.S.-led PRT was that most of the personnel in the Dutch PRT were going to rotate out at six- and four-month intervals, which stood in marked contrast to the usual yearlong deployments of U.S. personnel. The faster rotations would be tolerable if, for example, the personnel leaving were mechanics, but the fact that the PRT's core leadership would rotate out with such frequency was going to limit the overall effectiveness of the PRT as corporate knowledge regulary disappeared and relationships with local Afghans suffered.

Even though the challenges of establishing the Dutch presence in Uruzgan were not impossible, inadequate facilities and inappropriate vehicles did not make for a good beginning to the deployment. For all the criticism some of the Dutch leveled at us for being too kinetic, their mix of light, unarmored vehicles and extremely heavy armored personnel carriers gave conflicting signals to the population. If the goal was to communicate a less harsh approach by having lighter vehicles, then the heavier vehicles sent a completely different message; it was not one of strength but, as one colleague put it, of a fearful partner that was overly militarized. The Dutch had enough presence to claim participation in the war, but not enough to win the province. Years of demilitarization and lack of combat experience had made Dutch society less tolerant of casualties than the United States. In addition, they seemed to only want to operate in three of Uruzgan's now six districts. While technically they had responsiblity for the whole province, in effect, they had cut themselves off from half of it, and the areas they were going to operate in were historically considered among the safest in the area. Moreover, the Taliban were not ignorant of the differences between the United States and the Dutch and would aggressively confront them. Governor Monib was privately worried about the Dutch taking over and implored us to stay; but decisions and politics above our level governed our lives.

Although Lt. Colonel Tak and his staff were very kind to me personally, I had heard enough horror stories from my colleagues at other coalition PRTs to make sure they had to work with me and my replacement. Some of my colleagues were barely tolerated at other coalition PRTs; they were often excluded from meetings and trips outside the wire either from a conscious decision on the part of the coalition commander or from simply having been forgotten. When my replacement, Linda Specht, arrived, I made sure to give her the benefit of Frank Light's diligent work and my efforts to expand his personality profile so that she could have a deeper knowledge of the area than the Dutch. I eventually gave them a good portion of my files, but most I retained for Linda, hoping she could learn as much as she could to make sure the Dutch allowed her to participate.

The caustic command climate of the most recent U.S. PRT now gave way to the easygoing ways of the Dutch; it was a welcome reprieve. Nico was in my office using Kerry's old desk, and he and one of his staff used both of our Internet connections to do their work. The change-of-command ceremony was coming up, and Lt. Colonel Tak was having trouble finding a mullah to officiate the ceremony. I suggested the Afghan army's mullah and he welcomed the recommendation. He was also looking for a good interpreter, so I recommended Mohib to him who turned out to be a great choice.

The change of command was very impressive for Tarin Kowt. We went up to FOB Ripley and I sat next to the Dutch ambassador in the reviewing stand as the senior American in the province. A large crane used to move shipping containers had an Afghan, Dutch, and NATO flag hanging from it, but no American flag; things were already starting to change. I asked the Dutch ambassador about this oversight and he looked aghast at the obvious protocol error, but I indicated it was all right since the ceremony was about to begin; however, I had made my point. The PRT's soldiers, the Afghan army, and the Dutch were neatly organized in rows in front of the flags, and a small podium was facing them with the flags arrayed behind it. The Afghan army mullah opened with a prayer, then Governor Monib gave a speech, with Mohib translating. He spoke of the good work the United States had done in Uruzgan and that the residents of the province welcomed the Dutch presence and looked forward to working with them to improve the lives of the people. Various Dutch officers also gave speeches and we were done. The American presence was over; four years and a few months and we were now starting to become part of history. Although the Green Berets would continue to operate in the province—after all, they had been there since 2001— providing a clear sign of our continued dedication to fight the Taliban, the dynamics of the area had changed. The Special Forces were not viewed by the Dutch as their brothers but as "the Americans," and all sorts of friction started to bubble up in the ensuing months. While Dutch Special Operations Forces and the Green Berets got along just fine, the conventional Dutch military and its diplomatic corps were always complaining about the SF's "cowboy" ways—as if that's an insult to an American.

14   INTERREGNUM
   (2006–2008)

You must know something about strategy and tactics and logistics, but also economics and politics and diplomacy and history. You must know everything you can about military power, and you must also understand the limits of military power. You must understand that few of the problems of our time have been solved by military power alone.

   —President John F. Kennedy, at the U.S. Naval Academy Commencement, Annapolis, Maryland (June 7, 1961)

T wo months after I returned from Afghanistan in August 2006, I mobilized with the U.S. Navy for service in Iraq. As I went through the six months of training and the six-month deployment, I tried to keep abreast of how the province was doing. As the days and weeks rushed by and became months and years, I naturally started to focus on other endeavors and my personal life, but Uruzgan still showed up in the news. Reading diplomatic cables and other reporting, I tried to keep up with events and politics in the province as new names started to pop up that I didn't recognize. Governor Monib's great beginning had eventually turned into disappointment as he increasingly stayed in Kabul lobbying for a job in the central government because the intrigues of Jan Mohammed Khan and the now-unrelenting violence made governing too difficult. With his education and experience, he had too many opportunities for work in Kabul and the political intrigues of the province had proven too much. In 2007 Monib was replaced by another Uruzgan outsider named Asadullah Hamdam. At this point, the violence had gotten so bad that my interpreter Mohib moved his family to Kandahar City, following Jan Mohammed Khan who had done the same earlier.

While Farooq was doing well after his sacking from the PRT, continuing to tend his farm and enjoy his family of three wives and multiple children, his brother Sultan had not. The Taliban visited him late one night and beat him to death within sight of the school we had built for his village and his home where I had eaten my first Afghan meal. Dr. Rasool, who was head of our only nongovernmental organization in the province that provided local health care to the villages, was also killed when he traveled through Bamiyan Province. His vehicle had been ambushed and he and another doctor had been killed instantly. Throughout the province, suicide-vest and car bomb attacks increased precipitously, as did the number of fighters. In 2007 the Green Berets fought back a determined assault by 250 Taliban fighters against Forward Operating Base Anaconda in eastern Uruzgan. That same year, the Dutch also had to fight an intense campaign against the Taliban in Chora when hundreds of fighters tried to retake the district capital they had overrun in early 2006. From June 15 to 19, the Dutch struggled against the Taliban in what they eventually called the Battle of Chora, even lobbing artillery rounds from Tarin Kowt several miles into Chora proper to weaken the insurgents. The Dutch finally won the fight with the assistance of Rozi Khan, who had brought his militia fighters to their rescue. In May 2008 Rozi Khan was elected district chief of Chora District in an election engineered by Governor Hamdam to exclude Jan Mohammed Khan's meddling. It was a very successful election and seven candidates ran representing five of the main tribes in the province. About 2,000 locals participated in the voting, and Rozi Khan received 30 percent of the vote. In September 2008, however, just four months after his election, disaster struck. In response to pleas from his friend that the Taliban had surrounded his home, Rozi Khan rushed to his friend's home at night with his militia. In a flash, Rozi Khan was gunned down by Australian Special Forces who had mistaken him for a member of the Taliban. Rozi Khan's killing greatly destabilized the Barakzai Tribe, and out of respect for him, his young son, Daoud Khan, was put in charge of the tribe and the district of Chora with Rozi's brothers serving as his advisers.

Mohib and I had kept in touch over the next few years and in 2008 he sent me a desperate e-mail:

HI How Are You Daer Sir And How Is Your Family Say My Hay To Your All Family No Sir I Do not Visit To Pakistan I am Here In Afghanistan One Another Bad News The Taliban Are Cam To My Uncle House In The Mideal Of Night They Heard Mohib Is living Here At Night Whin They Are Cam To The House So That Night I Was Not There So They Are Shout My Sister Enla And One Is My Qauson They Bouth Are Dadth Now Here In The T K Suchwation is Whery Bad And There Is No Scurety What Do You Think Abut Me Can I Go To The Forur Ccuntryes In The Canada I Have Realetivs They Are Caling Me To Com Here In Canada So Give Me Your Sjustion Thank You My Best Frent

While I was able to clarify that his sister had not been harmed by the Taliban, the same could not be said of her fiancé and now she no longer needed the wedding dress Mohib had given her. It turned out this was one of the same dresses I had originally purchased for Mohib's wife in 2005. With her fiancé dead, she and her family also moved to Kandahar City.

The Dutch were doing a wonderful job promoting development in the province, while doing their best to fight determined Taliban resistance. They had constructed a number of schools, clinics, radio stations, and bridges in the province while expanding the number of patrol bases in the area to secure the Tarin Kowt District as well as Chora. However, the war they encountered when they arrived in 2006 was not the war they had seen in 2005 when they were making their plans. The relatively safe province of 2005 had been replaced in 2006–2010 with a battlefield of unrelenting combat. Moreover, the gap between what the Dutch government had presented to their people in 2005 and the reality of the deployment restricted the government's ability to speak honestly about the nature of the fight and reduced their opportunities to do it right (see Appendix B for my postdeployment report to the Dutch government).

Mullah Hamdullah was no longer on the Provincial Council, having resigned in 2008. Word on the street was that he had violently slapped a young man in a mosque who had been bad-mouthing him. In return for not sending him to jail, then-governor Hamdam forced him to resign, using the incident to get rid of a political opponent. The bad blood generated by Mullah Hamdullah's boast in early 2006 that he had been behind Jan Mohammed Khan's replacement as governor had also not gone away. The former governor publicly called for Hamdullah's arrest. Politics had broken the friendship they had forged during the mujahedeen. Hamdullah's resignation was a serious blow to the Provincial Council since he had a great deal of experience running the Provincial Shura and working with the coalition. However, the reality of the Provincial Council is that, while it had started to meet after I had departed, it quickly stopped because of surging violence and a lack of coalition support. It simply melted away, never becoming the viable institution we had hoped it would become, although with Jan Mohammed Khan's departure the urgent need for its checks and balances had diminished.

Support for the Taliban in Uruzgan Province came from a variety of sources. Some of it was the result of tribal grievances (the Gilzai against the Durrani), frustrated hopes for a better life, sympathy for their cause, and rank opportunism. At the outset, our (and Karzai's) strategy of relying on warlords to create security and hunt down Taliban and Al Qaeda fighters created a stultifying environment where, in the interests of security, justice was set aside. In addition, because of our surface-level understanding of Afghan history, tribal dynamics, and our own local partners, our support for these warlords blinded us to the transgressions they committed against their own population. As determined as we might have been to thwart some of the worst incidents, our lack of resources prevented us from truly knowing what was going on in the province. As our mission expanded to include reconstruction, development, and good governance, the potential for corruption increased, and our mandate to support the Afghan government translated into deferring to the governor's wishes; however, we were limited in what we could do because of Karzai's strong support for Jan Mohammed Khan. The practical effect of this policy was to deny certain tribes, villages, and key personalities access to development and reconstruction efforts.

Because the goal was to get "money on the street" and get projects moving, we often focused on "big ticket" items such as a women's hospital, provincial government building, district center, and schools that were capital-intensive. These initiatives often took a long time to finish and rarely affected the population in a direct way. If a more robust series of projects had been started in each village and district, these longer-term undertakings might have been all right. Even though the Twenty-fifth Infantry, Special Forces, and the PRT were conducting civil affairs missions from four different FOBs, the collective effect of these projects was not enough to meet the expectations of the people for quick and dramatic improvement in their lives. Furthermore, while much of the development was appropriately focused on building the physical infrastructure of the government and the province, a fully articulated and resourced plan for building human capital was never really adopted. Even if such a plan had been formulated, we simply did not have the staff or resources to implement it. Absent nongovernmental organizations and a capable central government, one State representative and USAID adviser were not enough for the whole province. When the Twenty-fifth Infantry redeployed to Hawaii and Iraq in the late spring of 2005, the only Western troops in the province were the PRT, Special Forces teams at each FOB, and an engineering group working on the Tarin Kowt–Kandahar Road. The active patrolling presence of the Twenty-fifth Infantry had created a security bubble for our development and reconstruction activities. When that disappeared and it became publicly known that the Netherlands was going to assume control of the province, the Taliban were ready to implement a significant offensive to retake the area. When the Taliban arrived in force in 2006, they found a supportive population ground down from the corruption and injustice of Jan Mohammed Khan's rule, disenchanted because of a lack of demonstrable evidence of an improved standard of living, and unprotected from Taliban intimidation from a lack of coalition and Afghan troops in the villages.

15   AFGHANISTAN
(2009–2011)

*The purpose in deploying static units is to establish a grid of troops so that
the population and the counterinsurgent political teams are reasonably
well protected, and so that the troops can participate in civic action at the
lowest level.*

    —David Galula, *Counterinsurgency Warfare: Theory and Practice*[1]

*I believe that government starts at the bottom and moves upward, for
government exists for the welfare of the masses of the nation.*

    —Philippine president Ramon Magsaysay

I arrived at Bagram Air Field on December 28, 2009. As I descended the
steps of the C-17, the familiar smell of jet fuel, dust, rubber, and concrete
filled my nostrils, odors I hadn't smelled in a long time, a unique mixture
that seemed only to exist in war zones. It was my first trip back in three and
a half years, and this time I was in the uniform of a serving military officer.
Even though I had served a year in Afghanistan with the State Department,
I never referred to myself as an Afghanistan veteran. For me, this phrase was
reserved for those who had served in uniform, and as I mobilized from the
reserves to active duty for service in Afghanistan, I welcomed the transition
from my civilian life to the military, joining the ranks of my brothers in camouflage. The drive to Kabul was familiar to me, and seeing smoke lazily float

out of the family-run brick kilns along the road was oddly comforting. Instead of traveling in the commuter van the embassy had used in 2005, I was now traveling in a huge MRAP truck (mine-resistant ambush-protected) and was carrying a side arm. The MRAP was increasingly being used because of the horrendously high casualty rate from IEDs that was magnified by use of the less-well-protected Humvee. The perimeter of Bagram Air Field had been considerably built up since I had left and as we departed, the driver navigating the uneven road through the Shomali Plain, I was extremely excited about having an opportunity to put some of my ideas and experiences to good use. I was joining a number of my friends who had previously served in Afghanistan and were now back, excited by the energy of Gen. Stanley McCrystal.

For many of us who had worked in Afghanistan, where its causes and concerns had become an integral part of our lives, this was the moment for us to have the decisive impact we had all wanted during our previous tours. Insufficient resources, limited thinking about the war, poor leadership, and the simple fact that it was the nation's second priority to the Iraq War had hobbled our earlier efforts. I eventually arrived at the north side of the Kabul Airport at the newly established ISAF Joint Command (IJC) and settled in. The IJC had gone operational in October and was busily getting itself established while attempting to actively manage the five regional commands into which Afghanistan had long been divided. The command had been created to free up General McCrystal to focus on strategic issues, or "up and out," as some put it, and for Lt. Gen. David Rodriguez, the IJC commander, to focus on operational and tactical issues, or "down and in." Because it had direct reponsibility to conduct the war and because of Lt. General Rodriguez's extensive experience in Afghanistan, I felt this was the right command for me. His perspective on the war was gleaned from firsthand knowledge, which meant his decisions would be based on wisdom about the country and our operations there rather than the newest intellectual fad coming out of Washington, D.C., or arbitrary political timelines.

Much had changed since I had been away, and I had to quickly update the acronyms and organizational charts in my head. Instead of NATO being a sleepy command in northern Afghanistan and around Kabul as it was in 2005, it was now in complete control of the campaign. A blizzard of different khaki and camouflage styles buzzed around IJC as our multinational partners went about their business at the international headquarters. In addition to our long-standing partners and allies of Great Britain, Australia, Canada, and the Netherlands were countries such as Latvia, Mongolia, Belgium, Estonia, Macedonia, and Luxembourg, to name a few. These countries were supplemented by many of our other allies: Italy, Spain, Germany, Sweden, Norway, and France. Plunging back into the world of military acronyms, with their oddly comforting certainty, I noticed that some had changed and many were new. The old acronym for Kabul International Airport, KIA, had been changed to KAIA out of concern that "KIA" be mistaken for "Killed In Action"; it was now the more innocuous-sounding Kabul Area International Airport. The acronym for the Government of Afghanistan had changed as well going from GOA to GIRoA, which stood for Government of the Islamic Republic of Afghanistan. While we'd never before had an abbreviation to describe our meetings with Afghan officials, this had become KLE, or key leader engagement. Whenever an organization assigns an abbreviation to some action, it clearly signals the routinized importance of the event. In the counterinsurgency we were waging, having the term KLE served to reinforce the need to always work by, with, and through the Afghan government. Others changes were not so anodyne.

Civilian casualties had clearly gone up in the intervening years. With the increase in Taliban and their strategic choice to fight the government and U.S. forces in the villages and to use suicide attacks, incidences of civilians getting killed had surged across the country. To represent these growing and frequent phenomena, the military assigned it an acronym, CIVCAS, or "civilian casualties." It was sad to see such a term come into existence.

Sometimes we made up our own definitions of acronyms. When U.S. soldiers were with their buddies, for example, they would sometimes swap other definitions for ISAF (International Security Assistance Force). Many said it stood for "I suck at fighting" or "I saw Americans fight" or "I sun at the FOB."

The gap between the reality of NATO "fighting" in Afghanistan and how it was presented to the public at large was so huge, it was embarrassing. In many ways, NATO was double the bureaucracy and half the commitment of U.S. troops. While exceptions existed to this perception, as a rule it tended to be generally accurate. During one firefight, for example, a German Joint Tactical Air Controller was involved in an ambush and called for German air cover. Because the German planes couldn't help due to national caveats, which are restrictions on what they can do in Afghanistan, a U.S. plane five hundred miles away was called in to help out the soldier. These limits have life-and-death consequences, but politicians in national capitals wouldn't know it.

Led by Lt. General Rodriguez, ISAF Joint Command was, as one colonel on his staff put it, "the big monster forcing mechanism" for the war. The IJC took General McCrystal's directives and guidance and translated them into action. Accordingly, Rodriguez had collected several handpicked officers and noncommissioned soldiers to help him change the direction of the war. As part of that effort, I was assigned to a section of IJC called Future Operations where many of these officers worked. We had former PRT commanders, civil affairs team leaders, commanders of infantry units, psychological operations officers, and trainers of the Afghan army and police, among others, all in one room as part of a cross-functional team (CFT). The thinking behind the CFT was that all too often bureaucratic processes or stove pipes inhibit creative thinking and a holistic approach to solving problems. Instead of having stovepipes of excellence, we sought to break down communications barriers and work as a team. It was a simple concept but revolutionary for the military and the civilian agencies. Lt. General Rodriguez's focus was clear and informed by his experiences in Afghanistan, experiences that many of us had also acquired from previous tours.

One of the enduring challenges of the war was the synchronized delivery of sustained population protection with robust good governance, development, and reconstruction efforts. All too often, our security forces focused on either short-term clearing operations or intelligence-driven raids for specific targets, or stressed the number of insurgents killed versus adopting a population security posture. In addition, good governance, development, and reconstruction efforts too frequently emphasized short-term programs, were insufficiently resourced, or were uncoordinated with military efforts. Another element to this challenge was the sometimes painful adjustment of bureaucratic structures, geared toward solving the problems of another era, to the unique demands of counterinsurgency warfare today. As great as these obstacles were to overcome in order to adopt a comprehensive approach to these insurgencies, the extra challenge of inadequate partnering with the Afghan government exacerbated them. In many respects, this was simply an outgrowth of having no government to partner with or one that was incapable of having an enduring presence at the local level.

The IJC was attempting to increase local security to the point where, once we had cleared an area of the Taliban, enduring security forces could remain there to prevent their return. This persistent security presence also allowed our interagency partners at the Department of State, USAID, as well as GIRoA to expand legitimate, capable, and effective government to the people. It was a tall order, but all of us were confident it could be done provided we were given enough time. The general always stressed that "there ha[d] to be a sequence," "you have stability waiting to go," and that everything had to be "integrate[d] and sync[ed] [along] all the lines of operations." This meant, as one colonel put it, "synchronization in depth," and that "shape and build happens all the time." We had to be "a doing organization [and] not a hand-wringing organization," as that same colonel put it. But saying this was the plan and getting others to do it, many of whom were part of State, USAID, and the Afghan government, proved extremely difficult. Although these groups were insufficiently organized to achieve it individually, the role they played in this comprehensive plan was central to our success in Afghanistan. None of their efforts would be possible, however, if not for an increase in U.S. and NATO troops.

Following the success of the surge in Iraq, coupled with the Anbar Awakening movement there, security conditions in Iraq began to improve to such an extent that additional military resources started to become available for service in Afghanistan. Reflecting this newfound success, the Bush administration initiated the beginning of a sizable increase of U.S. forces to Afghanistan, culminating in the early-2009 deployment of 17,000 additional troops by President Obama. These troop numbers were increased even further by roughly 30,000 in late 2009, although they wouldn't show up until late 2010, following the Obama administration's Afghanistan policy review and ISAF commander General McCrystal's strategic assessment. The added U.S. contributions were supplemented further by another increase of 10,000 troops from contributing NATO countries. These substantial increases in combat power were matched by a concomitant pledge to increase the size of the Afghan National Army and Afghan National Police (from 134,000 ANA in 2010 to 171,000 in 2011, and from 94,000 ANP in 2010 to 134,000 in 2011). Accompanying this pledge was a dedicated effort to expand these forces for the long term to allow Afghanistan to secure itself. While these new resources were the beginning of a solution to Afghanistan's security problems, it was General McCrystal's strong emphasis on positioning all military resources in a population-protection posture that allowed the extra forces the opportunity to confront the insurgency in a newfound way.

The challenge, however, was that even though the additional 30,000 troops authorized by President Obama significantly helped the military adopt a population-protection posture, they were not enough to do the job effectively and comprehensively. Because of limited resources, ISAF had to focus its efforts on eighty-one "key terrain districts" (KTD), rather than work throughout all the areas affected by the insurgency, which violated a central tenet of counterinsurgency warfare. These KTDs had been selected not only because a large part of the Afghan population there was being threatened by the insurgency, but also because they were key economic and logistics locations. Examples were areas along the Ring Road or those near an entry point to the country. Unfortunately, none of the KTDs were in Uruzgan Province. The plan was to focus on forty-six of these districts in 2010, twenty the following year, and then fifteen in 2012. The secret hope of the U.S. military in Afghanistan was that by demonstrating the extremely positive effects that could be achieved in the war, President Obama would be prompted to relax his July 2011 withdrawal timeline. Many of them recalled his opposition to the surge in Iraq and his willingness to curtail U.S. military involvement there, even if this meant defeat. They were hoping that decisive effects on the battlefield could buy them political time in Washington to continue those actions that were required for long-term success. It was already becoming difficult to communicate an unbreakable link between the United States and the Afghan people while simultaneously establishing a withdrawal date, regardless of conditions on the ground. In the interim, we focused on our task at hand and tried to do our best. This was now President Obama's war, although many of us regarded it as America's war, and already the soldiers were unsure of his commitment to victory.

While Coalition Forces were struggling to adapt to the unique challenges of counterinsurgency warfare in Afghanistan, our civilian interagency partners were experiencing a no-less-dramatic adjustment with far fewer resources. Reflecting the need for greater coordination between civilian and military operations, U.S. Ambassador Eikenberry and ISAF Commander

McCrystal signed the United States Government Integrated Civilian-Military Campaign Plan for Support to Afghanistan on August 10, 2009. Reflecting this campaign plan and a renewed focus on conducting operations in the field, the U.S. Embassy in Kabul made several changes to its organizational structure to make itself more central to conducting counterinsurgency operations. To improve the ability of its interagency field staff to contact both the embassy and the central government, the U.S. Embassy created the office of Interagency Provincial Affairs (IPA) in July 2009. The IPA office was not only focused on supporting the field and its operations, but it also participated directly in embassy decision-making bodies with ISAF and U.S. Forces–Afghanistan (USFOR-A) representatives, and liaised directly with GIRoA through its ministerial advisers and political section. When I was in Afghanistan in 2005 and 2006, we had a four-man PRT shop to support our work, and now we had eighteen to do it. Assisting overall coordination of civil-military efforts at the embassy, a series of working groups, such as the governance and subnational governance working groups, were created with military and civilian representatives to shape governance and development policy decisions, to evaluate competing proposals, and to decide on courses of action.

In order to complement U.S. Embassy efforts to take ministerial programs to the Afghan countryside, the IJC created a ministerial outreach program to the key ministries focused on providing services and positive government to the Afghan population, such as the Independent Directorate of Local Governance (IDLG), the Ministry of Finance, the Ministry of Rural Rehabilitation and Development, and the Civil Service Commission, among other bodies. This group was partnered with USAID and DOS advisers to bolster the central ministries of Afghanistan, as well as to assist them in rolling out their programs and services to local communities. Helping tie the central ministries to the field and improve civil-military cooperation at the operational level, the State Department created senior civilian representative positions at each of the regional commands and at each PRT. These positions both coordinated and led all non-DOD U.S. government civilians in their respective areas of responsibility, and they also acted as a single point of contact for military leaders to assist in the general unity of effort. (Often referred to as "little Caesars," the representatives seemed to have adopted most of the rigidity of the chain of command with few of its benefits, such as greater information sharing and superior coordination.) Ambassador Eikenberry and Lt. General Rodriguez further agreed to have liaisons between their respective organizations to both improve civil-military cooperation in Kabul and support greater participation in each of the overall planning efforts of their respective organizations. This was my job as IJC's liaison officer to the U.S. Embassy.

As security forces increased in Afghanistan, another complementary effort was undertaken to increase reconstruction and development assistance by U.S. government civilian agencies. Besides an absolute increase in development assistance to Afghanistan, State and USAID also initiated a civilian uplift and sought to adapt some of their organizational structures to the unique needs of the conflict in the countryside. Toward this end, they brought in additional staff at the embassy, including three new ambassadors, to increase the embassy's organizational muscle and support a more robust effort in the field. Moreover, they increased the number of personnel in the provinces to around four hundred and placed them at PRTs, military task forces, and in the districts.[2]

Reflecting the localized aspect of the insurgency, the State Department also created a specialized team focused on governance and reconstruction at the district level, called district support teams, which have three-man elements comprising representatives from the DOS, USAID, and the U.S. Department of Agriculture. These teams were embedded with military units and provided tactical expertise, resources, and mentoring to district GIRoA officials as well as other enablers to colocated military units.

The sum of all these efforts was that our civilian interagency partners were not only better positioned to assist military operations in good governance and reconstruction, but were now able to assume a leading position in these initiatives over a greater area of the country in an enduring manner.

The main reasons behind the military successes of the Taliban have been a lack of security forces in the Afghan countryside and a nuanced political program to secure the loyalty of the people to their government. Author Bernard Fall, in his book *Street Without Joy*, stated that the armed element of the insurgency was simply "a tactical appendage of a far vaster political contest and that, no matter how expertly it is fought by competent and dedicated professionals, it cannot possibly make up for the absence of a political rationale."[3] The goal of GIRoA and the coalition was to create this counter-political rationale for the people. Community support for the Taliban, therefore, was not only from coercion by the movement, but also from the lack of a viable, positive, and enduring government program that secured the loyalty of the people to their government. Because the Afghan government was so undeveloped in Kabul and many coalition efforts were focused on building central government capacity from the start of the war, local government capabilities were largely nonexistent, embryonic, or imperfectly mentored. The Taliban took advantage of these various weaknesses and stepped into the governance vacuum with their own political program. In addition, the adoption of a warlord strategy in many parts of the country alienated the population since the warlords were often corrupt and exhibited abusive behavior. As this behavior was not acted upon by GIRoA or the coalition in a sustained manner, some portions of the population either sided with the Taliban or tolerated their presence.

Beginning in 2007, GIRoA created a directorate focused exclusively on empowering subnational governance to address these abuses and to build local government capacity. The Independent Directorate of Local Governance, which answered directly to President Karzai's office; originally evaluated provincial and district officials; removed those who were corrupt, abusive, or incompetent; and nominated replacement candidates. It also focused on providing incentives for good behavior through performance funds and training programs. As part of the general effort to expand and improve GIRoA's presence in the countryside, President Karzai signed a directive in February 2010 giving the IDLG the authority to coordinate the central government's ministries to provide sustained services through a fully manned district government. To support this effort, international donors provided additional funding and also redirected their social service programs to support GIRoA's endeavors. The mechanism through which this was to occur was the District Delivery Program (DDP). The DDP consisted of three funding streams that supported the salaries of new and current civil servants as well as the operating costs of their directorates. It also funded the coordinated delivery of services through the alignment of existing coalition programs in such things as health and education to empower Afghan civil servants with initiatives focused on the population's needs. The third stream was a mixture of GIRoA and coalition funding, principally through the Commander's Emergency Relief Program, to build the physical structures that housed government officials and facilitated their work. All of these efforts at the local level were led and coordinated by an Afghan district chief in partnership with a local representative assembly such as a jirga or shura. GIRoA sought to create a positive alternative to the Taliban's shadow government and prevent their armed wing from returning to intimidate or control the population through these combined efforts of enduring local security, delivery and sustainment of Afghan-led government programs, and good governance focused on community participation. Further, by establishing the government's sovereignty in the countryside, thus winning the struggle with the insurgents over the political right to lead the population, Afghans saw that their future was with the government and not with whatever the insurgents could offer.[4] The end goal of these efforts was to create a legitimate, capable, and effective government that the people of Afghanistan would support, one that would deny the insurgents allegiance to a shadow government while simultaneously freezing out the armed insurgency's ability to intimidate the population.

We were also undertaking a huge effort to collect the kind of information my predecessor at the PRT, Frank Light, had collected and that I had expanded. A perennial challenge of operating in Afghanistan has been not only understanding the human terrain, but also having the wisdom to appreciate the sources of conflict the Taliban exploits to separate the people from their government. All too often, military intelligence efforts were focused on finding the enemy to kill or capture, on identifying threats to coalition troops, or on recruiting human sources for intelligence. Information gathered on leading indigenous personalities, tribal structures, and settlement patterns, as well as reconstruction and development projects, was either not captured or, if it was, was retained at a local level and lost once a unit rotated out of theater. An unfortunate example of this was when the Dutch took over the Uruzgan computer share drive with all of our information on Uruzgan and traveled with the PRT to Nuristan Province, where it did no one any good. While subsequent military training had adapted to this challenge, emphasizing the need to understand the local population, and some programs such as the Human Terrain System had provided tactical enablers to military units to study the population, the general effort of collecting nonintelligence information was undeveloped.

To begin the process of centralizing human terrain information and operationalizing it so that it was useful to military units as well as civilian agencies, General McCrystal initiated the Rich Contextual Understanding project in

Hazara school girls look on as Lt. Gen. Karl Eikenberry is welcomed to Dai Kundi Province in 2005.

ABOVE: Provincial Reconstruction Team Commander Lt. Col. Robin Fontes speaks to the Uruzgan Director of Women's Affairs.

LEFT: A Hazara conducts a karate demonstration in Dai Kundi Province in 2005.

Afghan voter prepares to cast ballot for the Provincial Council and the Wolesi Jirga in 2005.

Outgoing and incoming civil affairs teams in front of the Uruzgan Province Court House in 2005. COURTESY OF CIVIL AFFAIRS TEAM

(L-R, back row) Lt. Col. John Dayton, SFC David Henry, Staff Sgt. Travis Blundell, Capt. Doug Dillon, and Staff Sgt. Clint Newman

(L-R, front row) Maj. Gustav Waterhouse, SFC Maria Rivera, Lt. Col. Douglas Goodfellow, SFC Clifford Lo, and PFC Erik Robinson

Not pictured: Sgt. Jermaine Dillard, Master Sgt. Will Williams, PFC Jacob Sotak, PFC Robert Whitmire, and SPC Jesus Garcia

Remains of first car bomb in Uruzgan's history in 2006. COURTESY OF RICHARD REITER

LEFT: Night letter left by the Taliban for Mullah Hamdullah in Uruzgan Province in 2006. The text says: Islamic Emirate of Afghanistan, Ministry of Defense, Army Reserves. Hamdullah Pap, who is known as (Mawlawi), is being informed to repent for being a puppet of the infidels, if he does not, he will be faced with the consequences, by the "Soldiers of God Almighty." Allah Akbar

BELOW: Uruzgan Provincial Council getting sworn in by United Nations elections officials in 2005.

(L-R) Mullah Hamdullah (partially obscured), Haji Khairo Jan, Mohammed Hanif Khan, Haji Nazar Mohammed, Noor Mohammed, and Haji Gul

LEFT: Concealed antitank mine in road to Chora District in 2006.

BELOW: Captured Taliban fighter being lectured by an Afghan National Army soldier in Chora District in 2006.

ABOVE: Humanitarian
supply drop for the village
of Chenartu in 2006.

RIGHT: Front gate of
Chenartu militia leader
Akhtar Mohammed in 2006.

LEFT: Uruzgan Province governor Abdul Hakim Monib leans on author's AK-47 in 2006.

BELOW: U.S. convoy traveling through the Delanor Pass from Kandahar to Uruzgan Province in 2006.
COURTESY OF MIKE WALTZ

Populzai tribesman carrying a rocket-propelled grenade launcher in Chenartu in 2006.

First four U.S. Department of State political officers who worked at the Tarin Kowt Provincial Reconstruction Team covering the period of 2004–2006.

(L-R) Raphael Carland, Frank Light, Richard Reiter, author

Author with United States Department of Agriculture adviser Jeff Sanders at the U.S. Embassy in Kabul in 2010.

USAID development adviser Kerry Greene resting during a mission to the district of Chora in 2005.

Washington, D.C. This project utilized subject matter experts on Afghanistan and Pakistan to not only provide advice on the region, but produce research products on specific subjects for the military enriched by academic, archival, and field research. These efforts were supplemented by the military's adoption of a USAID program called the Tactical Conflict Assessment Planning Framework, or TCAPF. This tool had a series of questions and training programs military units could use to help them understand why communities were siding with the insurgency and to identify local sources of conflict within those villages that insurgents used against the government. It also assisted military units in finding traditional leaders and representative organizations to work with, such as shuras and jirgas. To collect and analyze this information, in November 2009 the newly formed IJC, led by Lt. General Rodriguez, created the Information Dominance Center (IDC).[5] The mandate of the IDC was to centralize as much information as possible on the human terrain and to undertake the kinds of assessments needed to support stability operations. In addition, the IDC endeavored to make this information available to relevant civilian agencies to facilitate information sharing and to create a common operating picture. Beginning in February 2010, under the leadership of Maj. Gen. Michael T. Flynn, chief intelligence officer for ISAF, the military began to create stability operations information centers at the regional commands to facilitate and encourage collection of this kind of information in support of the IDC. It was great to have these efforts but I wished we had had them at least five if not nine years previously.

As innovative as many of these efforts may appear to be, they were already in the mainstream of military thinking of how to gather the kinds of information needed to confront the insurgency. The major innovation, however, was the partnership developed between the military, specifically the IJC, and its civilian counterparts, such as the U.S. Embassy, on understanding the human terrain. The U.S. Embassy, through its office of Interagency Provincial Affairs, sent two detailed surveys out to its field staff to assess the status and requirements of local government, the leadership abilities and corruption of officials, and the freedom of movement for GIRoA officials to conduct their work. They also polled their members on the presence of district-level programs administered by GIRoA, the United States and other governments, and nongovernmental organizations to establish a common understanding of enabling capabilities to influence and sustain district government. All these data were included in the assessments of districts and provinces by the IDC as they undertook a regular review of the areas to measure progress. In many respects, these evaluations created a forcing mechanism for the military and civilian agencies to work together on understanding and evaluating how stability operations were going as General McCrystal's strategy was being implemented. Moreover, the embassy's efforts to gather this information from the field helped them focus on improving their own management structures in order to create a more viable organizational counterpart to the military and to develop as an institution tying the ministries more closely to the field. These various efforts by the military and civilian agencies to improve situational awareness resulted in decision-makers who were better empowered to evaluate progress along both kinetic (e.g. enemy dead, IEDs discovered) and nonkinetic (e.g. good governance, reconstruction, and development) lines. Toward this end, the IJC created a one-page matrix for both military and civilian agencies to use on each district, focused on capturing kinetic and nonkinetic information as part of a strategy to shape, clear, hold, and build the districts of Afghanistan. The synchronization and centralization of this information was a substantial improvement in the ability of the coalition to undertake counterinsurgency operations through a better understanding of the people and their needs.

Against this backdrop of energy and innovation, my superiors decided that I should work as a liaison officer to the IPA at the embassy. It was thought that this would be the best place to use both my State Department background and field experience. A deal was struck that I would visit the embassy five days a week and commute back and forth between IJC and IPA, which I jokingly referred to as my "combat commute," since I was now a headquarters guy and not a field guy. The embassy kindly had me picked up and dropped off each day. When I stepped on to the embassy's grounds for the first time since 2006, it was as if time had stood still. Everything was mostly the same, the buildings, the smells, and the problems. The only difference was the people. My assignment to the IPA office and my responsibilities there were somewhat murky. As a liaison officer for IJC, I needed to attend as many meetings as I could and help IJC better understand embassy thinking. The embassy, however, wanted me to act as their planner, doing the legwork they should have been doing to figure out how the civilian uplift was actually going to happen. Since relations between the main leaders in country were strained, this "talking past each other" was common now. The most unusual thing about being at the embassy this time was how I was perceived by the State Department and USAID staff. Many didn't even know my rank, navy lieutenant, and seemed to have ill-informed or stereotypical views of the military: either not too bright, too militaristic and unappreciative of other, less martial approaches, or trying to take over everything in the war. A deep-seated institutional insecurity existed at the embassy, which was often reflected in the types of people who worked there; they were always sure the military had a nefarious agenda, and they were not pleased at having their operations questioned. The embassy outpost I had originally experienced, with diplomats and others who craved improvisation, entrepreneurship, and flat organizations, had been replaced by too many typical Foreign Service Officers who seemed to only operate well in bureaucracy and hierarchy and who focused on process versus results. Instead of working as a team with the military, the staff drafted memorandums of agreement to formally establish relations between the military and civilians, similar to two foreign nations drafting treaties. There was little trust between them and even less of a feeling of teamwork; it had gotten to the point where innovation meant lack of coordination at the embassy. It was depressing.

I was hopeful IPA would be a repository of sanity at the embassy, full of people who had worked in the field and knew that the institutional State Department and the realities of the field were two different things—one was tolerated, and the other seized with urgency. Of the eighteen people who worked there, only two of the diplomats had ever worked in Afghanistan (one in the field, although he was on loan for a few months, and one at the strategic level); any others who had were a member of the military (me), a member of USAID, and a member of USDA, respectively. None of us was in a leadership position. The one upside of working there was that Jeff Sanders and I were together again after five years apart. Jeff had been the USDA representative at the Tarin Kowt PRT and he was back for a year's tour. It was great to have an ally and a friend in the office with whom I could commiserate about all the inanities of the embassy. Even with all of these challenges at the embassy, I hoped that the IPA members would be the resident experts on all things outside of Kabul, which is to say, where the war was. However, with the many new ambassadors and working groups at the embassy and the ever-present need to feed the information beast that was Washington, most of the work of the office was on processes in Kabul and D.C., not on making a decisive impact in the field. Nor was the office organized in any sensible way; there was no section to collect information on the human terrain, for instance, or a section on operations, or one on policy. It was not task-organized at all, and because of this it tended to jump from one hot topic to another as they fell on the office radar screen. For a long time they had been focused on supporting the initial civilian uplift, but this distracted them from working on operationalizing the District Delivery Program at the ministries and in the field. By the time they had focused on it, they had to play catch-up with the military, which had already started its own liaison work. Because they were poorly organized and had no decisive impact on the Afghan government regarding effects in the field, they would frequently blame the government's lethargy on the lack of Afghan capacity. While capacity was always an issue in the Afghan government, which often did not have enough literate and trained employees to undertake its crucial work, the true capacity development challenge was the U.S. Embassy. It was extremely disheartening to see so few changes at the embassy, as if they had learned nothing about the war and our operations there, while many of their leaders bristled at constructive recommendations to address problems.

My key focus was on ensuring that the civilian uplift was working and that as many of the efforts of the military and the civilian agencies were coordinated and synchronized in the field as Lt. General Rodriguez wanted. The initial civilian uplift was going to be about four hundred people from the State Department, USAID, and the U.S. Department of Agriculture. The challenge was in actually finding civilians who wanted to deploy, training them appropriately, and then assigning them to the right places so they could have a huge effect on the local population. Tied to this was the need to evaluate them effectively so that we knew they were having a positive effect. One of my duties was to brief each group of civilians as they arrived in country on what the IJC was and what the general military strategy would be for the next few years. I took this opportunity to ask them how they had been trained, whether they knew where they were going, and what problems they had had with the process of being hired. Their answers were very illuminating and supplemented my own knowledge of how the uplift was going. Far too many had no idea where they would be serving in Afghanistan and wouldn't learn until several weeks had passed. This situation often prevented them from reaching out to the person they were replacing in the field or to the military unit there to get a better sense of the challenges in the area and the nature of the work. Moreover, many of them had been hired through a temporary hiring authority the State Department had recently been given called "3161." This authority had been created to help State hire well-qualified people quickly so that they could undertake the crucial work needed in the field. The challenge was moving beyond the talking points about the program and getting to reality.

While the credentials of many of these new hires were very impressive and they had a less dogmatic approach to addressing the problems of Afghanistan than many of my FSO colleagues, the screening process for them, as well as for regular government workers going to Afghanistan, was a shambles. Large numbers of the civilians in the uplift were too fat, too frail, or too flaky to do the job effectively. One officer weighed 375 pounds and couldn't put on his body armor successfully, even with extensions. Another had had double hip replacement surgery; yet another had to purchase a walking cane because of a pronounced limp. One person had shown up at his command with hair down to his waist, wearing surfer shorts and Birkenstocks; the military command there called him Willie Nelson. Another recruit had had heart bypass surgery and, because he used blood thinners, had a bleeding wound during much of the training; these same blood thinners were prohibited by the military because they prevented blood-loss mitigation efforts if you were wounded.

Things had gotten so bad that the embassy had sent a cable out to all U.S. embassies stressing the need for people to be in shape. It was titled, "Keeping Our People Safe: Instituting Physical Assessment Drills for Service in Afghanistan." One notable passage, "We've Got to Go Now," proposed that civilians experience a simulated security incident where they would have to dash from a meeting with Afghans, don their armor, and get into the Humvee. The proposed distance from the meeting to the vehicle was seventy-five feet. However, legal considerations prevented them from establishing these standards. Another problem was that people at the embassy often mistook passing the State Department medical exam as constituting being in shape; they were related but not the same thing. The real challenge was that the State Department was unable to turn people away because of the Americans with

Disabilities Act (civilians from the Department of Defense were turned away if they didn't meet standards). The practical effect of this view was that it not only increased the likelihood of death for the civilian because of poor health and an inability to seek cover in a firefight, but it also put the lives of soldiers at risk because they would be obligated to protect these individuals. Moreover, all the DOS and USAID employees were allowed five breaks over a year of service in Afghanistan. They had to be in the country at least three hundred days in order for it to be considered a "year" in the promotion process. Most soldiers who did a year only got one two-week break home. They deeply resented the part-time nature of many of our civilian colleagues, especially when they heard of an inspector general's report that said embassy morale was low because of the long hours.

Things were not all bad, however, and we were muddling through on the civilian side as best as some thought we could. Although training had improved considerably since I had deployed to Afghanistan in 2005, it was still inadequate. I had basically received a brief packing list of things for my initial trip to Afghanistan and no other training or gear. This didn't bother me too much since I was used to rough living and operating with the U.S. military. In 2010, deploying civilians received several weeks of training, including practical exercises simulating actual situations in Afghanistan. They were given training in small arms as well as tactical driving, but the course was a closed track and the students drove a Crown Victoria, hardly comparable with conditions in Afghanistan. Civilians also received training in basic Afghan culture and about a week of language instruction. Thankfully, the State Department had also decided to provide psychological support as well, in order to address potential problems prior to the staff coming home; I had received no such support both times I had come home. The embassy also had a dedicated office focused on supporting the civilian uplift through management and life support. This was a much-needed and pleasant departure from my previous tour.

We still had many able State, USAID, and U.S. Department of Agriculture personnel in the field doing some great work, but their ability to get things done was largely an outgrowth of their personalities. Many of these men and women didn't need much direction to get their job done and enjoyed living in austere environments, focused on helping the people of Afghanistan and the U.S. military. For example, Eric Meissner, one of my close friends, had worked with USAID as a development adviser to the Special Forces command in

Afghanistan. Over the course of his sixteen-month tour, he experienced more than a dozen firefights with the Taliban and was in country for at least three different SF rotations. Very few USAID staff, State officers, or even members of the military had had that much combat experience. These unsung heroes were still not getting the support they needed from the embassy.

To help with training, I drafted a thorough review of our current efforts to prepare deployers and suggested a comprehensive six-month program to replace the five-week set of courses. To stabilize our manning challenges in finding people to come to Afghanistan, I also put together a cable on different management ideas to even out the disjointed nature of continual rotations, such as allowing people to bring their families, to complete one tour in the field and then move to Kabul to work at the embassy, and to institute an award for civilians who worked in the field and experienced combat or were injured. Once my tour had finished, I sent many of these ideas to Ambassador Holbrooke's office, hoping things would change a bit. In addition, I proposed a revised organizational chart to the IPA leadership, recommending a deepening relationship with the military whereby we would graft on several military planners, civil affairs officers, intelligence personnel, and foreign area officers to their staff to help them with their planning and the execution of the civilian uplift. It was painfully clear that the IPA office didn't have the right number of people or those with the right set of experiences to manage the civilian uplift, let alone work to make the Afghan government a reality in the villages and valleys of the country. This proposal was ignored, and several others I suggested were halfheartedly embraced but never implemented. The department wasn't serious about the civilian uplift.

In general, things were better than they had been, but it seemed as if the State Department was now ready to fight the Afghan War in 2003 and not in 2010 or in the future. If the military is often criticized for fighting future wars the way it fought the last war, the civilian interagency can be accused of doing the same. Even with all of these horror stories, I knew many of my colleagues in the field were doing just fine because that kind of work tended to attract the right sorts of people, those who got along well with others and didn't let a bureaucratic mindset limit their ambitions for the Afghans. I was incredibly mad that these same Americans, who were serving our country in the field and would be the key players in determining whether our strategy would work or not in Afghanistan, were often referred to dismissively by the

FSOs at the embassy. As a civil servant I had heard these comments before from FSOs in their less-guarded moments, but to see the exact opposite attitude at IJC, where every soldier desperately wanted to be in the field, was just too much to take at times. It was at least comforting to know that Ambassador Eikenberry always read the names of dead Americans at the Monday morning staff meetings to honor their loss. While it was good to know that a few people realized the human cost of war, it was maddening that very few seemed to have that same emotional connection to the war and with those who had to fight it, let alone a sense of duty to do their best work.

As my tour progressed, I tried to catch up on the personalities and events of Uruzgan. With the appointment of a new governor in 2007, there was hope that Governor's Monib's short-lived tenure from 2006 to 2007 would not be replicated by Governor Hamdam. Unfortunately, the new governor seemed to suffer from many of the same problems Monib had: too many offers in Kabul for better and safer living conditions, and the intrigues and politics of local powerbrokers such as Jan Mohammed Khan. On March 21, Governor Hamdam's three-year term ended when President Karzai fired him. The previous year's Provincial Council elections had also changed the local political scene. All the members who had been elected when I was there in 2005 had either quit, decided not to run again, or were defeated. The council hadn't met since 2006 because of the violence and the simple fact they had no real authority. It also didn't help that they received little support from the coalition. Violence levels were also decreasing in the province; things had improved considerably since the highs of 2006–2007. This did not mean the province was secure, just that the Taliban had made a decision to focus on other areas. The Dutch experience in Uruzgan had been very beneficial to the people of the province but they never extended their development activities beyond Tarin Kowt, Chora, and Deh Rawud. The province's other three districts were "no go" zones and the Dutch had decided not to operate there. Thus, geopolitics was once again splicing up the communities of the Pashtuns, not because of their interests but our own. I sometimes wondered if the Taliban thought we were deliberately trying to lose.

The Malalai Girls School in Tarin Kowt was still functioning and as of 2011, another school had been built for high school girls as well. Uruzgan still had only three judges out of the eighty-nine it was authorized and they were largely inactive. The number of radio stations had increased from one to five and the Afghans operated two by themselves. Although the district center in Chora that USAID had built and the Taliban had overrun in 2006 was still standing, its roof was leaking and it was becoming a money pit for the Dutch. The Tarin Kowt–Kandahar Road was finally completed and extended into downtown Tarin Kowt. The Dutch were slowly building a similar road to Chora District and had improved the road out to the western district of Deh Rawud. The number of civilians at the U.S. PRT still hovered around two to three, even though the Dutch had increased their civilian presence significantly. As I had feared, the U.S civilians were largely marginalized by the Dutch and had to rely on the Green Berets to get around the province. Other Americans at firebases in Char Chena and Khas Uruzgan Districts never saw the Dutch PRT and had to rely on their own assets, providing further proof that the NATO approach was not focused on victory. In light of a political crisis in the Netherlands, the Dutch would be leaving Uruzgan in August 2010; some of them bemoaned the fact that all of their work would soon be forgotten once they departed. I could definitely sympathize with that perspective. In the intervening years, the Dutch and the Australians had been supplemented by Slovaks, the French, and Senegalese, as well as soldiers from the U.S. Navy, Air Force, Marines, and Army. I can't imagine the difficulties they faced in trying to organize a coordinated approach.

Jan Mohammed Khan was still trying to divide and conquer the tribes, but local views had somewhat moderated on Matullah. He was increasingly seen as an "up and comer" who wanted to do good in the province and not play the zero-sum games the old guard clung to. Rozi Khan's son, Daoud Khan, was still the district chief of Chora following his father's death in 2008 and gave every sign that he was learning fast. There were rumblings in the central government to remove him, which suggested the sinister influence of Jan Mohammed Khan, yet Rozi Khan's popular election by the people of Chora implied a depth of support for him and his son that the central government needed to confront gingerly if it wanted to retain the support of the people in the area. I was pretty sure they weren't overly concerned with local sentiment. Even though Haji Malem Abdul Khaliq Khan had received the highest number of votes for the Wolesi Jirga in 2005, he was mostly unknown to the Dutch because he resided near Khas Uruzgan District and they had chosen to limit their war to the boundaries of Chora.

It was quite evident that Uruzgan Province was not a priority for the United States and, as one diplomat explained to me, "not strategic." The distant reaches of our interests stopped at Uruzgan's borders. That was the story of the province, the Soviets didn't consider it strategic and neither did the Taliban, at least in the 1990s. However, its history suggested that it provided the perfect place to launch an uprising to conquer the south. Hamid Karzai did it in 2001 and the Taliban sought to do the same in 2006 and 2007. It may not have been strategic, but it had always been part of the effort to topple the government of the south, whatever political stripe it came in. As the saying goes, if we ignore history, we are bound to repeat it. The future of Tarin Kowt and the local government was hopeful: USAID was set to launch a $50 million municipalities program throughout southern Afghanistan focusing on each of the capitals of the provinces, and the Afghan central government was opening a civil service academy in Uruzgan to train civil servants, finally focusing on the human capital needs of the area. It was unclear who would be the new governor, but I hoped it would be someone from Uruzgan who had the support of the people and the willingness to stay at the job and improve the lives of the population.

The successful killing of Osama bin Laden on May 1, 2011, was a momentous event for our country and for me. To know that the man who had launched the attacks against our nation was dead filled me with joy as well as with immense pride in the thousands of Americans who contributed to his death. While there would never be closure over the attacks of 9/11, Osama bin Laden's killing was at least one step in that direction. Much work remained to be done against Al Qaeda and the Taliban, but at least America could feel some sense of satisfaction at having killed the elusive leader who had murdered so many of our countrymen.

It is the end of an era. On July 17, 2011, former Uruzgan governor Jan Mohammed Khan was assassinated at his home in Kabul. A small team of assailants stormed his home after detonating a car bomb at his front gate and each of the attackers wore a suicide vest. They also killed Haji Mohammed Hashim Watanwall, who was still serving as a member of parliament from Uruzgan and who had come back from Sweden to run for office at Jan Mohammed Khan's insistence in 2005. He had subsequently been reelected in 2010. The Taliban claimed they had been following Jan Mohammed for a while and were happy to have finally killed him. I was saddened by the news because any death is tragic, but his passing also symbolized the end of a dark period of history. Jan Mohammed Khan's killing followed the death of Ahmed Wali Karzai on July 12, 2011. Ahmed was one of President Karzai's seven brothers and the head of the Provincial Council in Kandahar. While the circumstances of the killing are still uncertain with respect to whether it was a Taliban operation or a personal issue between him and his bodyguard, the practical effect is the same. If members of Karzai's inner circle could be killed by the Taliban, then what hope did regular Afghans have as the Taliban reasserted their control while the United States reduced its military presence? I felt as if these killings were the opening moves of the next chapter of Afghan history of who would control the country as the United States departed.

The death of Jan Mohammed Khan had an element of justice to it. He had killed many innocent people and had abused the residents of Uruzgan, driving many of them into the arms of the Taliban. His elevation to power in the province in 2002 as part of our warlord strategy also symbolized the short-term thinking of U.S. strategists. His removal from the political scene finally eliminated his dark presence in Uruzgan and, I hoped, would provide the political space for new voices to emerge looking to have a just, representative, and competent administration for the province's impoverished residents. Jan Mohammed Khan's life was so inextricably linked to the history of Uruzgan it was hard to think of the place without his presence. However, his cousin Matullah, who had added "Khan" to his name since I knew him in 2005, symbolizing his rise in status locally, was still there and was reportedly leading a militia of more than three thousand men. Even though I had heard that opinions about him had moderated, I was still suspicious of his intentions since Daoud Khan, former Provincial Police chief Rozi Khan's son, feared that Matullah and his men would kill him.

Since I had left Afghanistan in April 2010, events continued apace in Uruzgan. On November 13, 2010, the Rozi Khan mosque was officially opened and his son cut the ribbon at the ceremony. During the same month, Daoud Khan was removed as District Chief of Chora District, confirming my suspicions that Jan Mohammed Khan's malign influence was felt in

Kabul. On December 13, 2010, a new governor arrived in Uruzgan named Mohammed Omar Shirzad. Like the two previous governors, he was an outsider to the area, but he was educated, seemed responsible, and was motivated to do the job. I had hoped a local resident would be selected, but the new governor seemed dedicated. On March 25, 2011, a large new mosque was completed in the village of Sar Marghab, the same village in which I had been ambushed in 2006. This was a clear indicator to me that security had improved in the Tarin Kowt area due to the construction of patrol bases by the Dutch, Australians, and Americans in the valley from 2006 forward. It was an encouraging sign that security had not only improved in the area but members of the Gilzai tribe, who had typically been most aligned with the Taliban, were casting their lot in with Coalition Forces and the Afghan government. Additionally, U.S. forces were starting a new and innovative program in Afghanistan called Afghan Local Police (ALP), which sought to organize villagers into self-defense forces to resist Taliban intimidation. The United States had long attempted to enlist communities in their own defense, so when members of the district of Gizab in northern Uruzgan spontaneously kicked out the Taliban in June 2010, the United States saw an opportunity they quickly capitalized on. They sent in a team of Green Berets to partner with the locals and this successful episode mushroomed into a model for community engagement that the United States is expanding around the country. While the Afghan Local Police program predated the events in Gizab, the fact that the community had undertaken the effort to remove the Taliban themselves was distinct. I hoped these and other efforts of having local communities participate in their own security would become the model for a long-term but sustainable strategy of protecting Afghans from the Taliban and stopping Afghanistan from becoming an Islamist state.

In many ways, I was fearful we were going to "snatch defeat from the jaws of victory" in Afghanistan and that we would sacrifice our commitment to the people of Afghanistan—who believed our statements of support for the long haul—to the interests of "strategic" considerations. It was difficult for them to understand how a country could communicate an unbreakable bond between our two peoples and commit to stay in Afghanistan until the Afghans were self-sufficient, and simultaneously set a concrete date of withdrawal, in this case July 2011. My concerns came true when President Obama announced on June 22, 2011, that large numbers of U.S. troops would pull out of Afghanistan regardless of conditions on the ground. Additionally, he seemed to be using the killing of Osama bin Laden on May 1 as a reason to leave Afghanistan more quickly rather than finish the job. The fact that all U.S. troops would be gone by 2014 despite the level of security in the country didn't augur well for Afghanistan or the United States. So many of our efforts seemed to have an end point as a starting point, a point of departure regardless of the conditions on the ground. In addition, bureaucratic processes and career paths still strongly influenced our strategies, and possible solutions were approached from the limiting perspective of how the bureaucracy could or could not perform a task, rather than from the stance of how to achieve the solution and compelling the bureaucracy to adapt to it. This requires leadership, imagination, and a commitment to victory; many of these qualities have been in short supply in Afghanistan and in Washington, D.C. The victims of 9/11 deserve better.

EPILOGUE

We had been trained in an institutional culture that emphasized prudence, compromise, and careful drafting; not the bold executive decisions required to govern in a semi-war zone.

—Rory Stewart, *The Prince of the Marshes and Other Occupational Hazards of a Year in Iraq*[1]

My experiences in Afghanistan and Iraq have taught me many things about human nature, about how our government wages war and wins peace, and about politics. In many ways, we are prisoners of our prior experiences, both personal and professional, and the wars of counterinsurgency we have been waging in Muslim countries have given us the opportunity to realize that some of our concepts of how foreign populations think and what they truly desire are tragically incorrect or, at worst, deadly. Our country has become a theoretical empire where a generation of politicians, military leaders, diplomats, and development officials learned the wrong lessons of how the developing world functions and crafted bureaucracies reflecting this incorrect knowledge. They have created deductive theoretical models largely developed in the safety of national capitals, and then applied them by using experiences garnered usually in the relatively well-structured world of traditional state-to-state relations. Many of these constructs failed miserably in the isolated

213

valleys of Afghanistan and urban hothouses of Iraq. This was the generation that led our nation to war and executed our policies in Iraq and Afghanistan for many years. The institutions in which they came up never incorporated the real lessons of the Vietnam War. Even though humanitarian crises and limited wars took place in the intervening years, which one would think would have prepared us well for Afghanistan and Iraq, they never challenged the central tendencies of our civilian and military bureaucracies, the priorities of our political parties, or our general view of human nature. They were blips on the screen and our government continued to do what it had always done.

I have grown to appreciate the great wisdom of the John Bagot Glubb quote cited at the beginning of this book: "To enable one country to appreciate what another people really thinks and desires is both the most difficult and the most vital task which confronts us." It is so obvious, yet so little understood by those who are charged with the solemn duty of formulating and implementing our policy. This is not to say that policymakers, development officials, diplomats, and the military purposely sought to do the wrong things, but that they are creatures of their experiences and they process new information based upon that framework. How many diplomats have we sent to Afghanistan and Iraq who knew a great deal about analyzing the politics of a nation-state but were clueless when it came to discerning tribal politics or leading the development of a city council or tribal jirga? How many military units would rather do what they know, kill the enemy and destroy his support networks, rather than patiently build an indigenous security force? How many development officials can give you laundry lists of projects they have funded but can't tell you how these projects built capacity in the host government and whether the project will exist in a year? Following the Vietnam War, those parts of our government that had traditionally been best positioned to acquire this sort of knowledge and wisdom regarding people overseas atrophied, and the generation that rose up after them were limited both in what they knew and in the ability to do it. But it was not only the reduction of our capacity to deal with overseas problems in a holistic manner that created problems for us in Afghanistan and Iraq, the American will to do so had also changed after Vietnam. We retreated from the world and relied on imperfect surrogates and theoretical constructs to conduct our policies, showing an outsized respect for the self-limiting nature of national sovereignty yet simultaneously feeling no sense of duty to ensure that nations dealt responsibly with their populations. This is not to say that we must police every country or adopt some neocolonial policy overseas. It is only a recognition that we must not surrender to cynicism, but rise to our responsibility and appreciate the fact that there is no universalistic approach to the problems of the world; instead, there are a series of approaches that can only be adopted by rigorously analyzing our own preconceptions and prior experiences and realizing our duty to the world.

The experiences of our civilians and military veterans in Afghanistan and Iraq have irrevocably changed them, and they will take these lessons and apply them to how we see the world as a nation, how we formulate and implement policy, and how we conceive of our responsibilities as a global power. In addition to fighting insurgents, our soldiers have built hospitals and roads, mediated disputes between tribes, and run elections. Many of our civilians have been in firefights, have experienced the loss of comrades to enemy action, and have known the sound of incoming mortars and rockets. They have gotten to know parts of the world many of us have never heard of, while representing our country and defending our interests. They have also seen where our government has tragically failed and what the difference is between the slick brief delivered in Kabul or Baghdad and the reality of life in the field. This permanent line in the sand separating those who have served from those who haven't will continue to divide the leadership of our country for generations to come. Those who have served are better citizens for having gone through the experiences of fighting unconventional wars, and they will seek to hold our politics, politicians, bureaucracies, and civilian and military leaders up to the high ideals they fought for, so far away from home.

AFTERWORD

At isolated firebases tucked into the verdant valleys and desert plains of Afghanistan, a generation of Americans has received a brutal education in the nature of insurgency as well as in how our government wages war. For these young men and women, the challenge of working with local villagers, partnering with them on development projects, while also fighting an enemy hiding amongst the people, has tested their fortitude, compassion, and grit. The ability to simultaneously have an affinity for and sensitivity to the people and their concerns while aggressively pursuing insurgent fighters has produced a unique type of Soldier, Sailor, Airman, and Marine; adroit at waging war, they are equally capable at building local councils, constructing schools, and mediating tribal disputes. In addition, the traditional peacetime separation between civilian and military tasks has been blurred in these conflicts and, indeed, eliminated altogether in the face of an enemy that seamlessly merges lethal and nonlethal approaches. For many of these Americans, the difference between how the war is briefed in Washington, D.C., and in Kabul, versus how it is waged in the field, cannot be starker. It is through these thousands of unique personal experiences of counterinsurgency that our government's age-old verities of waging war will be changed.

Throughout our military campaigns in Iraq and Afghanistan, success was not determined solely by decisions made in distant national capitals by generals and admirals, diplomats, and political leaders, but more often by military units and their civilian colleagues figuring out local problems on their own. These civil-military partnerships sought to help local communities improve their governance practices, facilitate reconstruction and development, and establish the foundation for the eventual handing over of responsibility to government officials. This approach, of partnership through shared goals, a respect for cultural differences as well as similarities, and an affinity for local concerns, often determined the difference between success and failure.

The development of Provincial Reconstructions Teams in Afghanistan reflected this awareness that more had to be done to work with local officials to bring the benefits of stable government and capable administration to local Afghans. The PRT concept was an innovative approach to dealing with the problems of Afghanistan, where no government existed in the countryside and the population's development needs were great. Successful PRTs took an active interest in the concerns of locals and sought to master the micro-histories of key leaders, villages, and valleys and became adept at understanding and practicing local politics. Moreover, many PRTs developed a shared sense of common struggle with local communities as they also tried to resist Taliban intimidation while improving their livelihoods. This sense of a shared struggle helped to break down cultural, religious, and social boundaries, allowing a generation of Americans to know more about dusty adobe villages, the histories of ancient tribes, and the politics of arable land than they do the new social media.

As the irregular warfare challenge continues, the great innovations that have come from our experiences in Iraq and Afghanistan, and have been paid for by our soldiers' blood, must be continued. Many of these roots of reform are quite shallow in our civilian and military bureaucracies but they must continue to grow to face this enduring threat. The challenge of terrorist and insurgent safe havens, whether they are in Yemen, Somalia, Pakistan, Chad, or a number of other countries, must be confronted by a holistic approach that blends both military and civilian approaches seamlessly. It is only through providing a positive alternative to the political objectives terrorist groups offer that we can hope to penetrate the safe haven of a person's mind, to replace his interest in causing harm with one focused on a positive and constructive future. The lessons and experiences of our civilians and military personnel in such far-off places as Tal Afar, Fallujah, Ramadi, Tarin Kowt,

Khost, Hit, and Lashgar Gah have demonstrated that a sympathetic under-standing of local concerns, along with a willingness to aggressively pursue in-surgents, will usually accomplish more than any other approach.

Dan Green's book is a unique contribution to not only the great literature about Afghanistan, but to the canon of work written by soldiers, civilians, and adventurers working in isolated outposts furthering the establishment of stable government and pursuing human knowledge. This book reminds me of Bing West's classic *The Village* and Jeffrey Race's *War Comes to Long An,* as well as Wilfred Thesiger's *The Marsh Arabs* and Douglas Collins's *A Tear for Somalia.* Dan's sympathetic treatment of the hopes of the inhabitants of Uruzgan and his critical eye for where our efforts failed, as well as his hope for our success, is a great testament to the enduring American will to prevail in this conflict. There is no greater memorial to the victims of the attacks on 9/11 than this lasting determination to overcome the challenges of Afghanistan to secure the peace and to vanquish our foes; we owe this as much to them as to ourselves.

—Brig. Gen H. R. McMaster, USA

APPENDIX A

Tarin Kowt: Some Ideas on Leadership Change in Uruzgan Province

In 2005, I wrote this report for Amb. Ronald Neumann as I finished my tour. I hoped to pass on to him any wisdom I had gained during my tour before he spoke to President Karzai about Governor Jan Mohammed Khan's removal. Ambassador Neumann very graciously sent me a hand-written note thanking me for writing it and said it had helped him immensely in his meetings with the Afghan president.

Any effort to remove Jan Mohammed Khan as governor of Uruzgan Province must take into account the entrenched nature of his influence in the area. Furthering the goals of good governance and enhanced security while facilitating a more democratized decision-making process in Uruzgan will need to be accomplished while balancing tribal relationships, personal animosities, and factional disputes. To facilitate these goals, decision-makers should look to elevate honest and effective members of the dominant Populzai tribe while bringing in additional members of other tribes such as the Barakzai, Achikzai, and Noorzai. Educated and professional men should be promoted over illiterate leaders who are more attuned to the ways of warlordism than good governance. Additional leaders and personnel should also be brought in from outside the province who do not have a stake in local disputes. With proper planning, adequate consultation with local leaders, and a willingness to make bold moves, governance and security will be enhanced in Uruzgan Province and local residents will be better off for it. End Summary.

GOVERNOR JAN MOHAMMED KHAN— FAMILY, TRIBAL, AND PERSONAL RELATIONSHIPS EXTEND HIS POWER

Through family connections, tribal ties, and personal friendships, Governor Jan Mohammed Khan sits atop a latticework of relationships that serve to strengthen his position as provincial government head and leader of the Populzai tribe. Members of the Populzai tribe, which is also President Karzai's tribe, are located in almost every single key leadership position of Uruzgan Province. The district chiefs of Yachtan and Oshay, the commander and deputy commander of the Afghan Highway Police (AHP), the mayors of Tarin Kowt and Deh Rawud, the police chief of Deh Rawud, the chief justice of the province, the deputy director of the Directorate of National Security, the Afghan Militia Force commander of the southern Chora region of Chenartu, and the directors of communications, agriculture, transportation, public works, and finance are all members of the Populzai tribe and were appointed by the governor. Longtime friends are also in key positions such as the Achikzai district chief of Chora, its mayor, and the police chief. The governor is also connected to the chief justice of the province and the Tarin Kowt Bazaar Precinct Police chief through marriage (all of their wives are sisters) and the commander of the AHP and thirty of his men are related to the governor.

The governor has also made efforts to remove members of rival tribes or personal opponents from positions of influence helping to consolidate his control. The governor has tried to remove both ANP commander and Barakzai tribal chief Rozi Khan and his ally Yachtan police chief Haji Ibrahim and some will tell you he was also behind the planting of several improvized explosive devices that nearly killed both men. He has also removed a main political opponent, Malem Khaliq Khan, from his position as district chief of Chora and is making efforts to remove the local head of the Directorate of National Security, Col. Zakriya Aziz.

ENHANCING SECURITY—PROMOTE FROM WITHIN, PROFESSIONALIZE THE LEADERSHIP, MAINTAIN MILITIA SUPPORT

The Afghan Highway Police

The appointment of Jan Mohammed Khan as governor of Uruzgan Province in 2002 was due in large part to his Taliban fighting abilities. He does this by using a mixture of Government of Afghanistan and militia forces, but his primary tool for maintaining provincial security is the AHP. This force of approximately 360 men is led by the governor's former militia leader and cousin, Matullah, and roughly thirty of the AHP's men are related to the governor. The Populzai tribe dominates the senior leadership of the group. While their Taliban-fighting abilities are great, they also serve as the governor's "muscle" against his opponents and are known to intimidate, murder, and steal from local Afghans who are not friends of the governor. Replacement of Governor Jan Mohammed Khan also requires that the AHP leadership be replaced. To maintain their fighting abilities while seeking to professionalize their activities and redirect their focus to mainly protecting the Tarin Kowt–Kandahar Road, Poloff recommends that Matullah be replaced and his deputy Dil Agha be promoted to commander of the AHP.

Deputy Commander Agha is a member of the Populzai tribe and is an educated former military officer with close ties to the governor, President Karzai, and the president's brother, Ahmed Wali Karzai. Well educated with over ten years of experience as a military officer, he has a good working relationship with Coalition Forces. He has told Poloff that he is committed to professionalizing the AHP and seems to have had some success at achieving this goal. A portion of the AHP should also be moved to Forward Operating Base Pacemaker and/or FOB Tiger to protect the Tarin Kowt–Kandahar Road and to get them out of Uruzgan Province. With little to do, this armed militia creates a threatening environment for the governor's political opponents. With better leadership, and a stronger focus on their core mission of protecting the Tarin Kowt–Kandahar Road, the AHP will make significant progress in becoming a more professional police force.

The Afghan National Police

The Afghan National Police (ANP) is led by Barakzai tribal chief Rozi Khan. A generally honest man, he is not the most skilled administrator and is limited in his abilities due to his illiteracy and the fact that Governor Jan Mohammed Khan has so effectively checked his influence in the province. Chief Rozi Khan is one of the governor's two main political opponents (the other being Chora District resident Malem Khaliq Khan). Chief Rozi Khan would like to be governor of Uruzgan but lacks the aptitude to do the job effectively. Because he does not get along with the governor, his appointment as governor would significantly destabilize the area. To improve the effectiveness of the ANP in Uruzgan, Poloff recommends that Chief Rozi Khan be replaced by his deputy Haji Nabi.

Deputy Chief Haji Nabi is a member of the Achikzai tribe and is the most professional police officer in Uruzgan's ANP. He has completed twelve years of schooling and one year at a police academy in Russia in addition to training in Afghanistan. Competent and honest, he takes his responsibilities seriously and actively engages local institutions such as the Provincial Shura and works well with Coalition Forces. Because Nabi does not have tribal assets to call upon in Uruzgan, Poloff recommends that Yachtan District police chief Haji Ibrahim be installed as the new deputy chief of police for Uruzgan. Mr. Ibrahim has served as police chief in the districts of Deh Rawud, Chora, and Yachtan. Because of the contacts he has made throughout the province by serving as police chief of three districts, Mr. Ibrahim would help the ANP be more assertive in placing its own choices into the position of district police chief instead of having the governor do it. Though a member of the Populzai tribe, he is independent of the governor, has his own support from President Karzai, is an ally of Chief Rozi Khan, and is well regarded by the community. Though uneducated he is proactive and has a reputation for honesty and a commitment to killing Taliban. His placement as deputy of the ANP in Uruzgan would allow Haji Nabi to operate with a loyal group of police officers who are proactive, experienced, and can provide the kind of protection the province needs.

IMPROVING GOVERNANCE—PROFESSIONALIZE AND MAINTAIN TRIBAL BALANCE

Poloff recommends that Deputy Governor Haji Aziz Khan be elevated to the governorship of Uruzgan following the September elections. Mr. Aziz Khan is a well-educated former Kabul bureaucrat who has been in his present position for approximately three years. A member of the Mohammedzai tribe, he has a good relationship with the governor, Coalition Forces, and the PRT. Because he has no ties to militias and comes from a relatively small Pashtun tribe, there is a chance he won't have as much influence as he would need in order to do his job effectively. A key aspect of this is the reaction of Governor Jan Mohammed Khan to the elevation of Haji Aziz Khan. If the governor can publicly support the change and is willing to devote some security guards to Haji Aziz Khan, then the transition will be much easier. A separate security detail from the National Directorate of Security should also be assigned to Haji Aziz Khan to facilitate a successful transition. Additionally, members of other tribes will need to be brought in to democratize decision-making, increase the legitimacy of the provincial government, and give Haji Aziz Khan the militia support he'll need in order to make his decisions effective throughout Uruzgan.

WHAT TO DO WITH JAN MOHAMMED KHAN, MATULLAH, AND ROZI KHAN?

The success or failure of the leadership changes in Uruzgan following the elections will be determined by how thoroughly Governor Jan Mohammed Khan has been included in the process and how supportive he is of it. A decision to remove Matullah as head of the AHP can only be done with his support and assistance. Additionally, if the governor feels that his opponents are being put into positions that threaten his interests or personal safety, he will oppose the process and there will be destabilizing effect throughout the province. Ideally, the governor will be given a position in the central government that will remove him from the province and allow his replacement the opportunity to get a good start. Additionally, it would benefit the leadership transition process if Matullah and Rozi Khan were taken out of Uruzgan for a few months. This could possibly be achieved through some sort of education and training program. If Matullah is removed as AHP head, in all likelihood his influence will continue to be felt in Uruzgan because Governor Jan Mohammed Khan will probably give him a job. Even though this would be an imperfect solution it would still be an improvement over the current situation.

Rozi Khan's status following the proposed leadership changes is very sensitive. Because of his rivalry with the governor and his own ambition to be governor, he will probably not be happy unless his new position is sufficiently senior to allow him to save face. That said, it can't be too senior that it threatens the governor's interests. Poloff recommends that Rozi Khan be made one of two or three deputy governors of Uruzgan. Mr. Rozi Khan would serve with the current, second deputy governor who is a member of the Populzai tribe and a close friend of Governor Jan Mohammed Khan. The benefits of this proposal are that the Barakzai tribe would play a larger role in decision-making in the province, Chief Rozi Khan would feel that the position was a promotion and would support it, and Governor Jan Mohammed Khan would still have access to the executive leadership of the province through Haji Aziz Khan and his friend who would still be one of the province's deputy governors.

Comment: On several occasions Governor Jan Mohammed Khan has expressed his weariness at serving as governor of Uruzgan Province. He often remarks that he is an old man and would prefer to retire if not for President Karzai's insistence that he stay in his present position. If true, and there is some evidence to support it, the governor may be a more willing partner in facilitating leadership change and a successful transition in Uruzgan than many think. If the process is done respectfully, with the governor's participation in key aspects of it, and the community is consulted on possible personnel changes, leadership change can be successful in this deeply conservative and Taliban-plagued area. However the process moves forward, it is imperative that local community leaders, including newly elected Wolesi Jirga and Provincial Council officials, be part of the consultative process. Their support will lend credibility and legitimacy to the process. Poloff also recommends that other leadership changes be held off until the new leadership has had the opportunity to get established. This should also be done because if the governor's friends and allies in the Provincial Directorates feel threatened, they will join forces with the governor and Matullah and work against the newly established leaders. After about six months has passed, leadership changes in the Provincial Directorates and in the justice system should be attempted. If leadership change in Uruzgan is done following some of the approaches mentioned above, the goals of better governance and enhanced security will be furthered and a more democratic and professional provincial government will be established.

APPENDIX B

Counterinsurgency in Uruzgan Province: The Political Dimension

In 2006 I wrote this counterinsurgency political strategy for Uruzgan Province after I had returned home from my trip to the province. Passing it to the Dutch government, I hoped its insights and recommendations, along with any wisdom I had garnered in Uruzgan, would help them appreciate the grievances, hopes, and goals of the residents of the province.

Support for the Taliban in Uruzgan Province comes from a variety of sources. Some of it is due to tribal grievances (the Gilzai against the Durrani), some is due to frustrated hopes of a better life, some is due to sympathy to their cause, and some is due to rank opportunism. Regardless, the PRT has a number of things it can do on the political front that can serve to eliminate many of the sources of support for the Taliban by using nonkinetic means. Chief among these is bringing the Gilzai tribe into the Government of Afghanistan (GOA) and making sure the provincial government is broadly representative of the province's tribes and delivers results evenly across the province. A second component of this strategy is spreading the benefits of reconstruction and development more widely throughout the province by focusing on underserved villages. A third component is helping the elected representatives of Uruzgan do their jobs more effectively and building up representative institutions. The hope is that by making the government more responsive to its citizens and more effective, and having the community see tangible benefits from helping the GOA and the coalition, the local support networks the Taliban rely upon will dry up as more and more residents of Uruzgan see a better future with the GOA than with the Taliban.

BRINGING THE GILZAI INTO THE GOVERNMENT: ELIMINATING TRIBAL SAFE HAVENS

During the Uruzgan governorship of Jan Mohammed Khan (2002–2006), he pursued a policy of tribal preference whereby Populzai supporters were appointed to positions within the provincial government well above their numbers in the area. While members of other Pashtun tribes were nominally included among his appointments, most of them tended to be long-standing friends of Jan Mohammed from his days of fighting against the Soviet Union rather than being representatives of their respective tribe. Besides the appointment of Engineer Hashim, who is a Gilzai tribal member from the District of Deh Rawud, as director of the Directorate of Reconstruction and Rural Development, and Mohammed Naim, the police chief of Char Chena District, no other public official comes from the Gilzai tribe. Hashim was selected primarily because he was the most qualified among Uruzgan's directors and his talents could not be denied, and Naim was appointed because he and his family are the only Gilzai supportive of the GOA in Char Chena. Most of the population of the district of Char Chena is implacably hostile to the GOA and coalition forces. Jan Mohammed Khan also deliberately excluded members of the Gilzai from the Afghan Highway Police and from contracts and development money from the Provincial Reconstruction Team. A significant portion of past reconstruction and development money from the PRT was also spent in areas supportive of the governor. Due in large part to security and logistical considerations and lack of political engagement with the Gilzai tribe, little development reached Gilzai tribal areas such as the district of Char Chena, the Tarin Kowt District villages of Mirabad, Sar Marghab, and Deh Rushan, among others, and the western portion of the district of Deh Rawud.

With the appointment of Abdul Hakim Monib as governor of Uruzgan in March 2006, the Gilzai are increasingly feeling that their interests will be heard and acted upon by the provincial government. Governor Monib, who is a Gilzai, though not originally from Uruzgan, has aggressively sought to include the tribesmen in his government. He is deliberately seeking to construct security checkpoints in the villages of Mirabad, Sar Marghab, and Deh Rushan (all Gilzai areas) and has promised increased development in those areas as well. In the district of Char Chena, he is looking to appoint a Gilzai tribesman as district chief, which would be a first for that region since at least 2002. Additionally, he has been convening shuras with Gilzai tribesmen to hear their complaints; this rarely happened during Jan Mohammed Khan's rule. While no Gilzai tribesmen were elected to the Provincial Council or to the Wolesi and Meshrano Jirgas, there is hope in that community that with Gilzai tribesman Monib in power, they will finally be brought into the government and see an improvement in their standard of living.

- The PRT should actively support friendly Gilzai leaders. This can be done with recognition (attention, frequent meetings), development projects in their areas (making it very clear to the local population that these projects came about due to the friendly leader's efforts), and security (preferably local forces but periodic coalition patrols). If the Gilzai feel that they are being victimized by other tribes (such as the Populzai in the past) then the PRT should work with the local provincial leadership to intervene. It should be made known to the Gilzai that the PRT (do this privately) and the government intervened on their behalf. Broach the subject of having "ex-officio" members of the Gilzai tribe attend Provincial Council meetings and schedule meetings for them with the Wolesi and Meshrano Jirga members. (Note: Mullah Hamdullah wanted the highest Gilzai vote recipient for the Provincial Council made a member of the Provincial Council. Though the PRT could not support this because he did not receive enough votes, there is an openness to this idea.)

- The PRT should aggressively seek to spread its development and reconstruction money into the Gilzai tribal community. Assistance should be linked to information from that community on Taliban membership and movements and on weapons caches. We also have to see their active participation in protecting their communities. Make clear that we do not favor any tribe, village, or district. We do not discriminate and are eager to work with them. Begin with quick impact projects such as fixing up the mosques, distributing school supplies, etc., and initiate long-term projects such as schools, clinics, roads, etc.

SMALL VILLAGES STRATEGY: BEYOND A MILE DEEP AND A FOOT WIDE

Reconstruction and development spending in Uruzgan has typically been on large-scale development projects such as the Tarin Kowt–Kandahar Road, the women's hospital in Tarin Kowt, the district center in Chora, bridges, and schools (predominantly in Tarin Kowt). Most of it has been Tarin Kowt–centric due to security and logistical considerations. Past teams were also influenced by Jan Mohammed Khan, who came from the district of Tarin Kowt. Though much of this spending was definitely needed, many villages did not see tangible evidence of assistance. In a sense, the spending was a mile deep but only a foot wide, lots of money but little distribution of it throughout the community. Though many smaller projects have been finished, such as wells, MEDCAPS and VETCAPS, school supply and wheat seed distributions, etc., many of these took place in the largest villages of a district. Smaller villages did not see much tangible proof that working with the GOA brought them benefits. Some of the support for the insurgency comes from this frustrated hope. Past PRTs had one civil-affairs (CA) team and each ODA (Operation Detachment Alpha) in the province had a small CA team as well, a total of four teams. Though they worked very hard and accomplished much, it was not enough for the whole province. Outside of Tarin Kowt, most of these projects tended to be small in size and temporary. As said above, much of the emphasis was on wells, MEDCAPS and VETCAPS, and the distribution of wheat seed and school supplies. Because security was an overriding consideration in Char Chena and in Deh Rawud, development spending really only took place in a handful of villages, if at all.

- Select several villages for targeted reconstruction, development, and political engagement. Villages should be chosen based on tribal affiliation and tactical location. Some villages should be Gilzai and at least one should be selected from all of the other significant Durrani Pashtun tribes. We should concentrate our efforts on the following villages but also consider doing at least one small project for villages that have likely not seen anything. A little attention will pay lots of dividends. Stay at it and be consistent.

Below are some recommended villages. Add or delete names based on local commander's knowledge.

TARIN KOWT
Mirabad, Sar Marghab, Deh Rushan (Gilzai)
Chenartu (tactical)

CHORA
Kala Kala (Baluchi Pass) (tactical)

KHAS URUZGAN
Shakajoy (tactical)

DEH RAWUD
Any villages across the Helmand River (tribal)

CHAR CHENA
Any villages (start with those within sight of the FOB) (tribal)

Create a list of projects for each village with each project increasing in sophistication and cost based upon cooperation from the village (this approach is probably best for more hostile villages). Definitely try a friendlier approach with GOA supportive villages.

SMALL PROJECTS:
Mosque painting and prayer rugs, humanitarian supplies, seed distribution, school supply distribution, Koran distribution, radio distribution.

RESULT:
Identify location of Taliban and IEDs, provide early warning to coalition, provide actionable intelligence.

MEDIUM PROJECTS:

Checkpoints, schools, clinics, mosque refurbishment.

RESULT:

Identify arms caches and IED cells and components, turn in Taliban members.

LARGE PROJECTS:

Building mosques, building roads, humanitarian air drops, check dams.

RESULT:

Actively resist Taliban, man own checkpoints, patrol local area, provide recruits for the ANP, AHP, and ANA.

BUILDING THE PROVINCIAL COUNCIL AND EMPOWERING MEMBERS OF PARLIAMENT

Though it had met a few times after the September 2005 election, it is vital that the Provincial Council (PC) be stood up and become a viable institution. Any discontent that the Durrani Pashtun may have with Governor Monib should be channeled into peaceful institutions. Having the PC meet regularly, with its meetings played on the radio, and making it a useful tool for the community is important. Empowering Mullah Hamdullah, who has strong democratic legitimacy credentials, is important as a useful corrective to any excesses or oversights by Governor Monib. Though they don't get along, it is important that their problems with each other be turned into a useful tension whereby the public's interest is met through their political struggle with each other. Governor Monib needs to see the PC not as something to be avoided but as something to be embraced. No one likes to be criticized, least of all politicians, but creative and constructive comments, regardless of how critical they may be, are very useful to Monib.

- Reconstitute the Provincial Council. Prod Mullah Hamdullah and other PC members to convene for monthly, if not biweekly, meetings. The PC is ostensibly charged with advising the governor but what it actually does is quite malleable. Hamdullah has run these meetings before and they are generally well organized (see previous reporting on Provincial Shura meetings). The coalition may have to help some members travel to Tarin Kowt for the meetings due to security concerns. It is a worthy investment. Make sure the meetings are broadcast on the radio (give Ali Mohammed a ride) and make sure the PRT, Special Forces, and other military commanders attend to deliver presentations on their activities and be open to questioning from local officials. There are some grumblings that the PC is not that representative. Broach the subject of reconvening the monthly Provincial Shura meetings as a useful supplement to the PC. Purchase satellite phones and phone cards for each Provincial Council and Wolesi and Meshrano Jirga member who does not have one so that we can easily reach them. This will pay huge dividends and can also become a useful source of information for the PRT on what's going on in the province.

- Empower the Wolesi and Meshrano Jirga members. Part of the PRT's mission is to strengthen the central government in the provinces. We can do this by making Uruzgan's members of Parliament more effective in Kabul and in Uruzgan. Set up a meeting with the governor, the PC, and the members of Parliament to establish a list of priorities for the parliamentary members. Once the list is established, and the list should be small and targeted (let's get some successes under our belt first), it should be followed up by the American, Dutch, and Australian embassies in Kabul in order to help the members get their projects and policies passed. Once the Parliament is done meeting, we need to make sure the people of Uruzgan know about the successes of their members of Parliament and that their government is working for them. Try to organize events, ribbon cuttings, etc., where decisions in Kabul visibly created tangible benefits in the community.

STAYING CONNECTED TO JAN MOHAMMED KHAN AND HIS SUPPORTERS

There is no faster way of making a friend in politics than reaching out to someone who had once been in power when you don't have to, and consulting with him on a regular basis and valuing his opinions, wisdom, and feelings. Because of the removal of Jan Mohammed Khan by President Karzai and most of his supporters by Governor Monib in 2006, there is a strong feeling among some in the Populzai community that Monib's tenure may not be kind to their interests. Though their opposition to the Taliban is quite strong, many of the Populzai may turn a blind eye to their machinations if they feel it is not in their interest to support the governor or the GOA. It is vitally important that the PRT visit Populzai tribal areas, especially west and south of Tarin Kowt, to show the villagers there that though many of their leaders are out of power, they are still important to the PRT and the GOA. Of necessity, we need to limit our projects in their area because they have historically enjoyed the benefits of a significant amount of reconstruction and development spending but frequent meetings that allow them to complain about the new political status quo in Uruzgan are useful and we should continue to undertake small projects in their area. It is also useful to invite former Uruzgan leaders to the PRT to allow them to complain about things as well. Sometimes their criticisms will be a useful balance to information we receive from the provincial government. I'd also recommend that Governor Monib go with you to the village of Touri (Jan Mohammed Khan's village) in a few months to show that the Populzai have nothing to fear from his tenure as governor (let's hope this is true).

- Schedule a shura with the village of Touri. Initially go out there as part of a village assessment without any provincial leaders. You might want to prime the pump by inviting old provincial officials up to the PRT to do an initial sounding out of their concerns. Once this task is accomplished, then decide whether it is yet advisable for Monib to accompany the PRT on another mission there to demonstrate that the provincial government is their government too. You may want to bring him out there after a few trips to the village alone or after several months.

- Invite former provincial government leaders to the PRT. Make a point of inviting former government officials up to the PRT to chat. Give them lots of attention. Not only will this be a useful source of information for you, and a check against the actions of other leaders, but by giving them the respect they deserve because of their former service we will benefit from the good will this will generate.

NOTES

Chapter 2. Afghanistan

1   John Bagot Glubb, *Britain and the Arabs: A Study of Fifty Years, 1908 to 1958* (London: Hodder and Stoughton, 1959), 147.

2   Please read Mark Etherington's *Revolt on the Tigris: The Al-Sadr Uprising and the Governing of Iraq* (Ithaca, NY: Cornell University Press, 2005) for a great account of Tim's service in Iraq.

Chapter 3. Uruzgan: The Heart of Asia

1   David Galula, *Counterinsurgency Warfare: Theory and Practice* (Westport, CT: Praeger Security International, 2006), 66.

2   Neil Sheehan, *A Bright Shining Lie: John Paul Vann and America in Vietnam* (New York: Vintage Books, 1989), 503.

3   Glubb, *The Story of the Arab Legion* (London: Hodder and Stoughton, 1948), 238.

4   Dai Kundi was created on March 28, 2004, out of eight northern districts taken from Uruzgan Province. The province of Nimruz is considered the fifth southern province. It borders Iran and Pakistan and constitutes the western corner of Afghanistan.

5   Col. Kenneth F. McKenzie, Maj. Roberta L. Shea, and Maj. Christopher Phelps, "Marines Deliver in Mountain Storm," *Proceedings*, November 2004.

6   James W. Spain, *The Pathan Borderland* (New York: Columbia University Press, 1963), 72–74.

Chapter 4. A Provincial Affair (Tarin Kowt—Spring 2005)

1   Edward Geary Lansdale, *In the Midst of Wars: An American's Mission to Southeast Asia* (New York: Fordham University Press, 1991), 376.

2   John Bagot Glubb, *Britain and the Arabs*, 161.

3   Galula, *Counterinsurgency Warfare*, 55

Chapter 5. A Visit to the Green Zone (Chora—Spring 2005)

1   Galula, *Counterinsurgency Warfare*, 78.

2   Ernesto Guevara, intro. and case studies Thomas M. Davies Jr. and Brian Loveman, *Guerrilla Warfare* (New York: Rowman & Littlefield, 1997), 52.

3   Etherington, *Revolt on the Tigris*, 194.

Chapter 6. The New Regime (Tarin Kowt—Summer 2005)
1   Galula, *Counterinsurgency Warfare*, 64.
2   Quoted in Bay Fang, "A 'Reluctant Warrior' in Iraq," *U.S. News & World Report*, January 9, 2006.
3   Sheehan, *A Bright Shining Lie*, 107.

Chapter 7. Journey to Chenartu (Chora—Summer 2005)
1   Bernard B. Fall, *Street Without Joy: Indochina at War* (Harrisburg, PA: Stackpole Books, 1961), 375.

Chapter 8. The Thin Black Line (Tarin Kowt—Summer 2005)
1   Glubb, *The Story of the Arab Legion*, 245.
2   Ibid., 234.

Chapter 9. Bringing Democracy to the Pashtuns (Tarin Kowt—Fall 2005)
1   Alec Kirkbride, *An Awakening: The Arab Campaign 1917–18* (London: University Press of Arabia, 1971), 104.

Chapter 10. Uruzgan's Bloody Past (Tarin Kowt—Fall 2005)
1   Lansdale, *In the Midst of Wars*, 373.
2   Patrick Fruchet and Mike Kendellen, "Landmine Impact Survey of Afghanistan: Results and Implications for Planning," *Journal of Mine Action* 9, no. 2 (February 2006), http://maic.jmu.edu/journal/9.2/focus/fruchet/fruchet.htm.
3   Antonio Giustozzi, *Koran, Kalashnikov, and Laptop: The Neo-Taliban Insurgency in Afghanistan* (New York: Columbia University Press, 2008), 87.
4   Sheehan, *A Bright Shining Lie*, 552.

Chapter 11. The War Returns (Tarin Kowt—Summer 2006)
1   Giustozzi, *Koran, Kalashnikov, and Laptop*, 234.
2   Sheehan, *A Bright Shining Lie*, 535.
3   Ibid., 631.

Chapter 12. The Good Samaritan (Chora—Summer 2006)
1   Sheehan, *A Bright Shining Lie*, 317.
2   Ibid., 637.

Chapter 13. The Dutch Take Over (Tarin Kowt—Summer 2006)
1   Sheehan, *A Bright Shining Lie*, 668.

Chapter 15. Afghanistan (2009–2011)
1   Galula, *Counterinsurgency Warfare*, 78.
2   Though this increase has generally been beneficial, its overall effects have not been as great as anticipated because of a number of challenges with the uplift.
3   Fall, *Street Without Joy*, 375.
4   Galula, *Counterinsurgency Warfare*, 4–5.
5   See "Host Nation Information Requirements: Achieving Unity of Understanding in Counter Insurgency," by Col. George Franz, Lt. Col. David Pendall, and Lt. Col. Jeffery Steffen, smallwarsjournal.com, January 2010.

Epilogue
1   Rory Stewart, *The Prince of the Marshes and Other Occupational Hazards of a Year in Iraq* (New York: Harcourt, 2007), 182–83.

INDEX

abbreviations, xxv–xxvii, 191
Abdullah, Said, 26, 50, 92, 97, 101, 150
Abizaid, John, 110
Achikzai tribe
  about, 36, 70, 137
  Khaliq, 72, 123
  members, 48, 70, 72, 117, 135, 224
  tribal balance in government, 221
acronyms, 190–91
ACS (Afghans for Civil Society), 41
Afghan Diaspora, 27
Afghan Highway Police (AHP)
  about, 39–40, 47–49, 84–87, 223
  Hamdullah, 123
  Jan Mohammed Khan, 115, 222, 228
  tensions with ANP, 47–48, 72, 84
Afghan Local Police (ALP), 210
Afghan National Army (ANA)
  about, 82
  Chora, 168–69
  clearing operations, 158
  Jan Mohammed Khan, 153
  Khaliq, 72
  mullahs meeting, 64
  Provincial Shura, 56, 58–59
  Sar Marghab firefight, 170
  size increase, 193
  Tarin Kowt Traffic Circle, 60–61
Afghan National Police (ANP)
  about, 45–49, 223–24
  Chora, 68–71, 72, 167
  compound, 45–46
  corruption, 57, 116
  Dai Kundi, 108, 111
  presence in Uruzgan, 156–57
  Provincial Shura, 57

size increase, 193
  tensions with AHP, 47–48, 72, 85
Afghan Reconstruction Group (ARG), 14–15
Afghan Security Force (ASF), 24, 26, 32, 80, 82, 217
Afghans for Civil Society (ACS), 41
Afghanistan Landmine Impact Survey, UN, 128
Agan, Noor, 72
Agha, Dil, 123, 223
Agha, Khan, 156
agriculture, 35, 44, 58, 69, 104, 140–41
Agriculture Directorate, 52, 58, 156
Ahmad, Mir, 64–65
Ahmadi, Habibullah, 104–5
Ahmed, Haji Ali, 157
AHP. See Afghan Highway Police
airport procedures, 73
Akbar, Ahmed, 161
Akbari, Jan Mohammed, 106–7, 109, 111–12
Akram, 150
Alkhan, Haji Nimatullah, 136
Alkozai tribe, 36
Americans with Disabilities Act, 203–4
Amin, Hafizullah, 130
Amshah, Gul, 53–54
ANA. See Afghan National Army
ANP. See Afghan National Police
ARG. See Afghan Reconstruction Group
ASF. See Afghan Security Force
Atifi, Abdullah, 130, 131–32
Australia, 191
Australian Special Forces, 147–49, 169, 170–71, 184, 210
Awakening: The Arab Campaign 1917–1918, An (Kirkbride), 115
Aziz (interpreter), 62

Aziz, Zakriya, 222

badal, 36
Bagram Air Field, 8, 15–16, 163, 189–90
Baki, Abdul, 43–44, 64–65, 87
Baki, Atifi, 80–81
ballot counting, 108, 117, 120–21, 125
Baluchs, 103
Barakzai tribe
    about, 28, 36, 46, 137, 184
    Jan Mohammed Khan, 72
    members, 46, 52, 124, 135–36
    tribal balance in government, 221, 226
Battle of Chora, 184
behavior code, Pashtun, 36
Belgium, 191
Berader, Abdul Ghani, 138
bin Laden, Osama, 208
Blehm, Eric, 134
blockade, Chenartu, 172–75
Blue, 150
Blundell, Travis, 26
body disposal, 142
Bowden, Mark, 75
brides, Afghan, 61, 76
Bright Shining Lie: John Paul Vann and
    America in Vietnam, A (Sheehan), 27, 83,
    142, 153, 157, 165, 172, 177
Britain and the Arabs: A Study of Fifty Years
    (Glubb), v, 11, 42
Brown, Ryan, 26
Bryan, Julien, v, 42
bureaucracy
    NATO, 191, 192
    Washington, 15, 110, 143, 211, 213–14
Bush administration, George W., 1, 2, 5, 193
businesses, small, 35

camels, 29, 35, 36, 68
campaigning, political, 107, 118–19, 130
Canada, 191
Carland, Raphael, 143–44, 160, 161
carpets, 75
CAT-A. See Civil Affairs Team–Afghanistan,
    U.S. Army
caveats, national, 192
caves, 30, 31
cemeteries, 30
CERP. See Commander's Emergency Response
    Program
CF. See Coalition Forces
CFTs. See cross-functional teams
Char Chena district
    about, 85, 155, 161–62, 228
    police, 68–69, 155
    Taliban, 160, 161–63
checkpoints
    Afghan Highway Police, 47
    Chenartu, 175
    Gilzai area, 229
    Tarin Kowt–Kandahar Road, 86, 97–98,
        157
Chenartu, 90–93, 172–75

children, Afghan, 30, 31–33, 49–50. See also
    girls, Afghan
Chora district. See also Chenartu
    about, xix, 69, 158
    Battle of Chora, 184
    district center, 167–68, 207
    elections, 90
    Khaliq, 124
    police, 68–71, 72
    visit and firefight, 165–71
    Wali, 76
Civil Affairs Team–Afghanistan (CAT-A), U.S.
    Army, xi, 23, 26, 29, 48, 49
Civil-Military Operations Center (CMOC), 48
Civil Service Commission, 195
civilian casualties (CIVCAS), 191
civilian-military operations coordination, 193,
    194–96, 199–202, 218–19
civilian uplift program, 196–98, 202–6,
    237ch15n2
clearing operations, 81, 149, 158, 160, 192
climate, 34, 81
Coalition Forces (CF), 37, 57–58, 62–63, 117
code of behavior, Pashtun, 36
Commander's Emergency Response Program
    (CERP), 7, 23, 197
Communications Directorate, 156
Communist Party, Afghan, 81, 115, 129–33,
    136–37, 139
contractors, xiv, 98
corruption
    IDLG, 197
    Jan Mohammed Khan, 46–49, 54, 72, 123–
        24, 127, 155, 222
    Matullah, 86
    Monib's firings for, 156
    Provincial Shura, 57
    warlords, 197
Coulter, Michael, 6
counterinsurgency, 23, 59, 67, 79, 189, 194–95,
    200
Counterinsurgency Warfare: Theory and
    Practice (Galula), 23, 59, 67, 79, 189
counting ballots, 108, 117, 120–21, 125
cross-functional teams (CFTs), 192
Crumpton, Hank, 144–45
culture, Afghan, 33, 66, 141, 204

Dai Kundi Province
    about, 34, 36, 51, 160, 235n4
    first PRT visit, 103–10
    second PRT visit, 110–12
Dam Neck training, 75–76
dam projects, 30–31, 58, 81
Davies, Thomas M., 71
Dayton, John, 16, 17–18, 41, 42, 48
DDP. See District Delivery Program
Deh Rawud district
    about, 85
    development, 228, 230
    Dutch, 206, 207
    floods, 55, 63
    Soviets, 128, 129

Taliban, 24, 160, 161
Delanor Pass, 35, 86, 95–96, 137
Del Bianco, Gene, 14
delivery of services, 197, 202
Department of State, U.S. *See* State
    Department, U.S.
de Tocqueville, Alexis, 121
development and reconstruction efforts. *See
    also specific efforts*
  assessment of, 186–87
  Dutch, 185, 206
  link to security, 17–18, 28
  McCrystal strategy, 192, 195–97
  PRT role, xi, 57, 218
  Uruzgan Province, 186–87, 227–30
  USAID, 23, 28
Dillard, Jermaine, 26
Dillon, Doug, 26, 31–33, 49
diplomats
  change in role, xii–xiii
  relationships and perceptions, 201
Directorate of Agriculture, 52, 58, 156
Directorate of Communications, 156
Directorate of Education, 130, 156
Directorate of Finance, 53–54
Directorate of Haj and Religious Affairs, 53
Directorate of Health, 52, 58, 156
Directorate of Information and Culture, 55, 61,
    63
Directorate of Justice, 54
Directorate of Local Governance, Independent
    (IDLG), 195, 197
Directorate of Public Works, 52, 58, 156
Directorate of Reconstruction and Rural
    Development, 52, 54–55, 58
Directorates, Province, about, 47, 53–55, 57–
    59, 60–61, 83, 226. *See also specific
    directorates*
Dirkman, Nathan, 65–66, 81–82, 104, 125
disposal of bodies, 142
District Delivery Program (DDP), 197, 202
district support teams, 196
Doc, 27, 80, 150
donors, international, 197
dresses, wedding, 76, 81, 185
Dubai, 75, 77
Dubs, Adolph, 12–13
Durrani tribal confederation, 36, 87, 126, 153–
    55, 186, 230. *See also specific tribes*
Dutch and Tarin Kowt PRT
  assumption, 177–82, 185, 198
  progress, 206–8
Dutch Battle Group, 179
Dutch Deployment Task Force, 178
Dutch Special Forces, 147–49, 169, 170, 182,
    184

economy, Afghan, 35, 62, 104
education, 32–33, 35, 49–50, 104, 109
Education Directorate, 130, 156
Edwardes, Herbert B., 69
Eikenberry, Karl, 79, 110–12, 194–95, 196,
    206

elections
  2008, 184
  2005 ballot counting and results, 120–21,
      125–26, 135
  2005 Dai Kundi, 104, 106–9, 112
  2005 election day, 119–20
  2005 planning, 59, 89–90, 92–93, 115–19
  Provincial Shura, 43–44
Elections Operations Center, 117–18, 119
embassy at Kabul, U.S.
  changes between author's tours, 204
  description, 12–14
  human terrain understanding, 199–200
  military-civilian operations coordination,
      195–96, 200–202
  personnel and recruitment, 24, 201, 203–4
  relationship with military, 204, 205–6
Estonia, 191
Etherington, Mark, v, 74
experiences of civilian and military veterans,
    overview, 215, 217–18
Explosive Ordnance Disposal team, 73, 166–67

Faisal, King, 29
Fall, Bernard B., 89, 196
farming, 35, 44, 58, 69, 104, 140–41
Farooq, 24, 131, 184
fat-tailed sheep, 35
Fick, Nathaniel, 82
Finance Directorate, 53–54
flood mitigation and relief, 50–51, 55, 63, 96
Flynn, Michael T., 199
FOB Anaconda, 159, 184
FOB Cobra, 73, 158–59, 162, 163
FOB Kodiak, 97
FOB Pacemaker, 96, 97, 223
FOB Ripley
  about, 17, 21–22, 147
  attacks on, 62, 159
  Dutch PRT assumption, 178, 179, 181
  elections, 117
  medical aid, 73
  protection of, 85
FOB Tiger, 97–99, 100–101, 223
FOB Tycz, 158–59, 178, 179
Fontes, Robin
  about, 79–80, 148
  Eikenberry presentation, 110
  elections, 90, 92, 96, 106–7, 118
  lunch for Afghan leaders, 101–2
  Newman, 151–52
  suicide bomb attack, 143–44, 161
force laydown, 158–59
foreign fighters of Taliban, 161, 163
Foreign Service Officers (FSOs), about, 23–24,
    201, 206
forgiveness, 36
France, 191, 207
funding
  Iraq War as priority, xiii
  local Afghan government, 122, 197
  PRT, xii
Future Operations, 192

Gafarov, Kemal, 59
Galula, David, 23, 59, 67, 79, 189
Garcia, Jesus, 80
Gates, Joe, 148–49, 152, 169, 174
geography of Uruzgan Province, 33–34
Germany, 191–92
Gilzai tribe
  about, 36, 161–62, 172
  elections, 116, 126
  members, 153, 154
  Monib, 154–55
  strategy to bring into government, 227–30
  Taliban, 154, 160, 186, 210
girls, Afghan
  appearance, 12
  education, 32–33, 49–50, 109, 111, 207
Giustozzi, Antonio, 140, 147
Gizab district, 44, 51, 104–5, 106, 107–8, 210
Glubb, John Bagot, 29, 214
  Britain and the Arabs, v, 11, 42
  Story of the Arab Legion, 33, 95, 102
Goodfellow, Douglas, 80
Government of the Islamic Republic of
    Afghanistan (GIRoA), 191–93, 195–99, 208
governor's compounds, 40–41, 105–6
Great Britain, 191
Greene, Kerry, vii, 7, 17–18, 25, 28, 141, 148
Griego, Wil, 150
guerilla warfare, 33, 71, 89
Guerilla Warfare (Guevara), 71
Guests of the Ayatollah (Bowden), 75
Guevara, Ernesto, 71
Gul, Haji, 126

Haj and Religious Affairs Directorate, 53
Haj to Saudi Arabia, 47, 53–54
Hamdam, Asadullah, 184, 185–86, 206
Hamdullah, Mawlawi
  background, 43, 51–52, 136, 139
  Jan Mohammed Khan, 136, 151, 185–86
  meetings with, 51–53, 122–23
  Monib, 154
  Provincial Council, 125–26, 185–86, 229, 232–33
  Provincial Shura, 43–44, 52–53, 56–57, 59, 118
  Shaikh Mir Ahmad, 65
  Taliban, 124–25, 137, 139
Hashim, Mohammed, 55, 149, 228
Hays, Jared, 89–90
Hazaras, 36, 65, 72, 95, 103–5, 107–10
health care, 35, 107, 108, 118, 167
Health Directorate, 52, 58, 156
Helmand Province, 34, 35, 80–81, 103, 129, 159–60, 162
Helmand River, 34, 35, 50–51, 95, 103, 105
Helmand River Valley floods, 50–51
Henry, David, 26, 32
Herat Province, 130, 138
hiring authority of State Department, 203
Hoffman, Martin, 14
home, visiting and returning, 74–76, 142–45
hospitality, 36, 75, 102

Hotak, Colonel, 46, 48
Hotak tribe, 161–62, 172
humanitarian aid, 26, 52–53, 59, 149, 174–75
Human Terrain System, 198–200, 202
Humvees, about, 179, 190
Hunter, Jim, 14
Hunting Al-Qaeda, 138

Ibrahim, Haji, 24, 46–47, 68–69, 124, 222, 224
IED Alley, 98
IEDs
  boy burying incident, 73–74
  threat of, 8, 163, 190
  villager removing incident, 166–67
Inaugural Committee, 1
Independent Directorate of Local Governance
    (IDLG), 195, 197
Information and Culture Directorate, 55, 61, 63
information collection, human terrain, 198–200, 202
Information Dominance Center (IDC), 199–200
information sharing, 199–200
In the Midst of Wars: An American's Mission to
    Southeast Asia (Lansdale), 39, 127
Integrated Civilian-Military Campaign plan for
    Support to Afghanistan, 195–96
Interagency Provincial Affairs (IPA), 195, 199, 200–202, 205
International Security Assistance Force (ISAF),
    178, 191, 194, 195. See also ISAF Joint
    Command (IJC)
International Visitors program, 151
interpreters, 26–27, 80–82, 150. See also
    specific names
Iowa National Guard, 24, 67, 80
IPA. See Interagency Provincial Affairs
Iran, 103–4
Iraq War
  policies of, 214, 217–18
  as priority over Afghanistan, xiii, 177, 190
  PRTs, xi
  troop surge, 193, 194
irrigation, 26, 29–31, 35, 97
ISAF. See International Security Assistance
    Force
ISAF Joint Command (IJC)
  about, 190–91, 192–93
  human terrain understanding, 199–200
  military-civilian operations coordination, 200–201
  ministerial outreach program, 195–96
Italy, 191

Jan, Haji Khairo, 126, 136, 138–39, 141
Jan, Wali, 85–86
justice, 36
Justice Directorate, 54

Kabir, Engineer, 156
Kabul
  author's visit, 141–42
  description, 11–12, 15

Kabul International Airport, 73, 191
Kandahar Air Field (KAF), 16–17, 81, 128
Kandahar City, 16, 34
Kandahar Province, 34, 35–36, 97, 129, 159
Karmal, Babrak, 130
Karzai, Abdul Ahad, 134
Karzai, Ahmed Wali, 209, 223
Karzai, Hamid
  associates, 91, 106, 150
  background, 5
  Farooq, 24
  Jan Mohammed Khan, 28, 105, 123, 134, 151
  local governance, 197
  Monib, 157
  Tarin Kowt, 129
Karzai, Qayum, 41–44, 49, 56
Karzai: The Failing American Intervention and the Struggle for Afghanistan (Mills), 134
Kennedy, John F., 183
key leader engagement (KLE), 191
key terrain districts (KTDs), 194
Khaliq Khan. See Khan, Haji Malem Abdul Khaliq
Khalk Party, 130, 131, 132
Khan, Atiqullah, 87, 126
Khan, Daoud, 184, 207, 209
Khan, Haji Aziz, 50–51, 55, 224–25, 226
Khan, Haji Malem Abdul Khaliq
  about, 71–72, 135–37
  Dutch, 207–8
  elections, 116, 125–26
  Jan Mohammed Khan, 72, 222
  meeting with, 123–25
  Taliban, 137
  wife's injury, 151, 165
Khan, Haji Mohammed Akbar, 124
Khan, Ismael, 139
Khan, Jan Mohammed
  about, 27–28, 41, 71, 134–35, 223
  assassination, 208–9
  corruption and thuggery, 46–49, 54, 72, 123–24, 127, 155, 222
  elections, 115, 125–26
  firing of, 144, 153
  firing recommendations, 83, 112, 123, 221, 225–26
  Gizab, 105
  Hamdullah, 52, 136, 150–51, 186
  legacy, 155–56
  meetings, ceremonies, and lunches, 56, 60–61, 62–64, 101–2
  post-governorship, 151, 153–54, 157, 186, 207, 233–34
  Rozi Khan, 46, 122, 137, 222
  Taliban, 134, 136–38, 209
  Watanwall, 131
Khan, Mohammed Daoud, 132
Khan, Mohammed Hanif, 126, 141
Khan, Naqibullah, 126
Khan, Rozi
  about, 25, 46–47, 66, 136
  death, 184

elections, 115–16, 126, 135, 184
firing of, 112, 151, 156–57
Ibrahim, 68–69, 224
Jan Mohammed Khan, 28, 47, 122, 222
Khaliq Khan, 71–72
Monib, 154
Taliban, 137–38, 151, 154
Khan, Yar Mohammed, 70, 124, 138
Khan, Zahir, 70, 124
Khas Uruzgan district, 51, 55, 70, 90–91, 149, 159, 207–8
Kiran, 106, 160
Kilcullen, David, 145
Kirkbride, Alec, 115
KLE. See key leader engagement
Koran, Kalashnikov, and Laptop: The Neo-Taliban Insurgency in Afghanistan (Giustozzi), 140, 147
Kraemer, Marvin, 25–26, 45, 65
Kuchi tribe, 31, 35, 36, 68, 72, 108

LaFontaine, William, 15, 17–18, 24–25, 51, 58, 89, 148
L'Ancien Régime et la Révolution (de Tocqueville), 121
Lansdale, Edward Geary, 39, 127
Lashgar Gah, 81
Latvia, 191
leave, 74–76, 204
Light, Frank, 6–8, 18, 28–29, 53, 198
Lo, Clifford, 80
lunch for Afghan leaders at PRT, 101–2
Luxembourg, 191

Macedonia, 191
madrassas, 52, 54
Magsaysay, Ramon, 1, 45, 62, 189
Malalai Girls School, 49–50, 117, 118, 120, 206
male ballot counting teams, 120–21
marriage, Afghan, 61
martial arts, 112
Masoud, Ahmad Shah, 11, 15
Matullah
  about, 39, 70, 84, 207, 209
  Afghan National Police, 47
  corruption, 72, 84, 86–87, 90, 123
  firing of, 223, 225
  meeting with, 84–87
  Monib, 157
Mazdoryar, Sher Jan, 130, 131–33
McCrystal, Stanley, 190, 192, 193–95, 198–99
McElrath, Christopher, 65, 79
McMaster, H. R., 217–19
meals, 32, 44, 101–2
MEDCAPs (medical civil affairs project), 118, 157, 230
Meissner, Eric, 204–5
melmastia, 36
Metrinko, Mike, 75
military-civilian operations coordination, 193, 194–96, 199–202, 218–19
military power, 183

military vehicles, 178–79, 180, 190
Mills, Nick B., 134
mine-resistant ambush-protected trucks
    (MRAPs), 190
ministerial outreach program, 195–96
Ministry of Electricity and Power, 131
Ministry of Finance, 195
Ministry of the Interior, 28, 46, 116, 131
Ministry of Public Works, 130
Ministry of Rural Rehabilitation and
    Development, 195
Ministry of Transportation, 132
Mirabad, 64, 90–91, 92, 93, 155, 172, 174
Mission Program Plan U.S. Mission to
    Afghanistan, 28
Mohammed, Akhtar, 91, 92–93, 157, 172–75
Mohammed, Ali, 56, 63, 233
Mohammed, Dost, 63
Mohammed, Haji Nazar, 126
Mohammed, Haji Sardar, 156
Mohammed, Malim Faiz, 91, 157, 172–75
Mohammed, Mullah Yar, 70, 124, 138
Mohammed, Noor, 126, 135, 139
Mohammed, Pai, 135, 139
Mohammedzai tribe, 27, 36, 132, 133, 136,
    224
Mohibullah
    about, 27
    author's second Tarin Kowt tour, 150–51
    elections, 118
    engagement, 61, 76, 81
    lunches and ceremonies, 101, 181
    Matullah meeting, 84–85
    move to Kandahar, 184
    Provincial Shura, 56–57
    Taliban, 62, 185
Mongolia, 191
Monib, Abdul Hakim
    about, 144, 153
    challenges, 153–54, 157, 232
    Chenartu, 173–74
    Dutch PRT assumption, 180, 181
    Populzai, 234
    replacement of, 183–84
    successes, 155–57, 183, 228–29
morality, 62
MRAPs. See mine-resistant ambush-protected
    trucks
Muhammed, Taj, 54
mujahedeen
    Soviets, 12, 96, 127–29, 131, 133, 134–37
    Taliban, 129–30, 133, 138–39
mullahs, meeting with, 62–64

Nabi, Haji, 47–48, 55, 117, 224
Naim, Mohammed, 228
Najibullah, Dr., 130
nanawati, 36
national caveats, 192
NATO, 190–93, 207. See also ISAF; ISAF Joint
    Command
Nelson, Travis, 45–46, 48, 58, 66, 70, 72–73
Netherlands, 191, 207

PRT assumption, 177–82, 187
Neuman, Ronald, xi–xv, 221
Newman, Clint, 80, 96–97, 143, 151–52, 161,
    163
nights, Afghan, 29
Nili, 103–4, 108–9, 111–12
Nilofer, Sonia, 125
Nimruz, 235n4
nongovernmental organizations (NGO), 41,
    107, 140–41, 187. See also specific NGOs
Noorzai, Arif, 155
Noorzai tribe, 85, 87, 155, 161–62, 221
Norway, 191
Nyalas, 179

Obaidullah, Mullah, 156, 157
Obama, Barrack H., 193–94, 210
Office of Secretary of Defense (Policy), 2
Olson, Major General, 17–18
Omar, Mullah, 16, 36, 56, 128, 137–38
Only Thing Worth Dying For: How Eleven
    Green Berets Forged a New Afghanistan
    (Blehm), 134
Operation Mountain Thrust, 158, 160
operations coordination, military-civilian, 193,
    194–96, 199–202, 218–19
opium, 35, 44, 104, 140
Osmani, Aktar Mohammed, 138
Owen, Captain, 60

Pashtuns. See also specific members; specific
    tribes
    about, 27, 33, 36, 42, 65, 103–5, 173
    members, 87, 130, 154, 162
    uprising, 5, 24, 91, 129, 134
pashtunwali, 36
Patrias, 179
Pedersen, Colonel, 17
personnel carriers, 170, 179, 180
personnel rotations, 180, 205
physical fitness of civil recruits, 203–4
piss tubes, 82
police. See Afghan Highway Police; Afghan
    Local Police; Afghan National Police
police advisers, xii, 45. See also specific names
policymaking, 214–15
polling centers, 89–90, 107–8, 116–17, 119–20,
    158
pond projects, 29–31
poppy crops, 35, 44, 104, 140
population protection, sustained, 192–94
Populzai tribe
    about, 36, 85, 137
    Afghan Highway Police, 85, 223, 224
    Jan Mohammed Khan, 134, 228
    members, 24, 28, 91, 122, 130, 131, 136
    Monib, 153, 156–57, 234
    tribal balance in government, 155, 221–22
Prince of the Marshes and Other Occupational
    Hazards of a Year in Iraq, The (Stewart),
    213
property lines, 33
Provincial Council

elections, 107, 108, 123, 125–26, 135, 206
   political strategy for, 232–33
   role and support for, 122, 136, 226
Provincial Reconstruction Teams (PRTs)
   about, xi–xiii, 6, 23–24, 74, 195, 218
   Tarin Kowt description, 6–8, 22–27, 147–48
Provincial Shura, 42–45, 49, 51–52, 56–59,
   125–26, 233
psychological support, 204
Public Works Directorate, 52, 58, 156
Purcham Party, 130

Qasim, General, 154
Qatawazi, General, 132

radio
   Mullahs, 51, 63
   Nili, 108
   role and use of, 35, 42, 56, 118, 167
   Uruzgan stations, 35, 61, 185, 207
Rahman, Habib, 58–59
Rahmatullah, Malem, 122–23
Rasool, Dr., 110, 112–13, 184
Razag, Mullah, 139
reconstruction and development efforts. *See*
   development and reconstruction efforts
Reconstruction and Rural Development
   Directorate, 52, 54–55, 58
refugees, 104, 149
Regional Command–South Commanders
   Conference, 17–18
registration, voter, 89, 118
Reiter, Richard "Ruff," 143, 161
Republican National Committee, 1
revenge, 36
Revolt on the Tigris (Etherington), v, 74
Rich Contextual Understanding project, 198–
   99
Rivera, Maria, 80
roads, 34–35, 39, 207. *See also* Tarin Kowt–
   Kandahar Road
Robinson, Erik, 80
Rodriguez, David, 190, 192, 196, 199, 202
rotations, personnel, 180, 205
Rozi Khan mosque, 209

Samad, Haji Abdul, 139
Sanders, Jeff, 29–31, 201
sanitation, public, 35
Sardar, 139
Sar Marghab firefight, 169–71
schools, 32–33, 35, 49–50, 54, 109, 207
screening process for State Department
   recruitment, 203
security
   elections, 115–18, 119–20
   sustained population protection, 192–94
   Tarin Kowt PRT, 8
   Uruzgan Province, 153–54, 157, 210
seed program, 140–41
Sellers, Terry, 17–18, 42, 51, 60–61, 63
Senegal, 207
September 11 attacks, author's experience, 2–5

Seventh Special Forces Group, 144, 150
sewage systems, 35
Shah, Zahir, 132
Sheehan, Neil, 27, 83, 142, 153, 157, 165, 172,
   177
sheep, 35
Shiites, 36
Shirzad, Mohammed Omar, 210
small villages strategy, 230–32
Smith, Art, 45–46, 48, 70, 76
Sozak, Jacob, 26
Soviet invasion and occupation, 128–29, 133,
   136–37
Spain, 191
Specht, Linda, 181
Special Forces (SF), 187
   Char Chena, 162–63
   clearing operations, 81, 158, 160
   Dutch and, 181–82
   Provincial Shura, 52, 58
   at PRT, 80, 82, 100, 150
   Seventh SF Group, 144, 150
   stability operations, 199–200
State Department, U.S.
   embassy personnel and recruitment, 24, 201,
      203–4
   reconstruction and development, 195, 196,
      202–3
   resources of, xii, xiv
   security, 24, 193
Stewart, Rory, 213
Story of the Arab Legion, The (Glubb), 33, 95,
   102
strategy for Uruzgan, political, 227–34
   bring Gilzai into government, 228–30
   Provincial Council, 232–33
   small village development, 230–32
   using Jan Mohammed Khan, 233–34
Street Without Joy (Fall), 89, 196
suicide bombings, 144, 158, 161, 184, 191,
   208
Sultan, 32–33, 184
Sunnis, 36, 62–63
surge, troop, 193–94
Sweden, 191
synchronization of operations, 193, 194–96,
   199–202, 218–19

Tactical Conflict Assessment Planning
   Framework (TCAPF), 199
tactical operations center (TOC), defined, 22
Tak, Nico, 179, 180–81
Taliban
   about, 16, 30, 54, 59–60, 116, 128
   assassinations and attempts on Afghan
      leaders, 51, 63, 64–65, 184, 208–9
   Chenartu blockade, 172–73
   Dutch, 180, 184
   Hamdullah, 59, 124–25
   Jan Mohammed Khan, 134, 208
   Mirabad, 90
   Monib, 154
   Provincial Shura, 57, 59

PRT visit to Chora and Sar Marghab firefight, 166–71
rise of, 137–39
support for, 186, 196–97, 198, 227–28
threats to Mohibullah, 62, 185
Uruzgan presence, 2005 and before, 36, 106, 128, 140, 210
Uruzgan presence, 2006 and after, 147, 149–51, 157–64, 184, 186–87
Taraky, Nur Muhammad, 130
Tarin Kowt city
    about, 34, 36
    description, xix, 21, 30, 33–34, 39–40, 45
    traffic circle, 59–61
Tarin Kowt–Kandahar Road
    about, 35, 97–98
    Afghan Highway Police, 85, 223
    checkpoints, 85, 97–98, 157
    construction, 34, 96–98, 187, 207, 230
Tarin Kowt PRT description, 6–8, 22–27, 147–48
taxes, 54, 57
temperatures, 34, 81
Tenth Mountain Division, 147, 149, 158
Texas National Guard, 65, 69, 79, 92, 105
theoretical constructs of U.S. government, 213–15
3161 hiring authority, 203
Thurman, Tamara, 6
Tillman, Pat, 16
time line, Uruzgan Province, xxi–xxiii
Timmons, Tim, 13
traffic circles, 59–61, 69
training
    Afghan police, 48, 157
    GIRoA, 197
    U.S. civilian, xii, xiv, 23, 199, 204–5
transition team of Bush administration, 2, 5
transportation sector, Afghan, 35
tribal balance, 155, 221–22, 224–25, 226, 230
troop surge, 193–94
turnout, voter, 118, 119, 121, 184
Twenty-fifth Infantry, 17, 60, 69, 86, 158, 187

United Arab Emirates, 75, 77
United Nations
    Afghanistan Landmine Impact Survey, 128
    elections, 89–90, 104, 106–9, 116–21
    Khairo Jan, 139
United Nations Assistance Mission in Afghanistan (UNAMA), 52, 59
United Services Organization (USO), 16
Uruzgan Province. See also specific cities; specific districts
    about, 33–37, 208
    description, xviii–xix, 29–31, 95–96
    2007–2011 status, 206–10
U.S. Army Corps of Engineers, 86

U.S. Department of Agriculture, 29, 196, 202, 204
U.S. Forces–Afghanistan (USFOR-A), 195
USAID (United States Agency for International Development)
    ministerial programs, 195
    municipalities program, 208
    personnel, 141, 204–5
    reconstruction and development efforts, 49, 51, 108, 167, 196, 202
    resources of, xii, xiv, 187
    security, 193
    seed program, 140–41
    TCAPF, 199
USO. See United Services Organization

Vann, John Paul, 27, 84, 142, 153, 157, 165, 172, 177
vehicles, military, 178–79, 180, 190
Vietnam War, 21, 27, 142, 153, 157, 165, 172, 177
village development strategy, 230–32
voter registration, 89, 118
voter turnout, 118, 119, 121, 184

Wali, Haji Mohammad, 76
Walker, Kenneth "Ross," 65, 100, 107
Walker, Laura, 99, 100
Walt, Lewis, 21
warlords, 133, 186, 197, 209, 221
Watanwall, Haji Mohammed Hashim, 102, 115, 125, 130–31, 208–9
Waterhouse, Gustov, 80
weapon carrying, 24–25
Wheat Seed and Fertilizer Distribution Program, 140–41
White, George, 13–14
Whitmire, Robert, 80
Williams, Will, 26, 49
Wilson, Todd, 6
withdrawal timeline, 194, 210
Wolesi Jirga
    candidates for, 52, 89, 107, 108, 123, 130, 132
    elections, 119, 121, 125
    as part of local governance, 226, 233
women, Afghan
    brides, 61
    code of behavior, 36–37
    dress of, 12
    elections, 92, 108, 118, 120–21

Yassim, 162–63
Year on the Punjab Frontier in 1848–1849, A (Edwardes), 69

zan, zar, and zameen, 36–37

ABOUT THE AUTHOR

Daniel R. Green served as the U.S. Department of State political adviser to the Tarin Kowt Provincial Reconstruction Team in Uruzgan Province, Afghanistan, from January to November 2005 and from June to August 2006. For his work, he received the Superior Honor Award from DOS and the Superior Civilian Honor Award from the U.S. Army, as well as a personal letter of commendation from then chairman of the Joint Chiefs of Staff Peter Pace. Green has also received the Exceptional Public Service Award from the Office of the Secretary of Defense. He is a Soref Fellow at the Washington Institute for Near East Policy and trains military units through Aeneas Group International.

He had previously worked at the U.S. Department of Defense from 2001 to 2003 and at DOS from 2003 to 2008 before rejoining DOD in early 2008. Green left DOD in 2009, after working as a special assistant to the Assistant Secretary of Defense for International Security Affairs. The ISA office is responsible for formulating Middle East, NATO/Europe, and Africa policy. As a special assistant, Green participated in the formulation of DOD's Afghanistan policy through the NATO/European office.

Green is an active drilling reservist with the U.S. Navy, which he joined in 2003, and in 2007 he deployed to Fallujah, Iraq, for a six-month tour as a tribal and leadership engagement officer in Al Anbar Province. He also deployed with the U.S. Navy to Afghanistan from December 2009 to April 2010 as the ISAF Joint Command Liaison Officer to the U.S. Embassy's Office of Interagency Provincial Affairs.

Green has a strong record of writing and publication, including academic work, public policy studies, and military writing. He has published a scholarly article in *Politics & Policy*, received two best-paper awards at political science conferences, published numerous op-eds, and written several articles related to the global war on terror in *Military Review*, *Small Wars Journal*, *Strategic Studies Quarterly*, *Armed Forces Journal*, *Special Warfare Magazine*, *Marine Corps Gazette*, *Small Wars and Insurgencies*, the *Canadian Army Journal*, the *Australian Army Journal*, and *Proceedings*, three of which were cover articles. He also writes a monthly column entitled "Irregular Warfare" for *Armed Forces Journal*.

Green graduated cum laude from American University in 1998 with three majors—political science, history, and CLEG (communications, law, economics, and government)—and a minor in international studies, and he received the university's Outstanding Undergraduate Scholar Award. He was a George C. Marshall undergraduate scholar with the George C. Marshall Foundation and received research grants from three Presidential Libraries. Green also has a master's degree in international affairs from Florida State University. He is currently working on his dissertation for a PhD in political science at George Washington University, in which he is attempting to explain how the chairman of the Joint Chiefs of Staff is selected by examining the selection processes and candidates from the administrations of Harry S. Truman through Barack H. Obama.

Green has spoken about his wartime experiences at George Washington University, U.S. Central Command, the Marine Corps Intelligence Activity, various Canadian and U.S. military units, civic clubs, and at professional conferences in the Washington, D.C., area.

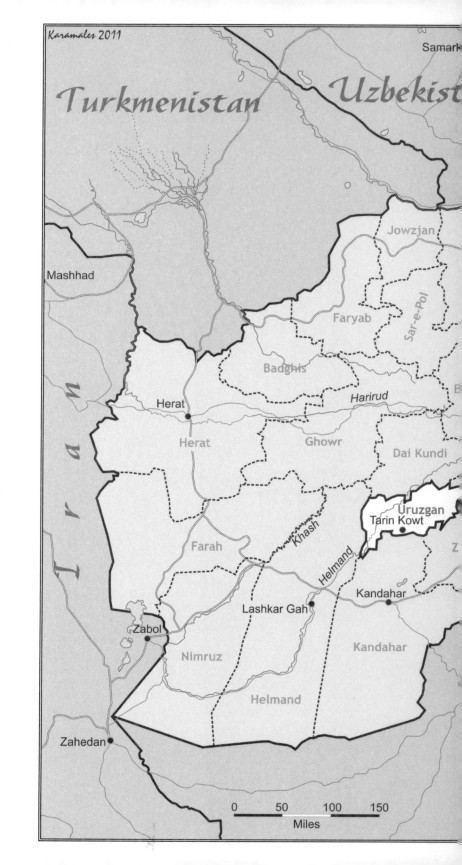